LEADERS
READY NOW

*Accelerating Growth
in a Faster World*

Matthew J. Paese   +   Audrey B. Smith   +   William C. Byham

Published by DDI Press, c/o Development Dimensions International, World Headquarters—Pittsburgh, 1225 Washington Pike, Bridgeville, Pennsylvania 15017-2838.

Manufactured in the United States of America.

Library of Congress Cataloging in Publications Data

Paese, M.J.

    Leaders ready now

    Accelerating growth in a faster world / Matthew J. Paese, Audrey B. Smith, William C. Byham

1. Business   2. Succession Management   3. Executives

4. Executive Development   5. Leadership   6. Promotions

ISBN 978-0-9761514-7-0 (hbk); ISBN 978-0-9761514-6-3 (ebk)

10 9 8 7 6 5 4 3 2 1

Dedication

Bob Rogers

For more than 37 years, Bob Rogers accelerated the growth of everyone at DDI. If we could simply show you how Bob operated on a daily basis, you wouldn't need this book. Not only was he an instrumental architect of many of the principles and best practices you will read in these pages, but he also did the hard work of building them into the way DDI operates. As this book goes to publication, Bob has completed his memorable run as President of DDI. His story doesn't end though, as the growth and development of people that are in his DNA will be his great legacy, both for DDI and the clients we serve. We are forever grateful, Bob.

You, Our Clients

Leaders Ready Now also is dedicated to our client partners around the globe. You are our North Star. Through fortitude and innovation, you continually show us how leaders and organizations truly grow, and you inspire us to follow your example and reach ever higher. We are deeply grateful for the wisdom, courage, and commitment you demonstrate as you energize growth in a world that desperately needs it.

LEADERS READY NOW
*Accelerating Growth
in a Faster World*

Table of Contents

GROW

SUSTAIN

SAPPED |

How Good Practices Drain Leadership Readiness

The CEO grimaced and kneaded his forehead as he and his senior team pored over the profiles of the organization's highest-potential leaders. Feeling the weight of ambitious growth targets, an impatient shareholder audience, and an agitated board, the team had confronted the urgent need for change, launching new performance imperatives. Soon they would have no choice but to push less-experienced leaders into broader, more formidable assignments.

Recognizing that their emerging leaders would need help, the top team had implemented an aggressive leadership-acceleration program, and now was the time to harvest its impact and begin deploying leaders to key assignments.

It wasn't going well.

After hours of studying profiles, debating requirements, evaluating progress, and confronting difficult truths, the CEO looked around the table at his team. *"We don't have the leadership to do this,"* he said flatly. *"We're not ready."*

Who was this CEO? The company? Their business issues? It doesn't matter. Take your pick. Countless business leaders are encountering their own version of this moment right now. They are feeling the same sense of alarm as they realize that the needs of the business stretch beyond the capabilities of the leaders inside it and, worse, that the investments they've made to build a stronger leadership bench haven't worked. It's a position no CEO wants to occupy, but it's one that many face as the competitive world hurtles forward. Too many are at a loss for how to respond. Too many are not ready.

Fast World, Slow Growth

This is not a book about how to lead. It's a book about how to grow great leaders. It will be valuable to you if your organization's future is in danger because of a lack of leadership and you've concluded that you must aggressively address the problem. Those who feel their leaders are growing at a satisfactory pace will not be inspired here. This book will be useful only if you feel it is time to take bold steps to prepare your leaders for bigger challenges—more quickly, more continuously, and fully enough so that they are ready—ready to lead in the competitive, chaotic world that we have come to know as the new normal.

Ready now.

> Is the energy inside your organization increasing or decreasing? When you say "Ready in two years" or "Ready with development," is it true?

Start by considering what it means to be ready. Are your leaders becoming more so, or are they struggling to keep pace? When weighing strategic alternatives, are leaders available, or do gaps create business risk? Is the energy and vitality inside your organization increasing or waning? And here's the tough one: When you say "Ready in two years" or "Ready with development," is it true? Will the time and effort create the readiness you need quickly enough?

Currently, the leadership-readiness curve is trending dangerously in the wrong direction, even as organizations worldwide are investing more than ever to try to turn it around.[i] The evidence has become so glaring that a grim recitation of statistics would be superfluous, so let's summarize instead: With leadership development consistently ranking among CEOs' top priorities over the last two decades, organizations have more than doubled their global investment, pouring billions of dollars into preparing the next generation(s) of leaders. But during this time, by every measure, leadership readiness has declined precipitously.[ii] Survey after survey, in virtually every sector (some far worse than others), reveals a deep erosion of confidence in leadership as well as a disconcerting lack of bench strength. Even the most optimistic estimates leave the typical organization leaderless more than half the time when needing to fill open assignments.[iii] For some, it is far worse: In the C-suite, executives routinely delay or withdraw from strategic priorities for lack of available leadership, and initiatives fail far more often than they would with a firmer hand on the tiller.[iv] As the rate of change accelerates, the efforts to help leaders keep up are themselves falling behind.

More than a decade ago, we published *Grow Your Own Leaders*[v] to help organizations address their leadership-readiness problems, laying down the practical foundations of how to identify and accelerate the growth of high-potential leaders to prepare them for higher-level assignments. We called these leadership groups *Acceleration Pools*[SM], and since that time, more than a thousand organizations across the globe—businesses in every industry, health care systems, government agencies, civil service groups, universities, churches, charities, and more—have implemented the Acceleration Pool concept. These organizations have been shown (via independent research) to outpace others in growing leaders and to have larger supplies of ready leaders and stronger performance among them.[vi] But as encouraging as these successes have been, the velocity of global competition has made it necessary not only to *grow your own leaders* but also to grow more of them, faster, in a far more complex world.

But is *faster* even possible? It's difficult to imagine asking leaders to learn any faster than what life requires already. However dire our leadership shortages may be, it is clear that we won't overcome them by attempting to cram more into the hyper-driven lives and overloaded minds of emerging leaders. Becoming *ready now* will not happen simply by trying to run faster.

Energizing Acceleration

To speed up in a frenzied world, one must first stop and rethink. But if you are a CEO or business leader seeking fresh insight on how to fundamentally change your organization's leadership equation, the quest can be exhausting. Two things are true about the current state of guidance on how to grow leaders faster:

1. The intense global need for leaders has sparked a proliferation of highly redundant ideas, often repackaging tried-and-true principles and best practices or making incremental enhancements that are pitched to sound revolutionary. CEOs and HR leaders, often in desperation, must read anything and everything to find any pearl of wisdom or insight that might boost their efforts.

2. The established guidelines for developing leaders now exist in a far more complex world, and many no longer have the impact they once had. This reinforces the need described in the first point and creates a vicious cycle in which the same ideas continue to be recycled, while the need for leaders further outstrips the ability of organizations to grow them.

Don't worry—we won't be promising a silver-bullet solution or warning that you can avoid disaster only by adopting our unique and perfect formula. You don't need us—not really. Everything you need to accelerate the growth of leadership is already inside your organization. You have the people, the resources, the budget, and, yes, the time to make your leadership grow. But if you're among the 74 percent of top leaders who say their succession management systems aren't functioning as intended, or the 85 percent who say they lack the leadership bench necessary to address emerging business challenges[vii], then you've stalled and could use a jump start or, at least, some fresh directions.

But figuring out your own formula can't possibly mean that things have to get more crowded with ideas than they are already. With all that has been learned, written, and applied, haven't we discovered enough of what we need to know about what it takes to grow leaders? The answer is both yes and no. Yes, we do know a great deal about the tools, technology, content, and methods that influence the speed of growth among leaders, and tremendous progress has been made.

But no, tools and technology do not grow leaders. *Leaders grow leaders.* And even the latest and greatest inventions do not change the prospects for closing the leadership gap. While the talent-

> Everything you need to accelerate the growth of leadership is already inside your organization.

management industry has poured incalculable resources into the advancement of tools and technology, the muscles of human effort for growing leaders have atrophied. It seems the more we invest in things, the less adept we are at investing in each other.[viii]

In our work throughout the world, we have asked executives countless times, *"What does it feel like when you're learning at high speed?"* Their responses are universally consistent: There is fear and excitement, worry and anticipation, terror and thrill, anxiety and experimentation, risk and possibility—all of which generates the energy for accelerated learning.

But as you're probably all too aware, most leadership-development programs fail to spark this brand of energy—or much energy at all. Participants may describe them as educational and interesting or even business relevant or strategically important. But these descriptors are a far cry from the fear, excitement, terror, and thrill that leaders associate with their moments of high-speed learning.

> There is fear and excitement, worry and anticipation, terror and thrill, anxiety and experimentation, risk and possibility—all of which generates the energy for accelerated learning.

Fear and excitement happen with risk, and that energy turns into growth when you take the right risks, at the right times. This means moving with alacrity and getting quickly to the heart of what really matters when building the skills and capabilities of your people. Speeding up growth will not happen simply by making learning activities happen more quickly. It will occur when you thoughtfully and systematically take risks that ignite energy in your leaders—in the form of uncertainty and enthusiasm. In our experience the leadership-acceleration efforts that fall short of their objectives are bound by a common description: They are aggressive in the pursuit of structure and application of tools, but anemic in the pursuit of energy.

If your acceleration efforts are falling short, you will not fix the problem with more process, tools, technology, or teams of smart consultants. The most fundamental barrier to growing leaders quickly is a lack of energy, and that energy can be generated by boldness—*your* boldness.

Make no mistake: You definitely will need some tools and processes to make the most of your efforts. But if you want more leaders *ready now* and you want them faster, you must use your acceleration toolbox far more shrewdly, and with a willingness to take on much more risk. As a management team, you must create and embrace the fear, excitement, anxiety, and experimentation that individual leaders experience in their moments of rapid learning. You must be willing to feel uncomfortable and remain open to uncertain outcomes as individuals and as a company. Only then will the leadership gap begin to close.

What Slows You Down

Having taken the time to open this book and read this far, chances are good that you too have read your share of books and articles and quite possibly have sponsored or created leadership-acceleration programs of your own. But if your investments are still coming up short, it's likely that one or more of the following circumstances describe your efforts.

Instead of creating energy, your processes are draining it.

The fastest, most powerful learning experiences convert fear and uncertainty into pride and wisdom. Consider several examples:

- A young, inexperienced leader takes on an assignment to lead a team of people older and more experienced than she.

- An operations executive is suddenly given responsibility to run the IT function, which he knows nothing about.

- A new CEO faces a sudden market crisis that requires a major strategic and cultural shift in direction.

Big first-time challenges like these administer a shock, instantly bringing the leader to attention. It's a jolt of uncertainty that carries a current of doubt; but with effort, discipline, and support, that doubt transforms into action and movement. Ultimately, if and when the challenge is conquered, a backward glance leaves the leader with confidence and insight that can be applied to the next challenge. It is in conquering difficult assignments such as these that leaders become ready to take on bigger leadership roles.

The challenge is scaling this concept beyond isolated, reactive incidents and creating a repeatable dynamic that causes entire cadres of leaders to become ready. For most organizations, scale becomes structure, but structure without energy kills acceleration. It's not uncommon for management to roll out learning initiatives to groups of anywhere from 10 to 10,000 people, after which those new processes become burdened with guidelines, meetings, documentation, mandatory events, and progress checks. Participants—often the company's busiest people—work diligently to make time for a process that has many moving parts but little connection to what they view as mission critical. Soon, what was built to generate the energy of growth dissolves into apathy and annoyance at processes that seem (and may well be) devoid of business importance.

It is not the process itself that is failing—it is the absence of energy to fuel it. Without energy, any processes you put in place will be unsustainable.

> For most organizations, scale becomes structure, but structure without energy kills acceleration.

How to rally the initiatives? By reexamining the architecture of your acceleration efforts and rewriting the rules of the game so that more is at stake, more is to gain, and all the players have a clearer understanding of their roles and how they will have an impact on success. You must be far more aggressive in the use and application of your existing approaches, setting bigger development targets for more people earlier in their careers.

There's no "why."

The business reason for acceleration is often summarized like this: *"We're running desperately short of leaders, and if we can't get more of them—good ones—very soon, we'll be in trouble. It's not an option to buy talent from the outside, so we have only two options: grow from within or fail."*

This usually causes management to sit up straight and pay close attention to the next part of the meeting: How to solve this? What most executives are thinking at this point is basically what's going through their heads when the organization faces a quality problem or a service problem or a cost problem: We need to analyze the causes, develop solutions, and execute a plan.

Except that acceleration is different. An organization can fix a quality, service, or cost problem with new and better processes that people learn to execute with discipline. But a leadership shortage will be filled only with energy for growth—fear and excitement—which then fuels the process and discipline that an acceleration system also requires. So, aiming to solve the talent problem demands a plan to solve the energy problem.

Energy will grow as you take on more risk with developing your people. But bigger risks require bigger *whys*. Why grow? Why accelerate? For management, the why is the business case for acceleration. In the absence of a strong one, it is

> Energy will grow as you take on more risk with developing your people. But bigger risks require bigger *whys*.

difficult to convince senior executives to take any risks (much less big ones) with development. In fact, acceleration isn't appropriate for every organization (e.g., companies in rapid start-up mode may need to emphasize talent acquisition, while others may be stocked with so much talent that the main challenge is retention).

For individual leaders, the why is the *personal* case for acceleration. Without one, it is difficult to convince individuals to take big chances with their own development. The typical conversation with an individual leader highlights the potentially exciting, lucrative, and influential future that acceleration can bring; the leader can—if the process works—learn, earn, and determine much more in the organization. For most, this would be enough to garner full interest and enthusiasm for whatever may come next. But *interest and enthusiasm are simply not enough.* Remember that the most powerful learning experiences—the ones that truly transform leadership capability—are characterized less by design than by necessity. When asked how they came into their moments of rapid learning, leaders routinely report reasons such as, *"They needed me, and I was the only one available who could do it,"* or *"I thought I could make a big difference,"* or *"My boss believed I could do it, so I agreed."*

When it comes to creating energy for acceleration, there is a vast difference between *"You could benefit from this"* and *"We need you."* To create a more powerful *why* for both management and individual learners, it is insufficient to make a case on behalf of only the business or the person. You will need to appeal to both. *"We* (the business) *need you* (the person) *to take a big chance."* Your case must be compelling to both management and each individual, conveying why the organization needs leaders to step up, what it needs from each leader, and why it's worth taking big risks to achieve faster, more significant growth.

You focus on doing things *to* leaders rather than *with* them.

As a business leader, you may speak frequently to individuals or groups of executives about the future of the business, and perhaps you review key leaders' development plans or even act as a mentor. All these activities are useful, but they are not what accelerated learners really want and need most from you—and they are not the activities that generate the greatest amount of energy in an acceleration system.

Ask any motivated, emerging leader what would truly ignite his or her energy, and the answer will likely involve working with senior leaders to solve current business dilemmas. As one acceleration-program participant put it, *"The leadership training is good, but what I really want is a piece of the action."* She wasn't talking about more money; she wanted a piece of the *business* action—to work more closely with leaders who were in the thick of it.

> If you aim to prepare more leaders—and do it more quickly—you must put them in the game much sooner than what might feel comfortable.

This doesn't mean that you have to put core businesses at risk by giving junior executives too much responsibility—it means that top leaders need to reframe the ways in which they spend time with accelerated learners and create development experiences that are truly transformational. Instead of offering a problem for an individual learner to solve alone (with tips and guidance from a senior leader), the organization needs to pinpoint a problem that a senior leader or team currently faces and then enlist the accelerated learner to help solve it. Leaders and learners should work on business challenges together, learning and growing simultaneously.

To learn the game, one must play the game. If you aim to prepare more leaders—and do it more quickly—you must put them in the game, and much sooner than what might feel comfortable. You must play *with* them, learning and growing together, faster than you otherwise would.

You are keeping your own growth to yourself.

Every acceleration effort you make will be limited by the amount of growth you display. This doesn't mean that everyone in the organization must observe your growth; it simply means that some must. Growth is an effect that cascades from leaders to teams, from the CEO down. The message is quite simple: If you want your organization to learn, then you will have to learn. If you are desperate to see faster growth, then you will have to grow. But your efforts cannot take place in private. You and your senior executive colleagues learn and grow every workday, but if the rest of the organization remains unaware of your learning efforts, you'll be missing a valuable opportunity.

For the energy of growth to become infectious, people at the top must model it. And because that axiom is no secret, many organizations create edicts that *"everyone will have a development plan."* Of course, this is a worthy objective that probably achieves some good, but it should not be mistaken for acceleration. Modeling growth is displaying experimentation with new approaches and hungrily gathering feedback so that the experimentation can iterate with a positive arc. Growth isn't a one-time effort, but rather a perpetual one.

Changes need not be profound, nor does self-disclosure need to cross the boundaries of personal preference. Development simply needs to be transparent *enough*. For acceleration to have the broad effect that businesses need, it must catch on. (If this makes you a little uncomfortable, you're on the right track.)

> For acceleration to have the broad effect that businesses need, it must catch on.

Your organization has an unhealthy relationship with failure.

Failure hurts. Crisis is painful and exhausting. Mistakes are costly. It's also true that inside the discomfort and loss, often profound wisdom, strength, and innovation may be gained. But finding these is not guaranteed. Without experimentation, purposeful risk taking, and a willingness to embrace uncertainty, there is little likelihood of better outcomes. What happens in your organization when a promising leader begins to struggle? In the aftermath of a leadership failure, does your senior management team seek to extract learning or to assign blame? Are developmental assignments qualification tests that leaders pass or fail, or are they opportunities for experimentation and application of more advanced leadership behaviors?

> Failure will work in your organization's favor only if you share risks with the leaders you seek to accelerate.

No one wants to fail, and even more unthinkable is failing alone. But that's often precisely the risk leaders face when they are asked to take on difficult assignments or participate in challenging leadership programs. When leadership shortages are severe, there is a temptation to adopt *sink or swim* approaches to development, pushing leaders into daunting challenges and assuming the best will survive and emerge from their experiences as better leaders. But it seldom works out that way. When leaders are left on their own to glean the lessons from risky assignments, learning becomes haphazard. The wrong lessons are often learned, and promising careers are ruined unnecessarily. It's true that failure is instrumental to growth, particularly *accelerated* growth, where so much is at stake. But failure will work in your organization's favor only if you share risks with the leaders you seek to accelerate.

Your senior leadership team's orientation and response to failure will either catapult or kill your acceleration efforts. It is essential for them to acknowledge that more risk means more failure. Leaders in rapid-growth mode will, by design, face situations that test their mettle. But if the expectation is that they need to succeed in each instance, risk taking will soon be strangled, and growth along with it. To learn and grow quickly, they will need to struggle through the ambiguity, discomfort, and loss of failed attempts, and come back again to try different, hopefully better ways. With the right support before, during, and after their experiences, your leaders will gain the insight and capability needed to be ready for larger assignments.

The Acceleration Imperatives and How the Best Use Them

Your organization may have some good processes in place to support learning, and because they likely took considerable effort to implement, they may be precisely what is preventing you from achieving the growth you

> You may have to question the efficacy of processes that were difficult to install. But relax, you don't have to be great at everything.

need. To truly transform the speed and efficiency of your acceleration efforts, *good* won't always be good enough. You may have to question the efficacy of processes that were difficult to install. But relax, you don't have to be great at everything, and you don't have to dismantle and rebuild your systems all at once (in fact, you shouldn't try). In this book we'll contrast good practices to great ones and outline those that have helped organizations radically improve

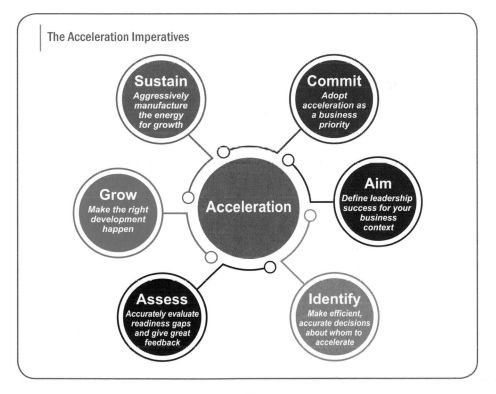

The Acceleration Imperatives

Sustain — *Aggressively manufacture the energy for growth*

Commit — *Adopt acceleration as a business priority*

Grow — *Make the right development happen*

Acceleration

Aim — *Define leadership success for your business context*

Assess — *Accurately evaluate readiness gaps and give great feedback*

Identify — *Make efficient, accurate decisions about whom to accelerate*

the results of their acceleration efforts. In each case they didn't try to do everything perfectly. They made choices about how to channel their efforts and focused on the specific aspects of their acceleration systems that were most essential in their context. We call these Acceleration Imperatives, and while you don't have to excel in each, you'll need to be aware enough about them to avoid system breakdowns.

A leadership-acceleration system is like an automobile, run by systems that operate in sync: ignition, transmission, suspension, exhaust, heating and cooling, and so on. The systems in the realm of leadership acceleration must complement one another, although many organizations are like a car that comes off the assembly line missing essential components—no matter how high-quality the car's elements, it simply won't run as it should. For example, an organization that focuses only on refining its talent-review process may succeed in establishing a good understanding of its leadership supply and demand, but it will not achieve accelerated growth. Making it work requires installing the rest of the acceleration system.

Other organizations resemble high-performance cars being driven far too cautiously. All the components are in place, but no one steps on the accelerator, leaving a potentially dynamic system idle. Assessments are superficial and offer little business-relevant data; feedback lacks impact; development plans lack creativity and risk. In the end, all the process elements fail to spark the energy and growth that are so badly needed.

> **Your job is to learn to drive faster.**

Whether the problem is missing components or overly conservative driving, the solution to poor performance is not to junk the machine; rather, it's to complete its assembly so that it's fully functional. Then, tune the car to suit your specific driving needs, and press down on the gas pedal. Your job is to learn to drive faster.

None of the Acceleration Imperatives are new concepts; the lessons they teach come from more than a thousand organizations worldwide with whom we have worked to implement them—many with great success, some not. If you are a veteran of leadership acceleration, you likely have had hands-on experience with most or all of them.

But while the descriptions of each imperative might seem like commonsense steps to success, organizations whose acceleration efforts are thriving have very different ways of describing what happens in relation to each of the six. There's a big difference between organizations that simply install system components and those that relentlessly pursue acceleration and achieve higher-impact results.

> There's a big difference between organizations that simply install system components and those that relentlessly pursue acceleration and achieve higher-impact results.

This book is organized into six sections aimed at illustrating the difference between good programs and exceptional efforts that dramatically improve leadership readiness. Remember, you need not be great in every area to achieve significant gains. Many of our most successful client partners have carefully chosen one or two Acceleration Imperatives and focused on being great in those areas (without completely neglecting the others). With respect to those Imperatives, they don't let "good" get in the way of "great."

Section I: Commit

We've seen senior management teams not only sanction and participate in leadership-acceleration efforts, but also take ownership of them and become intensely competitive about achieving real results that strengthen the business. Leadership acceleration is a central business priority, and it's managed that way.

Good	**Great**
When you have management's support and involvement	When management competes to make acceleration happen

Section II: Aim

Some organizations are satisfied to simply have a competency model in place. Others turn their model into an indispensable tool that management and individual leaders use routinely to point their efforts to where the business is going, how the context is changing, and what they must do to be ready for it.

Good	**Great**
When you have a competency model in use organizationwide	When your leadership model is an indispensable business resource

Section III: Identify

For some organizations the annual talent review isn't annual at all, nor is it simply a review. Great talent reviews are talent investment dialogs that happen routinely as part of business discussions. Informed by excellent data, they accurately isolate the most critical talent gaps, identify the individuals who have what it takes to grow as leaders, and secure resources to make it happen quickly so the leaders can be deployed where they are most needed.

Good	**Great**
When management participates in the annual talent review	When executives become shrewd and accurate in identifying potential

Section IV: **Assess** ─────────────────────────○

Most executives won't make big bets on the development of their people without a way to mitigate the risk. Nor should they. Organizations that make great use of assessment leverage methods that enable their executives to see how big bets (e.g., placing a young leader into a major leadership role) will play out and precisely how they can craft accelerated development plans that will make them pay off.

Good	**Great**
When you use assessment for key roles and high-risk scenarios	When management is addicted to objective talent data

Section V: **Grow** ─────────────────────────○

Helping emerging leaders learn new things isn't enough when trying to quickly convert them from not ready to ready now. New learning must be applied. Practice and experimentation need to become routine. The great ones don't just enable learning, they ignite the application of leadership approaches that are essential to business success.

Good	**Great**
When you have a wide array of learning options available for leaders	When you ignite application and practice of the leadership approaches your business needs

Section VI: **Sustain** ─────────────────────────○

Whatever form your acceleration efforts take, they should be built to outlast you and everyone else in the organization. A few organizations have figured out that this happens only when there is tension—positive tension—that builds passion, a common purpose, and devotion to ensuring that growth happens.

Good	**Great**
When you hold leaders accountable to fulfill their assigned roles	When you aggressively manufacture positive growth tension

Strap In; It's Time to Speed Up

Becoming *ready now* requires a decision to embark on a journey of continual acceleration. Coordination matters, but while the six Acceleration Imperatives imply a sequence, reality seldom adheres to it. Each organization—some with more experience than others—begins the journey from a unique starting point and makes progress by leveraging strengths and building in the areas that will create the greatest return within its unique business context.

> There is no perfect sequence, nor must you master every component before you begin to realize success.

Through the Acceleration Imperatives, this book offers six practical ways for you to challenge yourself and your organization to become bolder and to cultivate the energy, risk, collaboration, and ownership needed to sustain acceleration over time and produce tangible results. There is no perfect sequence, nor must you master every component before you begin to realize success. You determine the prescription and scale the challenge to your unique context.

Unlike some others, we don't view the challenge as a "war for talent." No war is necessary when the forces of energy, passion, and shared risk are rallied to the common purpose of growing yourself and your organization from within. That is how your organization can grow more *leaders ready now*.

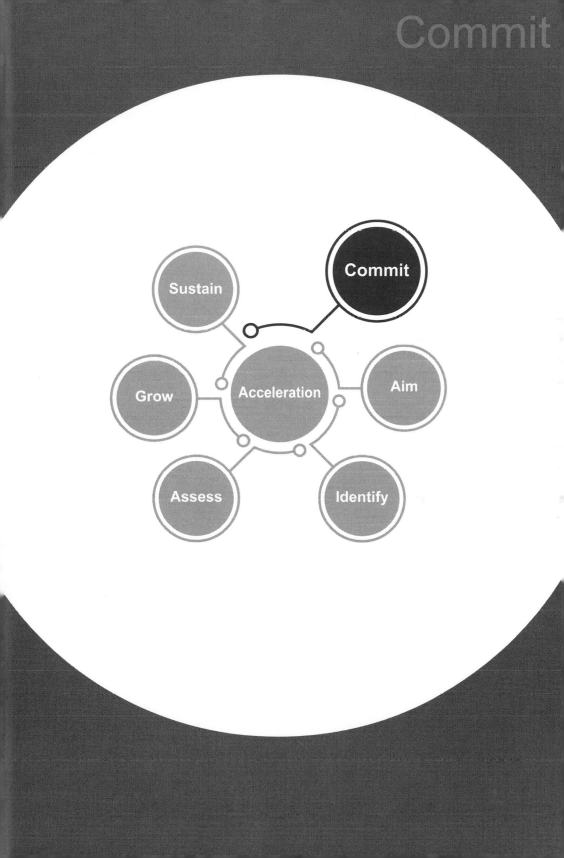

 **Commit** Adopt acceleration as a business priority.

In this section...

Chapters 1 and 2 outline how organizations become great at the COMMIT imperative. The practices they employ generate energy in the following ways:

- **Greater focus:** Isolation of the few most critical leadership priorities (Business Drivers).

- **A more competitive dynamic:** A business-level dashboard that the entire senior management team uses to track the most critical acceleration metrics.

- **A more compelling business case:** Clear articulation of the leadership gaps and exactly where they are in the business, including quantification of the leadership gap.

- **More enterprise-level ownership of growth:** Clear accountability for specific acceleration metrics at both the enterprise and unit levels.

- **More inspiring communications:** A clearer sense of direction that enables more positive communications to engage the entire organization around the goal of accelerated growth.

 Denotes that tools and information on this topic are available at the *Leaders Ready Now* website (www.leadersreadynow.com). Use this code to access content: LRN2016.

NAIL THE BASICS

1 | Defining the Essentials of Accelerating Growth

Taking a more aggressive approach to growing leadership capability is nothing new. Most organizations have tried or are in the process of doing so. In a recent study of 2,031 organizations worldwide, DDI found that 66 percent had installed programs to accelerate the growth of high-potential leaders. But of those, a startling 74 percent reported that their programs were not working.[i] Despite their efforts, leadership readiness remained stagnant. With trends like these, business leaders soon may conclude that programs and approaches espoused by HR are risky investments that stand no chance of improving leadership readiness.

> With trends like these, business leaders soon may conclude that programs and approaches espoused by HR are risky investments that stand no chance of improving leadership readiness.

But they would be wrong. While still a minority, many organizations do achieve significant gains. In contrasting research, a recent meta-analysis of 161 studies examining leadership acceleration programs showed that emphasizing the right practices boosts readiness by an average of 36 percent![ii] The key is the "right practices." That should not be taken to mean the "same practices" in each organization.

It would be a mistake for us to convey that acceleration is yet another new program in a world where too many already exist. It is not. *Acceleration* refers to the organizational effort to make leadership grow more rapidly, and the six Acceleration Imperatives are the categories of tactics to make that happen. Acceleration does not replace your talent-management or succession-management systems; it energizes them to maximize the velocity of growth and readiness for the future. Table 1.1 shows the key systems and processes that can be adjusted to enhance leadership growth. A brief scan shows that acceleration is not a cookie-cutter program or step-by-step recipe book.

What is acceleration, and how does it fit in a talent-management system?

Talent management refers to all organizational systems aimed at securing the talent needed to achieve business objectives. It encompasses all aspects of the employee life cycle, including recruitment, selection, performance management, assessment, development, succession planning, and career planning. Throughout this book we use the terms *Talent Management* and *Human Resources* interchangeably when referring to the department or function responsible for acceleration, assuming that both refer to the organization's collective effort to ensure that it acquires, develops, and retains the talent it needs.

Succession management describes the talent-management efforts aimed specifically at ensuring a steady supply of leaders who have been prepared for and are ready to take on critical business-leadership assignments. The principal outcomes of great succession management are a) the consistent, timely promotion of internal associates to open leadership positions, and b) their successful performance once in those roles. More leaders, *ready now*. There are two primary forms of succession management: *replacement planning* and the *Acceleration Pool approach*.

[continued at top of next page]

4

[continued from previous page]

Replacement planning is the process of identifying executives capable of filling critical roles—those that simply cannot be left vacant for any length of time—should any incumbents vacate their positions through retirement, departure, or job change. While replacement planning is essential as a component of a full-fledged succession-management system, taken alone it predictably falls short of generating a sufficient number of qualified leaders for today's more dynamic business environment.

The **Acceleration Pool approach** is the subject of our book, *Grow Your Own Leaders* (2002). In it, we set forth best practices for focusing on identifying high-potential leaders early in their careers and accelerating their growth toward general executive capabilities (i.e., without a specific position or functional destination in mind) to create a pool of agile leaders who are available and *ready now* for key posts when vacancies occur. The Acceleration Pool approach maintains the ability to secure replacements for key positions but provides organizations with more leadership agility by starting earlier, casting a wider net to identify hidden potential, and cultivating a larger supply of leaders who can step into more than one type of executive role.

We do not view the replacement-planning and Acceleration Pool approaches as *either-or* alternatives. Some crucial roles require clear, focused replacement approaches. But replacement planning alone cannot meet most organizations' broader needs. Effective succession management requires both. Acceleration is the organizational discipline of making growth happen faster, and as such, it goes beyond replacement planning and Acceleration Pools.

1.1 Table

The Acceleration Imperatives and Key Systems Associated with Each

Acceleration Imperatives	Key Systems and Activities
Commit *Adopt acceleration as a business priority* Chapters 1–2	**Acceleration Strategy** • Align talent needs with business and culture strategies. • Specify the highest-priority leadership growth initiatives and outcomes. • Complete Leadership Capacity Analysis to strengthen the business case for talent growth. • Determine short- and long-term talent system priorities (i.e., how capacity gaps will be addressed).
Aim *Define leadership success for your business context* Chapter 3	**Success Profiles** • Align competencies to the few leadership challenges that are most central to business success. This provides the business foundation for a success profile. • Align success profiles across all leadership levels, illustrating key transitional challenges. • Articulate knowledge, experiences, competencies, and personal attributes needed at each level of leadership.
Identify *Make efficient, accurate decisions about whom to accelerate* Chapter 4	**Talent Review (Identifying Potential)** • Efficiently review performance and growth of critical positions, units, or groups of leaders against business needs. • Accurately identify high-potential leaders. • Determine whom to accelerate and how.
Assess *Accurately evaluate readiness gaps and give great feedback* Chapters 5–6	**Assessment and Feedback** • Assess individual and group readiness for future leadership challenges. • Assess high-potential leaders and possible successors against critical positions, assignments, or levels. • Evaluate for Key Actions to enable precise, targeted development. • Gather analytics to objectively examine readiness against future business scenarios and common/critical leadership challenges. • Cultivate a dynamic, proactive feedback culture.
Grow *Make the right development happen* Chapters 7–11	**Development Solutions (Individual and Group)** • Secure a diverse array of development alternatives to support unique learning needs. • Align development solutions with both aggregate (business-level) needs and individual growth needs. • Foster the application and practice of leadership skill sets required for business success. • Make leadership development an ongoing process and blur the lines between learning anc performing.
Sustain *Aggressively manufacture the energy for growth* Chapter 12	**Measurement, Accountability, and Communication Tactics** • Ensure top-management modeling and active engagement in acceleration activities. • Drive global alignment and engagement. • Ensure system alignment and full accountability among senior management. • Secure skill-building opportunities for all process players.

The imperatives represent a lens through which any effort to grow leadership can be evaluated and enhanced, but they are most applicable where *speed* of growth is paramount. For that reason, most will find the imperatives particularly useful for succession, which directly addresses the urgency of an empty bench. And so, this book focuses primarily (but not exclusively) on succession management, discussing Acceleration Pools[SM] and replacement scenarios mainly to illustrate how the imperatives work. These imperatives also are highly beneficial to broader leadership-development efforts.

As you begin to prioritize your efforts to accelerate growth, you may target your succession-management process, key leadership-development initiatives, or your entire talent-management system. In any of these instances, it will be useful to consider the Acceleration Imperatives in terms of the impact each is intended to have and the talent systems that must be optimized to achieve it (see Table 1.1).

Whom Should You Accelerate?

Given that not everyone can (or wants to) be a leader, generating more *leaders ready now* requires you and your senior team to determine which individuals and groups will be the focus of your acceleration investments. Executives must make difficult choices about whom to accelerate and when. Some organizations struggle with this basic point of departure, maintaining that differential development is harmful to the culture because it excludes some people from participating. This point of view is a nonstarter, because acceleration is not an investment in the culture; it is an investment in the business.

> Acceleration is not an investment in the culture; it is an investment in the business.

Of course, acceleration can dramatically energize a culture, but that's not its principal purpose. As we mentioned at the outset, the goal of making more leaders *ready now* is most urgent for those businesses imperiled by inadequate or insufficient leadership. For that reason, the fear that a new system will

7

damage the culture must be answered with a clear business case and a strong communication plan to counter perceptions of exclusion. Later, we'll outline how to make that business case (Chapter 2) and how to make choices about whom to accelerate (Chapter 4) in a way that creates positive energy in the organization. Meanwhile, having gained a consensus that acceleration is a business necessity, you can anticipate at least some of the following general acceleration needs:

CEO and C-level acceleration: Naturally, having replacement plans in place for the CEO and members of the senior team is essential; nearly every organization with more than a handful of employees has considered the issue of succession, at least at the very top. But the replacement pool may be shallow, and again, the best way to ensure a strong succession plan is to set up an Acceleration Pool to develop and prepare potential replacements long before a position becomes vacant. Accelerating the growth of a small cadre of executives who can develop readiness for these critical roles is crucial to organizational stability and success.

Executive acceleration: The most common crisis that acceleration addresses is the absence of leaders capable of taking on executive-level roles. Because the responsibilities and required skills in these roles increase so dramatically, the transition represents one of the most significant and challenging jumps in the career of any leader. And because the feeder pool for these roles is often stocked with individuals several levels below the necessary levels of capability and experience, failure is common, heightening the need for effective acceleration.

Mid-level leader acceleration: Some organizations also create pools that prepare individual contributors and frontline leaders to fill mid-management roles, where much of the organization's execution energy resides and where many organizations have trouble building strength. Because population sizes are larger, these pools tend to be built and managed somewhat differently than executive-oriented pools, often with more cadre-based learning and growth options that equip leaders with core skills to apply to the challenges of mid-level leaders.

Global/Regional/Business unit acceleration: Multinational, multi-business, or multidivisional organizations often establish pools for each unit to meet the needs of the separate groups. In some instances these disparate pools are managed totally independently of one another; others build in review sessions to create insight into talent across boundaries and to find opportunities to share and grow leaders who have awareness and capability across the enterprise.

Critical role-acceleration efforts: Not all acceleration efforts should focus on traditional leadership roles. Many key positions are technical or functional in nature or require a unique brand of creativity or insight that gives the organization a competitive edge. These positions might require special project leaders or innovators of new concepts, products, or methods. They might have typical leadership responsibilities, or their leadership might be more nontraditional (such as thought leadership) or lateral. Acceleration efforts should target these roles as well and take a pool or individualized approach based on the nature of the role and size of the group. For example, one global social services organization established an Acceleration Pool for its Country Manager position. In another case, a technology firm cultivated the development of three high-potential players for the role of Product-Design Executive—a highly creative role without traditional leadership responsibility.

How Many People Can You Accelerate?

While the size of an Acceleration Pool or cadre of leaders should be proportional to the size of the resources available to develop the group's members, that doesn't mean that acceleration is for only a chosen few. We once received a call from an enthusiastic HR leader in a large professional-services firm, proclaiming that the firm had just accomplished something unprecedented: Senior management had assembled to review the firm's key talent and agreed

> While the size of an Acceleration Pool or cadre of leaders should be proportional to the size of the resources available to develop the group's members, that doesn't mean that acceleration is for only a chosen few.

on their highest-potential leaders. Seven senior leaders along with two HR leaders identified 250 individuals who would receive specialized development; recognition letters were sent to each person, welcoming the individual to this process. Indeed, those were big steps—yet, the top team failed to plan for what would happen next and didn't even commit to being involved in the development process.

Seven senior executives cannot make 250 leaders *ready now*, nor did this organization need them to. In fact, the organization was facing critical executive leadership needs for approximately 25 positions over the next three to five years. Only several were seen as prepared to step up, which meant that the firm needed to fill about 20 slots. The group of 250 was then stratified into those with the very highest potential (approximately 40) and the rest. Other top executives were asked to join the seven senior team members to support the acceleration of the 40, while the remaining 210 junior leaders participated in more scalable, group-level learning alternatives. All 250 were given development plans, but HR set out to develop the 40 highest-potential leaders far more directly. Their growth assignments aimed higher and pointed toward the urgent leadership needs inherent to the key executive roles. Over time, as leaders began to be promoted out of the pool, more and more of the 210 were brought into the more-focused acceleration process.

There is no magic number or formula for how many people you should identify for acceleration. It depends on the size of your leadership gap and the resources you plan to devote to closing it. (In Chapter 2 we outline how to quantify your gap.) A key point, however, is that converting leaders from *not ready* to *ready now* takes considerable support—much more than simply ensuring that leaders have development plans. The key is to analyze both your resources and acceleration needs to determine ideal pool sizes and stratifications based on the precise gaps you need to close.[iii]

Acceleration: Who Is Responsible for What?

We often hear phrases like, *"You have to own your development"* and *"Ultimately, growth is up to the individual."* And surely, little can happen without the buy-in of the person being developed. But acceleration cannot and will not occur if individuals are left to drive their own growth. To repeat our definition, *acceleration is the organizational discipline of making growth happen faster*. While easy to understand in concept, acceleration does require coordinated effort to ensure that the right growth happens for the right leaders at the right times; therefore, it is a shared responsibility. Top management, the Talent Management function, and individual learners—along with the key players listed in Figure 1.1—all must share in the commitment to acceleration:

> Little can happen without the buy-in of the person being developed. But acceleration cannot and will not occur if individuals are left to drive their own growth.

CEO/President/Business leader: Principal champion and advocate for acceleration.

Senior management team: The group of business leaders (typically reporting to the CEO or business head) who assume responsibility for acceleration and play direct roles in executing various elements of the process.

Talent Management (HR): Designer and facilitator of the acceleration system, providing strategy, tools, roles, and processes for ensuring sustainable progress and measurable outcomes.

Accelerated learners: Acceleration is not focused solely on high-potential leaders. While high-potentials may be the best example of accelerated learners, they are far from the only ones. Acceleration can and should apply to everyone in the organization, but the manner in which it is applied varies significantly and is determined by the organization's investment strategy (see Section III: Identify).

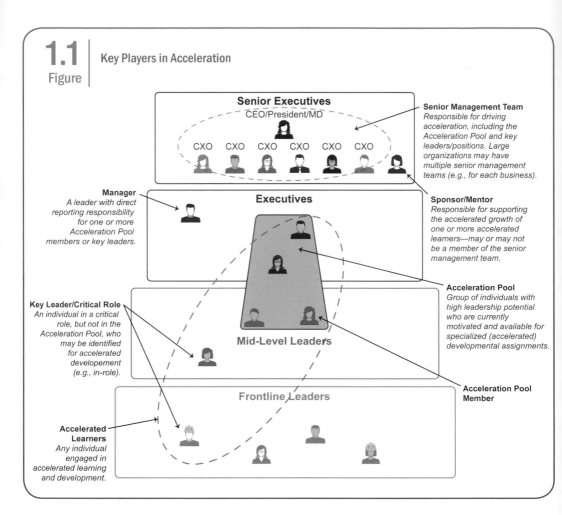

1.1 **Figure** | Key Players in Acceleration

Senior Executives
CEO/President/MD

CXO   CXO   CXO   CXO   CXO   CXO

Senior Management Team
Responsible for driving acceleration, including the Acceleration Pool and key leaders/positions. Large organizations may have multiple senior management teams (e.g., for each business).

Manager
A leader with direct reporting responsibility for one or more Acceleration Pool members or key leaders.

Executives

Sponsor/Mentor
Responsible for supporting the accelerated growth of one or more accelerated learners—may or may not be a member of the senior management team.

Key Leader/Critical Role
An individual in a critical role, but not in the Acceleration Pool, who may be identified for accelerated developement (e.g., in-role).

Acceleration Pool
Group of individuals with high leadership potential who are currently motivated and available for specialized (accelerated) developmental assignments.

Mid-Level Leaders

Acceleration Pool Member

Frontline Leaders

Accelerated Learners
Any individual engaged in accelerated learning and development.

The CEO's role: For an Acceleration Imperative to gain a strong foothold, the CEO must be the chief catalyst, establishing talent growth as a key topic on the executive agenda and ensuring that there is full commitment, alignment, and accountability among the top team. As the CEO, you must be the most vocal and visible champion, with the close help and partnership of Talent Management leaders. Many CEOs translate this as the need to advocate and support investment in talent initiatives, but that is only part of it: You also must be a strong manager of talent, taking personal action to build the strength of the senior team and other key leaders. This means playing an active role in identifying leaders with potential, reviewing assessments, evaluating job performance and development progress, and generating creative

> As the CEO, you must be the most vocal and visible champion, with the close help and partnership of Talent Management leaders. Many CEOs translate this as the need to advocate and support investment in talent initiatives, but that is only part of it.

development alternatives for senior team members and others.

The senior management team's role: The top team is responsible for the entire business, including allocating resources to accelerate the growth of leaders. If you are part of the C-suite, it is—or should be—in your job description to help review and approve the organization's talent strategy, participate in the talent-review process, identify critical positions and high-potential leaders, prescribe development solutions for key leaders, serve as a mentor or coach, and act as a model of personal development by executing your personal development plan. Like the CEO, you play a role in both advocating and sponsoring accelerated growth as well as having personal responsibility as a talent manager who is deeply involved in the growth and development of the organization's most critical and high-potential leaders.

The Talent Management (HR) role: For HR leaders tasked with ensuring that growth happens quickly, being provocative is more important than being popular: The relationship between talent growth and business success is not self-evident to all leaders, and it is your job to make and sustain the connection. This starts with a compelling business case for growing leadership capability, including the business consequences of doing nothing, and facilitating your organization's response to this business need in the form of a straightforward talent strategy that clearly articulates both your talent priorities and the initiatives that will be executed to meet them. With a strategy in place, your role then is to design the processes, build or acquire tools and technology,

> For HR leaders tasked with ensuring that growth happens quickly, being provocative is more important than being popular.

facilitate the key activities that the processes require, and ensure that all stakeholders understand and are equipped to fulfill their roles along the way. Indeed, the entirety of this book is a guide for you, the Talent Management leader, in your journey to answer this call.

The accelerated learner's role: The efforts of the CEO, top management, and HR all point to enabling individual leaders to engage in high-energy learning opportunities and walk away from them more prepared for the next leadership challenge. From that perspective the individual leader's role is simple: *to learn*. But being invited to learn has a decidedly different ring than being invited to *learn faster*. Learning faster means more

> Being invited to learn has a decidedly different ring than being invited to *learn faster.*

than participating in a seminar or attending a leadership-training course—it means taking on new, unfamiliar leadership assignments in order to cultivate new skills. For many, stretch assignments feel exhilarating; others find them terrifying. Delight or fear notwithstanding, the individual leader's role is to step up and take on new challenges and, while doing so, seek feedback and prepare to be confronted with the inadequacy of past approaches. While leveraging the insight gained from formal learning opportunities as well as from coaches and mentors, individual leaders must continually reinvent their leadership approaches to adjust for more complex and difficult scenarios. This requires openness and a sense of adventure along with humility and respect for the learning process. Finally, learning faster means embracing discipline. Setting specific, measurable development targets that fully capture one's unique growth needs requires rigor and courage; achieving them requires perseverance and no small amount of support. So, while the individual leader's role may be the simplest to understand, it also is the most difficult to achieve.

The Acceleration Credo

When committing to the journey of acceleration, a shared sense of purpose and a clear understanding of the implications help keep your communications clear and consistent and your progress free of confusion or dissent. The Acceleration Credo (see sidebar) summarizes the most fundamental assumptions that top management must share. Why have a credo? Because we find that some of the most important and foundational beliefs about leadership growth are frequently not foregone conclusions among senior leaders, and the potential differences in philosophy can (and often do) cause system breakdowns. This makes it all the more important to surface and confirm the basics. The Acceleration Credo rallies your top team around the fact that accelerated growth is possible, essential, beneficial, and a senior management responsibility. This unified point of departure enables clear communications, ensures perceptions of fairness, sustains progress, and ultimately helps to cultivate a healthy culture of learning and growth.

> Some of the most important and foundational beliefs about leadership growth are frequently *not* foregone conclusions among senior leaders.

The Acceleration Credo

*We (the senior management team) believe that **accelerated growth is:***

- **Vital to the business.** *It is a business necessity to grow leadership capability from within the organization, and we assume accountability for ensuring that growth happens—faster.*

- **Possible.** *We can positively alter the organization's leadership readiness by investing in the accelerated development of our people.*

- **Both a right and a responsibility.** *Everyone in the organization deserves the opportunity and must accept the responsibility to grow professionally.*

- **Not a democracy.** *Because resources are limited and needs are urgent, not everyone can or should be developed at the same rate or by the same means. Some will develop in place, while others will be offered special development to capitalize on opportunities to fill critical leadership needs.*

- **More than knowing who our best people are.** *It is not enough to retain our key players—we must grow new capabilities and equip leaders to succeed in assignments they have not yet encountered.*

1.1 Appendix | Acceleration at a Glance

Acceleration Imperative	CEO	Who Does What[1]		Individual Leader (High Po)
		Senior Management Team (SMT)	Talent Management (HR)	
Commit — Adopt acceleration as a business priority (Chapters 1–2)	• Establish importance of accelerated talent growth to the business. • Clarify expectations of all leaders with respect to talent management. • Charter the senior management team's role in the acceleration process.	• Discuss and agree on talent needed to execute business strategy. • Agree on SMT member accountabilities. • Agree on measures of success in talent management.	• Build a provocative business case for acceleration. • Facilitate development of a talent strategy. • Ensure that outcomes are measurable. • Establish routine for progress evaluations. • Ensure role clarity among all stakeholders.	N/A
Aim — Define leadership success for your business context (Chapter 3)	• Share insights on leadership needed to drive business and cultural success. • Ensure input from all appropriate senior leaders.	• Share insights on leadership needed to drive business and cultural success. • Review and approve final profiles.	• Facilitate development of success profiles for all levels of leadership. • Ensure stakeholder input, business relevance, and research foundations.	• Share insights on leadership needed to drive business and cultural success.
Identify — Make efficient, accurate decisions about whom to accelerate (Chapter 4)	• Champion the need to identify leadership potential. • Ensure that senior leaders adopt enterprise view. • Support use of objective data to support process.	• Prioritize organizational talent over unit-level talent. • Review and evaluate leaders with rigor and objectivity. • Support judgments with behaviors and examples.	• Design and facilitate rigorous processes. • Ensure use of objective data to support judgments. • Ensure focus on potential and growth, not only performance and results.	• Share personal motivations regarding development, advancement, and leadership.

1 Note that not every role is addressed in this table. Roles of managers (to whom high potentials report), mentors, executive coaches, and other key stakeholders are discussed in the specific chapters referenced for each mandate in the Acceleration Imperative.

1.1 Appendix | Acceleration at a Glance *(cont'd)*

Acceleration Imperative	Who Does What[2]			
	CEO	Senior Management Team (SMT)	Talent Management (HR)	Individual Leader (High Po)
Assess Accurately evaluate readiness gaps and give great feedback — Chapters 5–6	• Champion use of high-quality assessments to enhance placement and development decisions. • Support and become familiar with objective, valid readiness assessments for key leaders.	• Support and become familiar with objective, valid readiness assessments for key leaders. • Leverage assessment to enhance selection, succession, and development.	• Ensure valid assessment systems for all critical positions, assignments, and role levels. • Drive common application and high-integrity use of assessment to improve decision making.	• Step up to objective assessment to identify personal strengths and growth needs. • Invite feedback to understand growth opportunities. • Provide thoughtful and accurate self-evaluation.
Grow Make the right development happen — Chapters 7–11	• Ensure sufficient organizational resources to support development. • Hold senior management accountable for talent growth. • Devote personal time to catalyzing growth of key leaders and senior team.	• Support investments in development. • Devote personal time to catalyzing growth of key leaders and/or groups. • Be accountable for talent growth. • Apply creativity and risk in generating high-value learning opportunities for key leaders.	• Assemble diverse development alternatives to support unique learning needs. • Ensure role clarity and support for development. • Cultivate executives as mentors to enhance impact and business relevance of learning.	• Commit time and energy to growth opportunities. • Take on "stretch" assignments to cultivate new skills. • Seek feedback and input from colleagues and mentors to improve approaches.

2 Note that not every role is addressed in this table. Roles of managers (to whom high potentials report), mentors, executive coaches, and other key stakeholders are discussed in the specific chapters referenced for each mandate in the Acceleration Imperative.

1.1 Appendix | Acceleration at a Glance *(cont'd)*

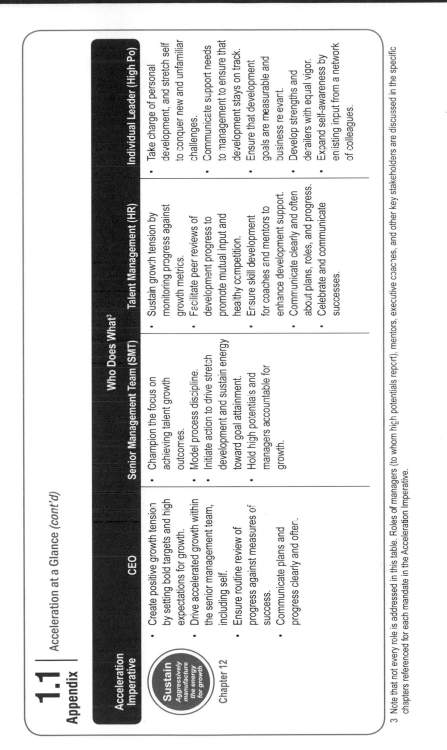

Acceleration Imperative	Who Does What[3]			
	CEO	Senior Management Team (SMT)	Talent Management (HR)	Individual Leader (High Po)
Sustain *Aggressively manufacture the energy for growth* Chapter 12	• Create positive growth tension by setting bold targets and high expectations for growth. • Drive accelerated growth within the senior management team, including self. • Ensure routine review of progress against measures of success. • Communicate plans and progress clearly and often.	• Champion the focus on achieving talent growth outcomes. • Model process discipline. • Initiate action to drive stretch development and sustain energy toward goal attainment. • Hold high potentials and managers accountable for growth.	• Sustain growth tension by monitoring progress against growth metrics. • Facilitate peer reviews of development progress to promote mutual input and healthy competition. • Ensure skill development for coaches and mentors to enhance development support. • Communicate clearly and often about plans, roles, and progress. • Celebrate and communicate successes.	• Take charge of personal development, and stretch self to conquer new and unfamiliar challenges. • Communicate support needs to management to ensure that development stays on track. • Ensure that development goals are measurable and business relevant. • Develop strengths and derailers with equal vigor. • Expand self-awareness by enlisting input from a network of colleagues.

3 Note that not every role is addressed in this table. Roles of managers (to whom high potentials report), mentors, executive coaches, and other key stakeholders are discussed in the specific chapters referenced for each mandate in the Acceleration Imperative.

MAKE GROWTH MATTER

2 | Elevating Acceleration to a Top Business Priority

Astrategy is not the game itself. It is a plan for how to win it. Call it a road map, blueprint, outline, or whatever term works in your context; but, like the rudder on a boat, a leadership-acceleration strategy that is embraced and operated by you and your senior management team will steer your actions and the actions of your highest-potential players, their managers, your HR function, and your entire organization. It's not rocket science, but if you try to operate without a strategy or with an incomplete one, expect mediocrity.

> As a senior management team, it won't be enough for you to sanction learning and development activities and then watch from the sidelines. You need to get into the game.

Acceleration is a discipline—a way of operating that makes your talent-management systems work better and faster by getting more people in the game, earlier in their careers, with the learning and guidance they need to develop the capabilities that your business needs. It's more than simply helping people learn. It's helping them *grow* by applying what they've learned to the problems your business is facing. There's a big difference. As a senior management team, it won't be enough for you to sanction learning and development activities and then watch from the sidelines. *You* need to get into the game. And so it requires that you *commit* to a plan for acceleration and manage it as a priority equal to your other top business objectives.

Committing to a leadership-acceleration strategy means securing five components of a plan, around which your senior management team must be fully aligned:

1. **Leadership Priorities (Business Drivers):** When we say *Business Drivers,* we don't mean the external forces that affect your business; we mean the *leadership* hurdles or challenges that must be overcome to grow your business and build a healthy culture (i.e., drive the business). Because focus is so crucial, it is essential to isolate the three or four most critical challenges that leaders must meet to execute your organization's strategic and cultural priorities. These are your leadership priorities (Business Drivers), and as we illustrate below, they are fundamental to an acceleration strategy.

2. **Leadership Capacity Gap(s):** Simply knowing that you need more leaders is not enough. You'll need to specify precisely where you need them (e.g., levels, positions, units, regions), how many you'll need, and when they will need to be ready. This is your business case for acceleration. You will refer to it constantly and update it continually.

3. **Growth Engine:** Based on your leadership priorities and gaps, you will make choices about which programs and initiatives to build or improve upon so that you can stock and grow your pipeline of leaders. These choices include how to identify leadership potential, assess readiness, accelerate growth, and drive performance.

4. **Acceleration Dashboard:** As with any key strategic objective, you need a clear means of charting progress. You won't be able to measure everything, so choose the few make-or-break metrics that most readily demonstrate that

22

growth is happening. Find a way to display and discuss them regularly. Do not skip this.

5. **Sustainability Tactics:** This is the Achilles' heel of so many systems. Don't start without a few tactics that strengthen communications, align efforts, build skills, clarify accountabilities, and measure progress. Together, these tactics ensure that the strategy has a practical routine that fits your business routine, continuously improves, and delivers on its promise to strengthen your leaders' capability.

While it is not senior management's role to execute each of these components, you do need to come together to chart a course that prioritizes efforts. If you're concerned that a focus on acceleration might result in too much time spent discussing leadership and not enough on your core business, you might consider putting this book down now. Acceleration definitely will result in more time spent on leadership. But that does not mean adding more hours to your day. A good acceleration strategy integrates your leadership priorities with your strategic priorities so that they can be addressed together. This chapter describes how to make that happen.[1]

1. Isolate Your Top Leadership Priorities (Business Drivers)

The most successful business strategies identify the few most-critical priorities and relentlessly pursue them. But somehow, leadership strategies don't seem to receive the same rigor. Focus is the issue. Many organizations struggle to clarify the few leadership priorities that arise from the business strategy, but pinpointing them is at the foundation of effective acceleration. We refer to these leadership priorities as

> The most successful business strategies identify the few most-critical priorities and relentlessly pursue them. But somehow, leadership strategies don't seem to receive the same rigor.

---

1 If you think you may already have this aspect of your acceleration system well in hand, the checklist in Appendix 2.1 can help you quickly evaluate the strength of your acceleration strategy and identify opportunities for enhancement.

Business Drivers. They are the few (no more than four) challenges that an organization's leaders must conquer in order to *drive the business* forward.

Business Drivers simplify and strengthen the connection between leadership and business success. For every business strategy, changes and improvements in the organization are needed, and these changes naturally require leadership. But the type of leadership needed varies with the nature of the effort. *Dominate the market in Southeast Asia. Become the highest-quality player in a segment. Beat the competition to developing economies.* And so on. Every business strategy is different, and each interacts with the organizational culture in distinct ways, placing unique requirements on leaders and creating a specific leadership *context*.

The traditional manner in which HR has defined these unique requirements (contexts) has been with competencies. While competencies are absolutely a key component of a great talent-management system, the comprehensive lists of competencies are usually too long and detailed to be useful within boardroom conversations about talent. In response, many organizations seek to reduce the list of competencies to a select few, but this leaves critical skills unaddressed and reduces the competency model's utility for feedback and development.

So, what to do? How can we articulate an organization's unique leadership context—both business and cultural aspects—without creating a list of variables that is too long for practical use? The answer: Business Drivers. Or, if you prefer, Leadership Priorities or any other term that suits your lexicon. Regardless of the name, they are the few broad leadership hurdles that an organization must clear to execute its strategy. Examples include *Drive Efficiency, Launch New Products, Execute a Competitive Strategy,* and many others. Note that these are not business strategies; they are the leadership challenges that arise from the business strategy. Each Business Driver requires multiple competencies for success, which means that competencies can and should be connected to Business Drivers but need not be the primary descriptors. In Chapter 3 we share more detail about Business Drivers, how to identify and define them, and how to connect your competencies and success profiles to them.

2.1 Table
How Business Drivers Simplify the Connection Between Leadership and Strategy

STRATEGIC PRIORITIES	CULTURAL PRIORITIES (VALUES)	BUSINESS DRIVERS	COMPETENCIES
Company Q will be the low-cost provider of high-quality products across the world by executing these **strategic priorities**…	…while modeling the core values that define our **culture**…	Therefore, our leaders must be prepared to step up to these **key leadership challenges**…	…by drawing on these key **competencies:**
• Continue to aggressively penetrate existing markets where we dominate. • Relentlessly pursue new ways to operate more efficiently and reduce cost. • Make the transition from regional/local operations to global operations. • Maximize market share in select emerging markets.	Innovation Integrity Reliability Service Teamwork	**Drive Process Innovation:** Create systems and processes and make decisions that effectively use organizational resources and enhance operational efficiency.	• Establishing Strategic Direction • Operational Decision Making • Empowerment/ Delegation
		Execute a Competitive Strategy: Lead and drive the execution of a customer-centered business strategy aimed at realizing Company Q's competitive advantage and brand promise as lowest-cost provider of high-quality products.	• Entrepreneurship • Driving Execution • Business Savvy • Influence
		Create a High-Performance Culture: Develop an organizational culture that leads to ongoing excellence and effective growth of the business while maintaining the highest integrity.	• Building Organizational Talent • Passion for Results • Coaching and Developing Others

For now, we'll focus on how Business Drivers can make your leadership-acceleration strategy clearer and more compelling. Table 2.1 shows how one large consumer products organization did it. After defining strategic and cultural priorities in columns 1 and 2, it specified the high-level leadership needs (Business Drivers) in column 3 and the competencies in column 4. At a glance, one can clearly see the connections between this organization's business and cultural priorities and the leadership capabilities it needed to achieve them.

Clearly, the consumer products company in Table 2.1 is aiming to grow leadership to accomplish three primary objectives: Drive Process Innovation, Execute a Competitive Strategy, and Create a High-Performance Culture. Referring to the strategic talent need by discussing only these three Business Drivers, as opposed to 10 or more competencies, presents an immediate economy of language. The other advantage is that the Business Drivers speak more to leadership *context* than the characteristics of leaders, which is how business leaders naturally think and speak. Your acceleration strategy is your plan for getting more leaders ready. Business Drivers provide a clear, concise answer to the question, *"Ready for what?"*

2. Size Your Leadership Capacity Gap(s)

> This facet of your strategy crystallizes the business case for acceleration by being brutally honest and specific.

With your leadership priorities defined, the next task is to get specific about what you currently have in terms of leadership talent, precisely what you will need, and exactly where it will be needed in the organization. This facet of your strategy crystallizes the business case for acceleration by being brutally honest and specific about where the organization stands now with respect to talent and illustrating what will happen if no new action is taken.

Start by clarifying the factors that affect the supply of and demand for talent in your organization:

Capacity projections: Given your strategic priorities, Business Drivers, and critical roles, how do the current supply and quality of leadership stack up? For example, how many new sales leaders will be required to drive the global launch of a new blockbuster drug? Are you growing or downsizing certain businesses? Are you creating differential focus in emergent markets or other geographies? If so, do you need to ramp up staff in new markets?

People trends: What are the external and internal trends influencing your organization's supply of leaders? For example, demographic trends may include an aging population approaching retirement, the need for greater ethnic and gender diversity, turnover risk, differences in ability to attract and retain talent in different geographies, and unique issues associated with new expectations from emerging generations.

Organizational situation: What is the current maturity of Talent Management (HR) within your organization? Is there clear ownership of and support at the top? What people systems (recruiting, selection, development, performance management, compensation) are currently working, or not? What is the strength of the current HR team to build a case for, and then execute, a new strategy? Are they seen as credible by the senior executives they must challenge and influence?

Critical roles: What are the critical roles or positions commonly regarded as essential to strategic execution and that have unique impact on an organization's most fundamental sources of value? For example, a global retail company may view the position of store manager as one of the most pivotal roles in executing the strategies formulated at the corporate level. A manufacturing company might perceive the role of product manager as similarly consequential. While each organization must carefully examine its own roles and determine the factors that define *critical,* the primary considerations include:

- Impact on core business outcomes: revenue, profit, quality, customer satisfaction, etc.

- Impact on major business priorities or strategic initiatives.

- Unique or specialized skill sets that make it difficult to find candidates or replace incumbents.

- Large/Wide span of influence, affecting large employee populations and the organization's culture.

- Expected increase in demand for the role due to growth, expansion, or shifting priorities.

Critical roles have uniquely high impact on the variability of organizational performance, which means that defining them is essential in prioritizing leadership capacity needs and in making decisions regarding talent deployment and development.

Leadership needs by level: Every organization has its own leadership pipeline through which individuals progress as they climb the ladder or traverse the organization laterally. As roles and responsibilities increase in complexity from individual contributor on up to CEO, there are common transition points at which role requirements increase. This makes it particularly important (and difficult) to ensure a steady supply of ready-now leaders for those transitions and to include these segments of the organization in the leadership capacity calculation. Through job analyses we have found that there are typically three to four major leadership transitions in an organization's pipeline.

Some organizations employ as many as seven or eight levels; however, with regard to leadership growth strategies, we have seen more success with flatter hierarchies consisting of four to five levels (e.g., C-suite, strategic leaders, operational leaders, people leaders, individual contributors). This is a simpler framework that more clearly depicts the most challenging transitions as leaders progress. Figure 2.1 shows a common example of how leadership levels (transitions) are defined.

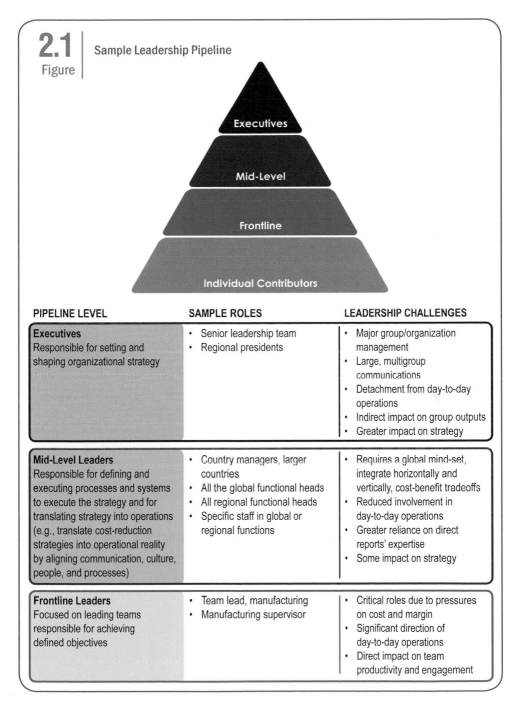

2.1 Figure   Sample Leadership Pipeline

PIPELINE LEVEL	SAMPLE ROLES	LEADERSHIP CHALLENGES
Executives Responsible for setting and shaping organizational strategy	• Senior leadership team • Regional presidents	• Major group/organization management • Large, multigroup communications • Detachment from day-to-day operations • Indirect impact on group outputs • Greater impact on strategy
Mid-Level Leaders Responsible for defining and executing processes and systems to execute the strategy and for translating strategy into operations (e.g., translate cost-reduction strategies into operational reality by aligning communication, culture, people, and processes)	• Country managers, larger countries • All the global functional heads • All regional functional heads • Specific staff in global or regional functions	• Requires a global mind-set, integrate horizontally and vertically, cost-benefit tradeoffs • Reduced involvement in day-to-day operations • Greater reliance on direct reports' expertise • Some impact on strategy
Frontline Leaders Focused on leading teams responsible for achieving defined objectives	• Team lead, manufacturing • Manufacturing supervisor	• Critical roles due to pressures on cost and margin • Significant direction of day-to-day operations • Direct impact on team productivity and engagement

2.2 | How to Calculate Your Leadership Capacity Gap
Figure |

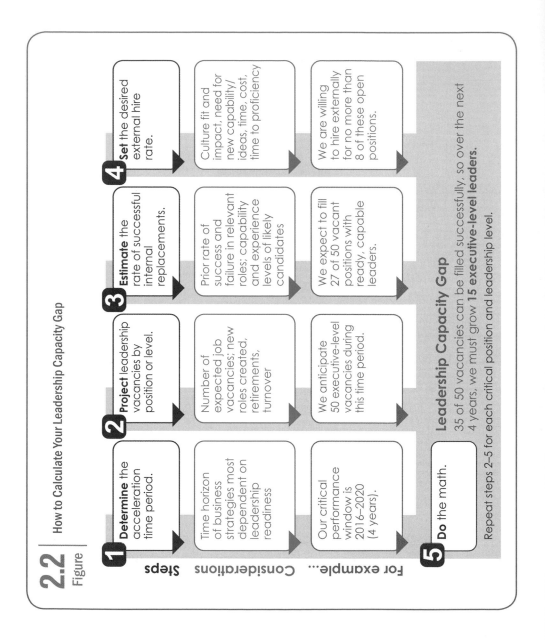

Steps

1 **Determine** the acceleration time period.

2 **Project** leadership vacancies by position or level.

3 **Estimate** the rate of successful internal replacements.

4 **Set** the desired external hire rate.

Considerations

Time horizon of business strategies most dependent on leadership readiness

Number of expected job vacancies; new roles created, retirements, turnover

Prior rate of success and failure in relevant roles; capability and experience levels of likely candidates

Culture fit and impact, need for new capability/ideas, time, cost, time to proficiency

For example...

Our critical performance window is 2016–2020 (4 years).

We anticipate 50 executive-level vacancies during this time period.

We expect to fill 27 of 50 vacant positions with ready, capable leaders.

We are willing to hire externally for no more than 8 of these open positions.

5 **Do** the math.

Leadership Capacity Gap

35 of 50 vacancies can be filled successfully, so over the next 4 years, we must grow **15 executive-level leaders.**

Repeat steps 2–5 for each critical position and leadership level.

Capacity Gap: All of these inputs are considered in the calculation of your Leadership Capacity Gap. You can quantify your leadership gap by using a straightforward calculation

> A quantitative illustration of the talent need builds a far stronger business case for acceleration.

process like the one shown in Figure 2.2. More detailed guidance for using the calculator can be found in Appendix 2.2. Certainly, this is one of many forms that a capacity calculation might take. You may have experimented with your own, either informally or perhaps as part of more advanced workforce planning efforts. The core point is that a quantitative illustration of the talent need coupled with the qualitative illustration (Table 2.1) paints a vivid picture of what will happen if growth efforts fail, and it builds a far stronger business case for acceleration. Quantifying your company's leadership needs bolsters the business case for acceleration and informs how to equip the *growth engine* to ensure that the right systems and processes are in place.

3. Tune Your Growth Engine

Once you pinpoint the leadership gaps, your next step is to plan how to close them. This means building, adjusting, or replacing programs and initiatives aimed at growing leaders—*your growth engine.* The time horizon of your engine's impact should be aligned to the timing of your business objectives. We routinely see talent strategies that are rebuilt from year to year, while business objectives are rooted to much longer-term goals. Your plan should direct the people-related initiatives that help you achieve both your short- and long-term business goals and deliver outcomes in step with them. It also should outline the specific actions required, including prioritization of initiatives, timing, accountability, and defined milestones that require stakeholder involvement and/or communication.

Your growth engine should define both *what* will be among the talent initiatives and how those initiatives will be executed. It should address the following areas:

Success profile: At the center of the growth engine is the success profile, which articulates in detail what great leadership looks like at each level, stemming from the organization's Business Drivers. This includes the required *knowledge, experience, competencies,* and *personal attributes* (e.g., motivation, personality). In Chapter 3 we outline how to define and build success profiles that align the elements of the growth engine around a common business purpose and unique organizational context.

Filling the pipeline: This element includes approaches for external recruiting and selection as well as identification of high potentials who will receive differential focus and investment of time and resources to accelerate their development. Chapter 4 details approaches to your talent review that will produce a clearer view of your organization's leadership along with a larger pool of high-potential leaders who likely will grow quickly and succeed at higher levels.

Assessing readiness: This part of the game plan includes assessment methods that gauge the extent to which individuals are *ready* to make the jump to the next level of leadership and isolates the top development priorities that will accelerate their growth. Assessment mitigates the risk of big development assignments and helps to determine which specific development approaches (e.g., executive coaching, formal learning, assignments) will be most useful. Chapter 5 provides details on how to optimize your assessment systems for acceleration.

Accelerating growth: What are the best approaches for developing talent to enhance their performance in current positions along with their readiness to move to the next level? Processes should be crafted to meet people's various learning needs as well as the expectations of associates and leaders at different levels in the pipeline. In addition, development strategies should be defined at both the individual and cadre level, and they should encompass formal training and other approaches—including action learning, learning journeys, and peer/executive coaching. Best practices for determining ideal development strategies are described in Chapters 7–11.

Driving performance: This element of the growth engine is typically characterized by cascading performance management processes designed to connect individual and team goals to the organization's business goals (strategic priorities).

4. Build an Acceleration Dashboard

Having distilled your leadership priorities to the few drivers that will fuel business success, you will need a way to track progress. This is often where things get sticky. What you do next will differentiate lip service from meaningful action. It's one thing to talk about the leadership you need and another to display progress in actually achieving it. We have seen organizations conduct rigorous evaluations

> It's one thing to talk about the leadership you need and another to display progress in actually achieving it.

of their acceleration systems and make verbal commitments to faster growth, only to arrive at weak measures of system success that do nothing to create the energy and tension that are needed.

The experience of a financial services organization illustrates a classic mistake. It faced a desperate talent shortage in a business that was being positioned as the most likely source of near-term profit and, in fact, the potential savior of the whole company's future. The business model was promising, but the organization needed more leadership capability to make it work. After designing a highly accelerated leadership growth initiative, senior management landed on two metrics as key indicators of progress: 1) retention of key players, and 2) the creation of development plans for each person. While the business needed real growth, the senior management team made a commitment that fell far short of assuring it. There were no metrics associated with actual growth of leadership capabilities or increases in readiness. In less than two years, the business floundered, and management was forced to make a painful pivot, divesting major business entities and making significant personnel reductions.

Contrast this with a food services company that faced a similar business challenge—a market with excellent prospects for growth amid a devastating wave of leadership retirements. It too launched an aggressive acceleration program for a group of 35 high-potential leaders, but elected to track their progress in very different ways than the financial services organization. Senior management focused on six dashboard metrics:

Progress against development plans: It wasn't sufficient to have a development plan. Each plan was reviewed quarterly by management and evaluated for whether the agreed-upon objectives had been met and if further development was needed. Management then tracked the overall proportion of plans that showed progress versus those that did not.

Difficulty of development: Because less-experienced leaders needed to develop quickly, management knew that incremental steps would mean failure. Each development plan was reviewed for the extent to which it would stretch individuals' capabilities and result in important new capabilities that the business needed. Aggregate difficulty was shared on the dashboard.

Speed to completion of development plans: Plans were given a start date, and when objectives were completed, end dates were recorded. HR tracked completion times, which were discussed and evaluated in management review meetings. Over time, speed increased.

Business impact of development: As development plans were constructed, they were evaluated to determine the extent to which they would have positive impact on the business. Many plans that were initially crafted with retention or more general development were rebuilt and integrated into specific business initiatives. This meant that more was at stake, but also that more was to be gained if the plan succeeded.

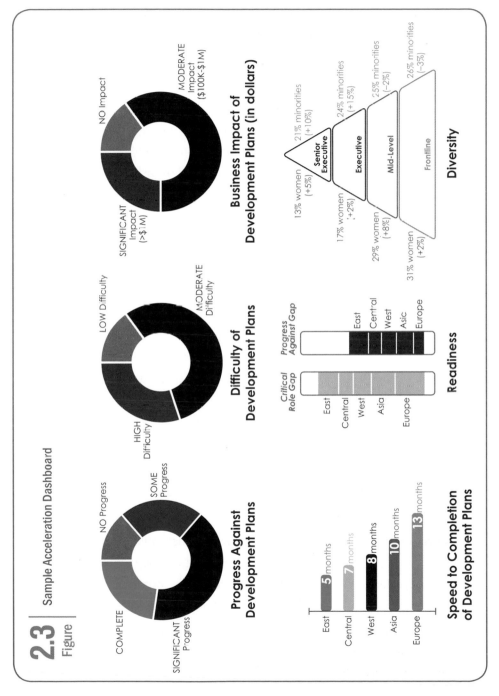

2.3 Figure | Sample Acceleration Dashboard

Progress Against Development Plans

NO Progress
SOME Progress
HIGH Difficulty
COMPLETE
SIGNIFICANT Progress

Difficulty of Development Plans

LOW Difficulty
MODERATE Difficulty

Business Impact of Development Plans (in dollars)

NO Impact
MODERATE Impact ($100K–$1M)
SIGNIFICANT Impact (>$1M)

Speed to Completion of Development Plans

East — 5 months
Central — 7 months
West — 8 months
Asia — 10 months
Europe — 13 months

Readiness

Critical Role Gap
East
Central
West
Asia
Europe

Progress Against Gap
East
Central
West
Asia
Europe

Diversity

Senior Executive — 21% minorities (+10%), 13% women (+5%)
Executive — 24% minorities (+15%), 17% women (+2%)
Mid-Level — 25% minorities (–2%), 29% women (+8%)
Frontline — 26% minorities (–3%), 31% women (+2%)

Readiness: Having quantified the Leadership Capacity Gap, senior management reviewed progress in closing it quarterly. As high-potential leaders completed their development plans and became more immersed in higher-level leadership assignments, management adjusted readiness levels, and overall leadership readiness was expressed relative to both critical roles and against the corporate gap. (See Figure 2.3.)

Diversity: As it did with readiness, senior management identified diversity targets and reviewed progress against them periodically to sustain focus on the objectives relating to gender, ethnicity, and technical/functional background. This data informed subsequent efforts to identify leadership potential and mined increased proportions of leaders from the underrepresented subgroups.

While other outcomes could be tracked on a dashboard (Appendix 2.3 lists other measures that are commonly employed as indicators of progress in acceleration), the food services organization began by articulating the specific outcomes that were highest priority and that demonstrated progress in accelerating growth and producing more readiness. And it worked. Two years following the launch of its initiative, the organization had secured ready replacements for more than 80 percent of its key positions, made significant gains against its diversity goals, and enjoyed steady business growth by successfully capitalizing on opportunities.

5. Build in Sustainability Tactics

Your acceleration strategy isn't complete until you know how you will stay focused on it and how you will avoid being seduced by the urgent at the expense of what is most important.

Align your leadership discussions with your business discussions. If your leadership-acceleration conversations are separated from your business discussions, they eventually will be edged out of mind entirely. Annual talent reviews almost certainly are not frequent enough. To sustain the focus on acceleration, leadership must be a routine topic in your discussions around strategy and business execution. Of course, each organization has its own approach to planning, and you likely have confronted the challenge of altering those processes. (Turning an aircraft carrier or moving a mountain might seem easier.) But in fact, the best approach

> If your leadership-acceleration conversations are separated from your business discussions, they eventually will be edged out of mind entirely.

is *not* to fundamentally change your strategic business-planning processes. Better to augment them with relevant conversations about talent.

A pharmaceutical corporation that sought to reinvent its focus on leadership made the following changes to its annual processes for discussing talent:

- At the start of each performance cycle, one-on-one expectation-setting conversations between business unit (BU) leaders and the CEO added a specific segment on leadership. The CEO and each BU leader agreed on the top leadership priorities and set specific goals for leadership growth, which then became part of monthly updates. Performance against these goals became a factor that influenced each BU leader's annual bonus.

- The strategic-planning process was augmented to include a specific goal-setting segment related to leadership growth. As priorities were finalized for each business unit, leadership needs were summarized as well. Overall corporate and business unit leadership requirements were then declared at the end of the strategic-planning session, resulting in both corporate and BU-level leadership growth goals for the coming year.

- Quarterly operational reviews (between the CEO and leadership team of each business unit) were adjusted to include progress updates on BU-level leadership growth targets as well as more in-depth updates on high-potential leaders receiving specialized (accelerated) development.

- An explicit discussion of the Leadership Capacity Gap (quantified) at the corporate and business unit levels as well as in relation to critical roles became part of the annual talent review. This included a review of progress against targets along with recommended adjustments to growth engine initiatives.

- The overall process for strategic-planning and business-operational reviews kept the same schedule and routine, but the discussion of talent became much more deeply integrated into those reviews. New strategies were considered at once with the leadership needed to execute them. If insufficient leadership was identified as a barrier, senior management set goals to close the gaps, which then became part of the business plan.

In this way this pharmaceutical company reshaped its conversations about leadership without having to dismantle its business processes. We revisit this topic in Chapter 4 when we discuss the talent review.

Communicate *why* **often.** Good talent initiatives clarify how all processes will be completed. Great talent management systems do so as well, but only after they communicate *why*. A well-designed learning program will be little more than an insomnia cure if it is presented without a compelling narrative about the reason for its existence. A strong communication strategy should create a persuasive case for acceleration and the initiatives undertaken to drive it as well as a story that links the importance of each initiative to business objectives.

> A well-designed learning program will be little more than an insomnia cure if it is presented without a compelling narrative about the reason for its existence.

For example, a long-tenured leader from a major automotive corporation appealed to his colleagues on the senior management team, *"If all our young leaders do is learn to imitate us, the future of this company is in big trouble."* He went on to make a case for how the prevailing approaches to leadership were precisely what was preventing the organization from achieving a competitive advantage. They, the senior management team, needed to find a way to encourage emerging leaders to become students of leadership and to outdo their predecessors by finding new, better ways to lead the corporation forward. This appeal served as a powerful platform on which to engage senior management and high-potential learners. It also connected the details and activities that were soon to come for all of them.

Hold one another accountable. As acceleration activities (e.g., talent reviews, assessments, development planning) unfold, it is not only acceptable, but essential for your senior management team to feel (and apply) some pressure within the group. Asking challenging questions of one another about whether progress is sufficient or appropriately targeted can fuel extra effort and create strong commitments to meeting goals and living up to accountabilities. Naturally, this must be espoused and modeled by the CEO, but it becomes self-sustaining as the group becomes more accustomed to holding one another to a high standard of excellence. Mutual tension in pursuit of growing talent benefits everyone in the organization, which serves to reinforce the healthy pressure that is applied to the system.

Build your skills as leaders of acceleration. As coaches and mentors, you will need to support the development of others. But very few senior leaders are naturally gifted in these areas.[i] There may need to be interventions to equip mentors, coaches, HR professionals, or others with the skills needed to support development efforts. These might include training around coaching others, building and monitoring development plans, and developing organizational talent. Also common is training for Human Resources to elevate its ability to be a strategic partner with business leaders. Much of this chapter informs how HR and talent management professionals can enhance their relevance and value to business partners who need their expert guidance to address crucial business needs.

Measure progress. Conventional wisdom says that "you can't manage what you don't measure." This is particularly true when elevating a leadership-acceleration strategy to a level equal to other business strategies. Measurement creates the focus, tension, and tangible objectives required to execute a talent strategy. The most effective measurements go beyond mere statistics to quantify what's working in talent management, why those initiatives are effective, and

2.4 | Leadership Acceleration Strategy Model
Figure

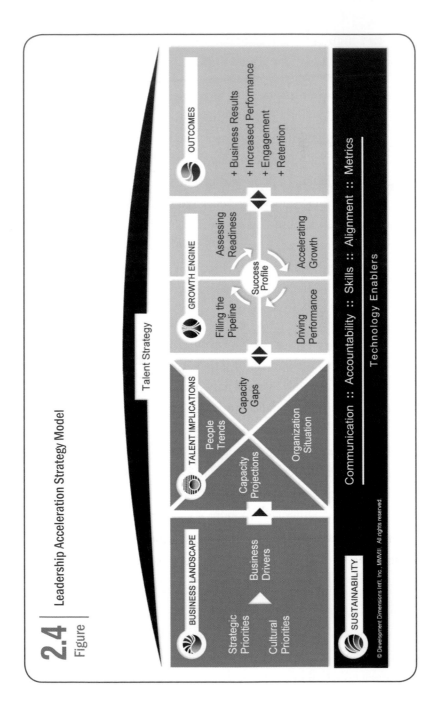

Talent Strategy

BUSINESS LANDSCAPE

Strategic Priorities

Cultural Priorities

▲ Business Drivers

TALENT IMPLICATIONS

People Trends

Capacity Projections

Capacity Gaps

Organization Situation

GROWTH ENGINE

Assessing Readiness

Filling the Pipeline

Success Profile

Accelerating Growth

Driving Performance

OUTCOMES

+ Business Results
+ Increased Performance
+ Engagement
+ Retention

SUSTAINABILITY

Communication :: Accountability :: Skills :: Alignment :: Metrics

Technology Enablers

what impact they are having on the organization. Many organizations include hard talent-management outcome metrics in their balanced scorecards and review these indicators at the C-suite and board levels. One interesting trend for many organizations is to consider metrics for longer-term strategies that span more than one year (e.g., 18 months, two years). Appendix 2.3 lists a series of common acceleration system metrics.

Leadership Acceleration Is a Business Priority

CEOs who achieve true success through the growth of people view talent management as a preoccupation. Organizations that employ the actions discussed in this chapter (and depicted in the Leadership Acceleration Strategy Model in Figure 2.4) are more effective in executing their development strategies and outperform organizations that fail to do so. With high-quality leaders these organizations are more than six times more likely to be top financial performers than organizations with weaker leaders.[ii] They are obsessed with talent metrics. They are

> With high-quality leaders these organizations are more than six times more likely to be top financial performers than organizations with weaker leaders.

in perpetual pursuit of ways to maneuver people, processes, and strategy to more quickly and comprehensively change the complexion of leadership in their organizations. They don't default to looking outside the organization to recruit new talent or to delegating the entire job to HR. They do so by adopting a strategy for how they will accelerate the growth of their own, and then elevating that strategy to a top business priority. Having outlined the basic structure for such a strategy, we now turn to the second Acceleration Imperative, Aim, which starts our journey into the realm of how to best define leadership success for your business context.

Appendix 2.1

Has your senior team committed to a leadership-acceleration strategy that will produce more leaders ready *now*? Check all that apply.

Leadership Priorities (Business Drivers)

☐ Our senior leadership team has clearly defined our top business priorities (strategic and cultural) and has identified the few most critical leadership challenges that will need to be conquered to meet them.

☐ Our senior leadership team has committed to being personally involved and accountable for the growth of leadership in our organization.

☐ Leadership requirements have been clearly and simply articulated in language that management can easily recognize and use over time.

Leadership Capacity Gap

☐ We have analyzed and clearly summarized the specific roles, units, and/or businesses where gaps in leadership capability exist.

☐ We have identified our most critical roles in the organization.

☐ We have specified both the quality and quantity of leadership needed, where we need it (e.g., units, roles, levels), and by when.

☐ We have a strong business case that articulates the business value gained from growing our leadership capability as well as the loss that results from doing nothing.

Growth Engine

☐ We have reviewed all of our talent initiatives (existing and planned) and determined the highest priorities relative to our business objectives.

☐ Our investments in talent initiatives are commensurate with our business and talent priorities.

☐ Our talent initiatives include effective efforts in all the following areas: identifying leadership potential, assessing readiness, accelerating growth, and ensuring performance.

☐ We have a clearly articulated leadership success profile that cascades across all levels and is tied directly to the most critical leadership needs identified by our senior team.

Acceleration Dashboard

☐ We have identified the most important outcomes of success in our talent-management system, and we are able to gather the data and information needed to track them.

☐ We visually display and routinely review progress against our top leadership growth targets.

☐ Our talent growth metrics are directly tied to our business objectives.

Sustainability

☐ Our discussions of leadership growth are integrated with our business reviews.

☐ There is energy and tension that pushes management to focus on leadership growth.

☐ Senior management team members hold each other accountable for accelerated growth.

☐ The communications around acceleration are clear and compel people to action.

☐ Our technology is sufficient to support the talent growth we need.

Appendix 2.2

Guidelines for Calculating the Leadership Capacity Gap

The following provides additional detail on the Leadership Capacity calculator (Figure 2.2):

Target leadership levels and/or critical roles: Start by isolating the segments of the organization in which a shortfall in leadership would be most consequential. For most organizations this means key *levels* of leadership at which significant increases in responsibility (transitions) occur and *critical roles* that require high levels of experience and capability and/or have uniquely high impact on organizational success. It will be important to calculate the gaps for each level and role.

Acceleration time period: Select the desired time period for which projections will be made. This likely will be dictated by top business priorities and their respective time horizons (two to four years is typical).

Preliminary leadership vacancies: For each level and critical role, list the current and planned head count as well as the gap between the two. If exact numbers for planned head count have not been determined, estimate them. You may wish to consider people trends, such as future skill demands, or organizational situation variables like velocity of growth, pending acquisitions, market shifts, and so on. The goal is to arrive at a sound estimate of the number of vacancies in key roles that will occur because of changes or growth in the organization. Then, for each level and critical role, estimate the number of role vacancies that will be added due to promotion, retirement, and resignation/ termination or unexpected turnover rates.

Estimate the internal replacement rate: Consider the organization's historical rate of filling key roles through successful internal promotions, and project the expected rate for the relevant time period (assuming that rate continues). Again, if this data is not known, estimate or adjust historical rates based on what is known about the talent that will be available for key levels and roles in the relevant time period.

Set the external hiring rate: Specify the proportion of vacant positions that will be filled through external hiring. Depending on your organization's business and cultural priorities, you may be more or less willing to increase the rate of external hiring to close the leadership gap. Understand, however, that these approaches have far higher risk to both business performance and cultural acceptance. High rates of external hiring can demotivate aspiring leaders.

Additional talent needed: The result of all these estimates, which should be repeated for each critical role and key job level, is a specific number of positions that will be unfilled unless the organization can accelerate the growth of internal associates to help them become ready now more quickly. This adds powerful clarity to the business case for acceleration and helps to establish more concrete metrics against which progress can be tracked.

Appendix 2.3

Sample Acceleration System Measures

Lead (process) Measures

- Talent reviews completed.
- High-potential leaders identified.
- Individual readiness assessments completed.
- Learning courses, events, processes conducted.
- Reactions to acceleration programs/processes (assessment, development, etc.).
  - Accelerated learners
  - Managers/Mentors
  - Senior management team
  - Talent management
- Development plans established.
- Development plans completed.
- Speed of development plan completion.
- Number of development plans completed—by mentor/sponsor.
- Average speed and business impact of development—by mentor/sponsor.
- Sustained application of development (demonstrated repetition).

Lag (outcome) Measures

- Percentage of ready-now leaders for critical roles or senior leadership positions.
- Ready-now leaders in key Business Driver areas.
- Business impact of development.
- Retention of key talent (relative to target).
- Ratio of internal/external hires.
- Success rates (performance) of new incumbents, including speed to productivity.
- Diversity (by role, level, ethnicity, gender, functional background, etc.).
- Time to fill key positions.
- Percentage of planned moves executed.
- Performance of newly placed leaders.

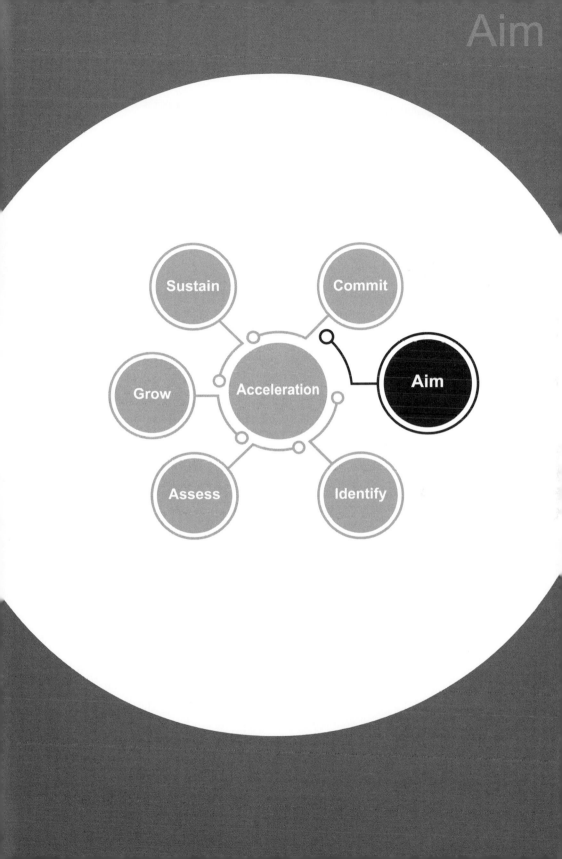

Aim Define leadership for your business context.

In this section...

Chapter 3 outlines how organizations become great at the AIM imperative. The practices they employ generate energy in the following ways:

- **More relevance to the business context:** Business Drivers provide a clear, simple connection between business and cultural priorities and the leadership needed to meet them.

- **Greater usability:** A common language that can be used with any application at any level of leadership—broad business context, competency focus, and Key Action precision.

- **More precise, accurate guidance for skill development:** Key Actions describe exactly how competencies can be practiced to achieve proficiency or mastery.

 Denotes that tools and information on this topic are available at the *Leaders Ready Now* website (www.leadersreadynow.com). Use this code to access content: LRN2016.

BECOME FLUENT IN THE LANGUAGE OF GROWTH

3 | Defining Leadership Success for Your Business Context

Gandhi, Churchill, Lincoln, Mandela, Joan of Arc—what made them great? Wait. Don't answer. We have not devoted this chapter to yet another attempt to define the perfect leader. Let's ask a different question instead: If we put Churchill into India circa 1930 or Gandhi into the United Kingdom at the start of World War II, would each have achieved the same success? No one can say, but we can assert that for most of history's great leadership successes, the leader was uniquely suited for the task at hand. For many, in fact, it has been said that the task was what made the leader (e.g., Dr. Martin Luther King, Jr.). A lesson illustrated throughout the history of leadership is that when defining what it takes to be successful, it's not enough to describe the person. Context matters.

If your leadership-acceleration system can establish a common, usable language to accurately describe both your leaders and your business context, you will arrive more quickly at the best ways to accelerate growth and avoid the costly failures of placing the wrong people into key roles.[i] Unfortunately, the predominant approach to defining leadership success focuses exclusively on the characteristics of the person and applies little or no rigor to clarifying the business context. Entire talent-management systems routinely are built this way, which helps to explain why they are so often viewed by line leaders as out of touch with the business.

Business and HR leaders tend to speak different languages. Ask a CEO what she needs from her soon-to-be-hired COO, and most likely she will quickly state two or three high-priority, business-related needs such as, *"We need our new COO to drive operational efficiency, establish more accountability and alignment, and cultivate a more customer-focused culture."* This way of expressing leadership requirements is almost universal among senior leaders. They think (appropriately) in terms of business requirements and the broad challenges leaders face while striving to meet them. Ask an HR leader the same question about the COO role, and the response likely would include a much more detailed list, including competencies, personal attributes, experience, and knowledge—all important predictors of success and failure.

> **The language you use to focus and communicate the profile for success must clearly articulate the top few leadership priorities in your business context.**

So who's right—the CEO or the HR leader? The answer: both. The language you use to focus and communicate the profile for success must clearly articulate the top few leadership priorities in your business context, yet supply the precision needed to fully represent the requirements for leadership success. Doing so starts with identifying *Business Drivers*.

Business Drivers—The Language of Your Leadership Context

Business Drivers are the broad leadership challenges or obstacles that must be hurdled to execute an organization's strategic and cultural priorities and to *drive the business* forward. Some common examples include Execute a

Competitive Strategy, Drive Process Innovation, and Build a New Organization. Business Drivers work in tandem with *Success Profiles*SM, which is our term for the combinations of components that define the specific requirements for successful leadership in a given job (see Figure 3.1).

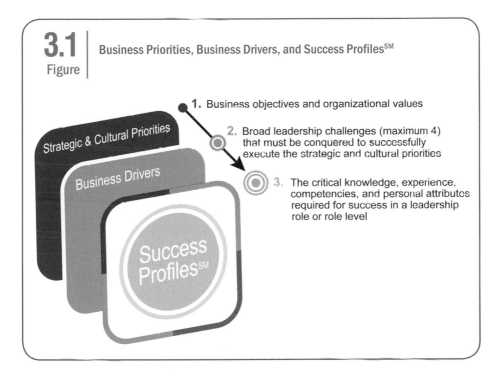

3.1 Figure | Business Priorities, Business Drivers, and Success ProfilesSM

1. Business objectives and organizational values
2. Broad leadership challenges (maximum 4) that must be conquered to successfully execute the strategic and cultural priorities
3. The critical knowledge, experience, competencies, and personal attributes required for success in a leadership role or role level

Strategic & Cultural Priorities

Business Drivers

Success ProfilesSM

Completing a simple three-part statement helps to clarify how business strategies, Business Drivers, and success profiles fit together:

- Part 1: *For our organization to be successful over the next two to four years, we must* (insert strategic and cultural priorities).

- Part 2: *Therefore, we will need our leaders to focus on* (insert 3–5 Business Drivers).

- Part 3: *Which means we will need leaders with specific skills and capabilities that include* (insert success profile).

Because they help define context, Business Drivers change the way leadership language is used. Take, for example, a global petroleum services organization in the midst of a multiyear effort to elevate companywide performance. Raising performance standards became a central thrust of the transformation. Not surprisingly, this led to revisions in the leadership competency model. There was a need for *Inspiring Excellence* to set higher performance targets, establish the right metrics, and drive to goal completion. Leaders also would need to spend more time and effort *Coaching and Developing Others* to ensure that employees were growing and cultivating new capabilities. *Strategic Influence* also increased in importance due to significant shifts in how people would need to operate. Following this logic, Figure 3.2 shows the Business Driver that was identified (*Build a High-Performance Culture*) and the associated competencies wired to it.

3.2
Figure | Wiring Competencies to a Business Driver

Business Driver
Build a High-Performance Culture
Develop an organizational culture that leads to ongoing excellence and effective growth of the business while maintaining the highest integrity.

Associated Competencies
Inspiring Excellence
Coaching & Developing Others
Strategic Influence

Table 3.1 illustrates how our petroleum partner articulated the top four leadership priorities (Business Drivers) that emanated from its entire business strategy and how those drivers connected to its competencies. In a single page we are able to see the connection from the organization's strategic and cultural objectives to the behavioral leadership requirements needed to execute them. Note that the Business Drivers are not simply the product of clustering competencies; rather, they are direct outputs of the business and cultural priorities.

3.1 Table

Relating Strategies, Values, Business Drivers, and Competencies

STRATEGIC PRIORITIES	CULTURAL PRIORITIES (VALUES)	BUSINESS DRIVERS	COMPETENCIES
*We will execute our vision by delivering on these **strategic priorities**...*	*...while modeling the core values that define our **culture**...*	*...Therefore, our leaders must be prepared to step up to these **key leadership challenges**:*	*...by drawing on these key **competencies**:*
Increase business in "crucial" segments.	Discipline	**Shape Organizational Strategy:** Develop a long-range course of action or set of goals to ensure successful realization of the organization's vision.	• Establishing Strategic Direction • Financial Acumen • Business Savvy • Energizing the Organization
Develop/Provide proactive solutions and profitable growth opportunities.	Integrity & Honesty		
	Respect		
Become our customers' preferred provider.	Safety	**Build a High-Performance Culture:** Develop an organizational culture that leads to ongoing excellence and effective growth of the business while maintaining the highest integrity.	• Inspiring Excellence • Coaching and Developing Others • Strategic Influence
Deliver efficient, incident-free operations.	Technical		
Continuously improve business effectiveness and efficiency.	Leadership		
Deliver on asset strategy.		**Execute Competitive Strategy:** Lead and drive the execution of a business strategy aimed at gaining a competitive advantage.	• Entrepreneurship • Driving Execution • Business Savvy
Build the industry's most competent and capable workforce.			
		Create Alignment & Accountability: Establish clear goals that align a unit's efforts with the organization's vision; ensure synergies between people, processes, and strategies to drive flawless execution of business objectives.	• Establishing Strategic Direction • Driving Execution • Sharing Responsibility (Delegating)

Additionally, the use of Business Drivers enables senior management to use fewer words to translate, understand, and articulate those leadership requirements without having to navigate a long list of detailed competencies. In communications to the board of directors, for example, succession-management objectives were communicated by using only the Business Driver labels (see Figure 3.3). When necessary, board members or other stakeholders can clearly see and understand the competency "wiring" underlying the Business Drivers, but they are not required to routinely operate with that level of detail.

> The Business Driver framework simplifies and focuses the entire talent-management system.

As you will see both here and in subsequent chapters, the Business Driver framework simplifies and focuses the entire talent-management system. It also elevates the business relevance of HR activities, including system design, talent reviews, assessment, development, succession management, and more. With specific regard to acceleration, Business Drivers also introduce a means for evaluating both group and individual leadership readiness.

Figure 3.3 shows a partial view of how our petroleum partner displayed readiness to lead against its four Business Drivers. Colors indicate levels of leader readiness based on an assessment built to assess the competencies wired to the four Business Drivers. While only six leaders are shown here, the same data was generated for dozens of senior leaders to enable broader business decision making against the organization's top leadership priorities.

The senior team was able to quickly address questions such as, *"Are we ready to Build a High-Performance Culture?" "Do we have the leaders we need to Shape Organizational Strategy?"* and so on. Acceleration strategies, both for individuals and the group as a whole, then were crafted to address the competencies and behaviors that underlie the Business Drivers, while data collected over time enabled management to better understand current readiness and determine whether progress was being made in closing gaps.

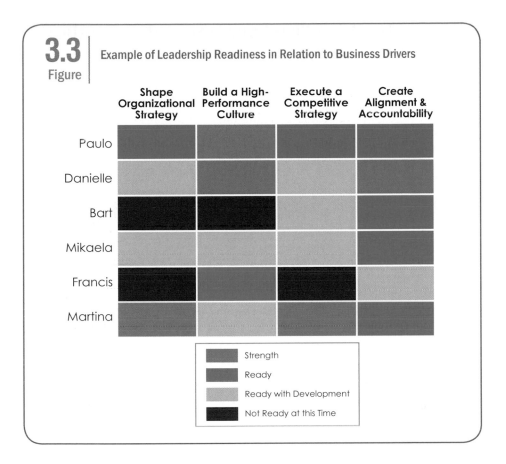

3.3
Figure

Example of Leadership Readiness in Relation to Business Drivers

While Business Drivers provide language that management can remember and use, they are useful only to the extent that their underlying components are precise and define the specifics of what it takes for leaders to be successful. We call these components a *success profile*.

Success Profiles—The Language of Assessing and Developing Your Leaders

Having articulated your context, you next need to define what it takes for leaders to succeed within it. These definitions comprise the language you will use in discussions about whom to deploy to key roles and how to aggressively accelerate development so that people can be ready sooner. You probably have at least some elements of a success profile in use already, but to guarantee accuracy, consistency, and insight, make sure your success profile measures each of the four components on the next page (see Figure 3.4).

- **Competencies**—Clusters of related behaviors that are associated with success or failure in a job. *(What people can do.)*

- **Personal Attributes**—Stable individual dispositions or abilities—including personality, cognitive ability, and motivation—that are related to job success. *(Who people are.)*

- **Experience and Job Challenges**—Job assignments and situations that one is likely to encounter in a given role or job family or that must be experienced and mastered before taking on a role. *(What people have done.)*

- **Business and Organizational Knowledge**—Requisite knowledge, business understanding, and awareness of how the organization and industry operate, including markets, technology, systems, processes, functions, products, services, and other stable elements of the organization and business sector. *(What people know.)*

As one business president once put it, *"We have a tendency to hire based on knowledge and experience, but we fire based on competencies and personal attributes—mainly derailers."* Knowledge and experience are the most easily observed and developed elements of the success profile. Traditionally, these draw the most management attention when leadership capability is being evaluated. Career track record, prior roles and assignments, accomplishments, initiatives led, results achieved, and academic degrees all tend to be quite well

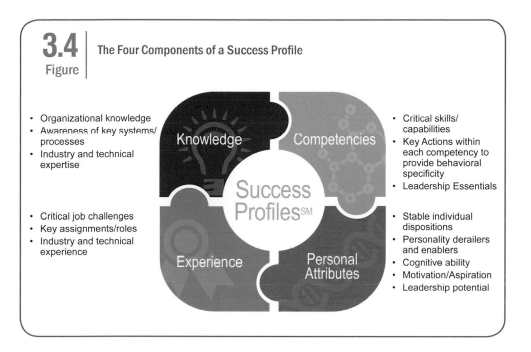

3.4 Figure The Four Components of a Success Profile

- Organizational knowledge
- Awareness of key systems/ processes
- Industry and technical expertise

Knowledge

Competencies

- Critical skills/ capabilities
- Key Actions within each competency to provide behavioral specificity
- Leadership Essentials

Success ProfilesSM

- Critical job challenges
- Key assignments/roles
- Industry and technical experience

Experience

Personal Attributes

- Stable individual dispositions
- Personality derailers and enablers
- Cognitive ability
- Motivation/Aspiration
- Leadership potential

known and, traditionally, have played the biggest role in driving decisions about potential and readiness. The irony is that, although they are the easiest to develop, they are less important determinants of success, particularly at higher levels. More critical to discern as one accelerates toward higher levels of leadership are competencies and personal attributes—the variables that more significantly differentiate success from failure. For that reason, this chapter focuses more on those two success profile components. In Chapter 9 we delve more deeply into knowledge and experience.

To Grow Greatness, You Will Need Great Competencies

Great competencies are possible only when the starting point is a focus on the broad business context—Business Drivers. And they are complete only when the end point is a specific behavioral definition that illustrates precisely how competencies are mastered. This three-point structure—broad business perspective, competency focus, and Key Action precision—is crucial to the development of great competencies.

Start by making sure your list is the right length. Competencies should define all critical skills and no more. Having conducted thousands of job analyses in organizations across every industry throughout the world, from production worker to CEO, we have found that the biggest challenge when identifying competencies for a success profile is to keep the list short. All competencies tend to look important (and job analysis survey ratings often prove it). The key, of course, is to arrive at the shortest possible list of competencies that represent the most critical skills needed for success in the role. While there is no magic formula to determine the right number, it is helpful to understand four skill domains and to ensure that your competency model represents each:

- **Interpersonal Effectiveness**—Interpersonal and communication behaviors that facilitate successful one-on-one and group interactions. Examples include Strategic Influence, Cultivating Networks and Partnerships, Building Customer Relationships, and Compelling Communication.

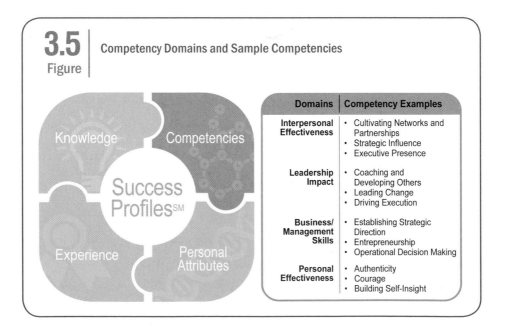

3.5
Figure

Competency Domains and Sample Competencies

Domains	Competency Examples
Interpersonal Effectiveness	• Cultivating Networks and Partnerships • Strategic Influence • Executive Presence
Leadership Impact	• Coaching and Developing Others • Leading Change • Driving Execution
Business/ Management Skills	• Establishing Strategic Direction • Entrepreneurship • Operational Decision Making
Personal Effectiveness	• Authenticity • Courage • Building Self-Insight

Knowledge — Competencies

Success Profiles℠

Experience — Personal Attributes

- **Leadership Impact**—Leadership behaviors that guide others in the successful execution of their assigned responsibilities and help them aspire to and achieve organizational outcomes. Examples include Energizing the Organization, Coaching and Developing Others, and Leading Change.

- **Business/Management Skills**—Management behaviors that guide or direct the business unit or project in achieving the outcomes necessary for success. Examples include Establishing Strategic Direction, Operational Decision Making, Entrepreneurship, and Building Organizational Talent.

- **Personal Effectiveness**—Individual styles or behavior patterns that facilitate success or failure on the job. Examples include Positive Approach, Courage, Authenticity, and Personal Growth Orientation.

Examples of executive-level competencies in each domain are shown in Figure 3.5. We have found that 8–10 competencies are sufficient for lower-level, less-complex roles, while 12–15 competencies are appropriate for complex executive roles. Having more than 15 competencies introduces so many variables that utility and interpretability decline considerably.

Example Competency Definition with Key Actions

COACHING AND DEVELOPING OTHERS

DEFINITION: *Providing feedback, instruction, and development guidance to help others excel in their current or future job responsibilities; planning and supporting the development of individual skills and abilities.*

KEY ACTIONS

Clarifies performance—Seeks information and opinions about an individual's current performance as well as long-term development needs.

Provides timely feedback—Gives timely, specific, and appropriate feedback about performance, development needs, and development progress; reinforces efforts and progress.

[continued at top of next page]

[continued from previous page]

Conveys performance expectations and implications—Communicates high expectations; links performance improvement and skill development to relevant personal and business goals; checks for understanding of and commitment to performance and development goals as well as follow-up activities.

Evaluates misalignment—Diagnoses gaps in knowledge, experience, skills, and behavior that underlie current and future performance; continually modifies evaluation based on new information.

Facilitates development—Leverages environmental supports and removes development barriers; advocates for individual to higher levels of management to create development opportunities; provides guidance and positive models; seeks suggestions for improving performance; collaboratively creates development plans that include activities targeted to specific goals.

Fosters developmental relationships—Helps people feel valued and included in coaching and development discussions by expressing confidence in their ability to excel, maintaining their self-esteem, empathizing, and disclosing own position.

If you're confident you have the right list of competencies, do not accept them as sufficient until you also know that they reflect precisely the behaviors—Key Actions—needed to master each competency. Most of us have, at one time or another, received poor instructions—whether from a boss, coach, teacher, or product manual—and it's unproductive and frustrating when these directions don't work. Competencies without the correct Key Actions are like misleading instructions. The sidebar above illustrates a well-defined competency: Coaching and Developing Others. The definition generally characterizes effective coaching, but the Key Actions break down the broad concept into observable behavioral elements that can be reliably assessed and more easily developed.

Here's a crucial point that only a few organizations truly understand: Your goal actually is not to develop competencies; it is to develop Key Actions. The most significant barrier to mastery is the lack of insight into "what I'm doing or not doing" that is inhibiting effectiveness. Leaders quickly achieve better results when they get the right guidelines. This has two important implications:

1. To assess competencies, start with Key Actions and combine those judgments into competency ratings—not the other way around. Leverage scientifically derived algorithms and/or trained assessors or interviewers to rate competencies and thereby ensure accuracy and reliability.

The Interaction Essentials—Key Actions Found in Most[ii] Competency Models

Across millions of leaders and hundreds of millions of behaviors that our assessors and interviewers have rated, several Key Actions have emerged as important to success in most competency models. Like a painter's grasp of color and medium or a tennis player's grip on the racket, there are fundamentals that are essential in every leadership job. We call them **Interaction Essentials,** and we believe every leadership success profile should include them.

Managing Relationships' Key Actions:

- Maintain or enhance **self-esteem.** *(to build social bonds)*
- Listen and respond with **empathy.**
- Ask for help and encourage **involvement.** *(to enhance collaboration)*
- **Share** thoughts, feelings, and rationale. *(to build trust)*
- Provide **support** without removing responsibility. *(to build ownership)*

Guiding Interactions' Key Actions:

- **Open** the discussion by stating the purpose and importance.
- **Clarify** the situation by seeking and sharing information.
- **Develop** others' ideas.
- **Agree** on specific actions.
- **Close** by summarizing actions and next steps.
- **Check** for understanding.

2. To develop competencies, focus on the Key Actions that have been identified as most important for the individual. Remember, the only way your leaders will master competencies is to practice and hone the Key Actions.[1]

As you define your competencies, you also may face the challenge of aligning them across the levels of your organization's leadership pipeline. Table 3.2 illustrates how competencies can be clearly cascaded to all levels of leadership. This is a useful means of simplifying your model and illustrating learning pathways so that accelerated learners more clearly understand how skills build across the pipeline.

This cascading model marks the hazards that emerging leaders must consider as they advance. The four-level structure in Table 3.2 represents a framework that works for many organizations; however, some require different configurations, with more or fewer levels of leadership. Regardless of the number of levels, when all competencies and job families (levels) are displayed at a glance, the junctures at which *transitional* competencies are introduced become apparent. Horizontally across Table 3.2 (from right to left), each successive move upward in the organization introduces competencies that reflect the changing requirements as one takes on more leadership responsibility.

Creating success profiles that illustrate these transition points serves two key purposes. First, individuals seeking to understand or develop their skills for higher levels of leadership get a clear picture of what is necessary at each level, clarifying the skill requirements of career progression and enabling more well-targeted self-development. Second, this framework provides a blueprint for the design of an organization's assessment and development systems. We can see, for example, why the operational leader level (e.g., vice president, director, function head) is where so many leaders struggle for the first time, having been successful in prior roles.[iii] The transition into the operational leader ranks

---

1 **Caution:** We've seen many competencies with subparts that don't function as true Key Actions because they can't be reliably observed (e.g., Imagines creative solutions; Understands the most important alliances to maintain). If it's not observable, you won't be able to assess or develop it. You'll also need to be thorough. Don't leave essential Key Actions out of your definitions (e.g., mastering *Influence* won't happen without skill in asking good questions to understand others' needs).

introduces the most significant addition of new skills required for success. HR leaders can design for this by building assessment and development processes that enable emerging leaders to begin learning about and preparing for the transition before it occurs as well as receiving guidance during the transition. (For more details on these approaches, see Chapters 7–11.)

3.2 Table | Sample Cascading Competency Framework

Strategic Leaders	Operational Leaders	People Leaders	Individual Contributors
Interpersonal Effectiveness			
Compelling Communication	Compelling Communication	Communication	Communication
Strategic Influence	Strategic Influence	Influencing	Influencing
Executive Presence	Executive Presence		
Leadership Impact			
Coaching and Developing Others	Coaching and Developing Others	Coaching	Coaching
Sharing Responsibility	Sharing Responsibility	Delegation and Empowerment	Planning and Organizing
Leading Change	Leading Change	Facilitating Change	
Driving Execution	Driving Execution	Execution	
Energizing the Organization	Energizing the Organization		
Business/Management Skills			
Operational Decision Making	Operational Decision Making	Decision Making	Decision Making
Building Organizational Talent	Building Organizational Talent	Selecting Talent	
Establishing Strategic Direction	Establishing Strategic Direction		
Entrepreneurship			
Personal Effectiveness			
Building Self-Insight	Building Self-Insight	Leveraging Feedback	Leveraging Feedback
Authenticity			

What's in a Transition?

Each step up in leadership responsibility introduces new challenges, some more than others.[iv] But what, specifically, causes roles to become so much more difficult? What is it that changes to create such seismic shifts in requirements for success? Below are the most significant aspects of change in executive-level leadership transitions and the common reactions of leaders who are unprepared to respond to them.

Transition Factor	FROM	TO	Common Reactions
Span of Influence	Single team/function management	Multiple team/function management	Sets unclear expectations; creates strategic confusion
	Focused objectives; resources determined by senior leadership	Complex, conflicting business objectives; competition for resources	Slow to build partnerships, alliances
	Small-group communications	Large, multigroup communications	Difficulty navigating political environment
Tactical Control	Involvement in day-to-day operations	Detachment from day-to-day operations	Reluctance to delegate
	Direct impact on group outputs	Indirect impact on group outputs	Desire for personal recognition for group success
			Do-it-yourself solutions
Consequences of Failure	Limited-scale consequences	Large-scale consequences	More personal stress
	Unit-specific countermeasures	Organizationwide countermeasures	Unrealistic demands on others
			Negative outlook
Business Scope	Basic P&L responsibility	Enterprise accountability	Financial "cramming" to ensure business fluency
	Limited number of inputs/variables	Many inputs/variables	Overemphasis on financial variables
		Broad business judgment needed	Poor business judgments

[continued at top of next page]

[continued from previous page]

Visibility	Limited visibility	Wide visibility	Cultural damage; propagation of derailers
	Personality derailers disguised	Personality derailers visible	
	Less cultural impact	Greater cultural influence—behaviors and approaches mimicked by many	Unwanted turnover
			Public executive failure
Constituents	Focus on team/ small group	Focus on organization, market, and customer	Narrow focus; lack of enterprise vision
	Objectives set by supervisor or manager	Objectives self-imposed	Incremental objectives (absence of "stretch" assignment)
			Organizational stagnation, lack of progress

Personal Attributes—The Most Difficult Success Profile Component to Develop

A complete success profile defines both the behavioral ingredients to success and the dispositional characteristics that underlie behavior. There are many possible permutations of factors and traits that could be discussed within this broad category, but for the purposes of talent management, there are four primary categories of *personal attributes* (see Figure 3.6):

- **Personality**—The stable, enduring aspects of one's disposition or nature, including performance enablers, such as Sociability or Interpersonal Sensitivity, and performance derailers, such Arrogance or Volatility.

- **Motivation**—Fundamental motives or preferences in the workplace, such as the desire for leadership and advancement; work values, such as quality, collaboration, affiliation, or altruism; geographic mobility; and technical, professional, or industry interests.

- **Cognitive Ability**—Intellectual and reasoning abilities, such as critical thinking, business judgment, logic, and quantitative and qualitative analytical capacity.

- **Leadership Potential Factors**—Behaviorally defined factors related to the likelihood that one will develop and grow quickly as a leader, accelerating readiness for higher levels of responsibility. While behavioral in nature, the potential factors are much less developable than competencies and are therefore considered elements of personal attributes.

> Knowing why we do what we do often is the most useful asset in preparing to take on a task or responsibility we've never attempted.

While many personal attributes represent towering strengths for some leaders, personal attributes that derail or inhibit performance are a unique challenge because they are difficult to develop. That said, the difficulty in developing personal attributes should not be a reason to avoid measuring them. Understanding the stable attributes that underlie capabilities and tendencies

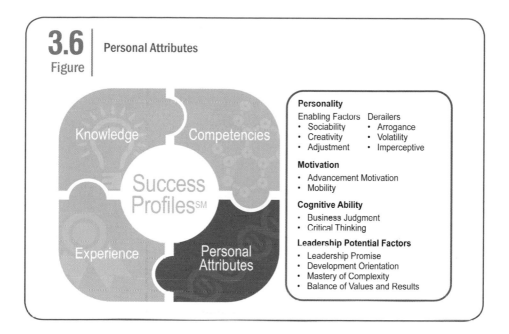

3.6 Figure | Personal Attributes

Personality

Enabling Factors
- Sociability
- Creativity
- Adjustment

Derailers
- Arrogance
- Volatility
- Imperceptive

Motivation
- Advancement Motivation
- Mobility

Cognitive Ability
- Business Judgment
- Critical Thinking

Leadership Potential Factors
- Leadership Promise
- Development Orientation
- Mastery of Complexity
- Balance of Values and Results

is crucial to enabling leaders to adjust and adapt to changing circumstances. Knowing why we do what we do often is the most useful asset in preparing to take on a task or responsibility we've never attempted. For this reason, personal attributes represent an essential component of a well-defined success profile.

Personality: Increasingly Important as Leaders Accelerate

Try as we might, we simply can't change our personalities—not significantly or quickly, which is precisely why we shouldn't try. In truth, there is no right or wrong personality. People are not better or worse human beings for their hardwired characteristics—it's what they do that matters. In making our life's work about human growth and development, we are bound to the notion that everyone has great potential, and we have observed this to be true. But to be sure, not everyone is equally

> As the demands on leaders become more complex and roles require ever-deeper and broader capabilities, personality becomes a more significant determinant of success.

suited for leadership. As the demands on leaders become more complex and roles require ever-deeper and broader capabilities, personality becomes a more significant determinant of success.

Why? Any leadership role at any level can be difficult, but several factors elevate the impact of personality in acceleration. First, more complex roles demand a wider range of skills. This inevitably means that leaders will need to stretch their capabilities into untested areas and apply unfamiliar behaviors. Strong personality characteristics, such as confidence or overconfidence, creativity or eccentricity, and prudence or perfectionism, can either enable or derail a leader's ability to adapt to more difficult challenges. A senior corporate finance manager, transitioning into the role of vice president of finance for a large business unit, might struggle to craft a comprehensive finance strategy because of risk aversion (a common derailer), which causes him to dismiss sound ideas for fear that they will fail. In his prior role his risk aversion might have been seen as appropriately careful and attentive to cautions that others should consider. The consequences of failure in his prior role were less severe, and so his risk aversion did not limit him until the scope of his new responsibilities activated the derailer.

Second, as leaders advance, their personalities become more visible and have a direct impact on the organization's culture. As leadership responsibility expands, particularly into executive roles, a larger proportion of time is spent attending or leading meetings, speaking to groups, making decisions, providing guidance and direction, and generally thinking and speaking with others—with little time to reflect and prepare. The result is that the leader's disposition becomes more publicly apparent. Moods, reactions, demeanor, thinking style, preferences, and emotions all fuel perceptions in the workplace. An extroverted leader with a light sense of humor and a desire for rapid action will garner very different reactions than the more stoic, introverted leader who prefers more thoughtfulness and clear execution plans. Over time, norms and habits become programmed into the culture as a direct result of the leader's personality. Obviously, these norms can either enable or inhibit job performance.

Third, the overall volume and complexity of work, exertion levels, unexpected challenges, and sheer stress make it difficult for leaders to monitor and adjust their natural behavior. Much of leadership action becomes reaction, and reactions are more

> Try as we might, under conditions of significant stress, most of us are unable to hide our true nature.

instinctual—driven in large part by fundamental dispositions. Under conditions of significant stress, most of us are unable to hide our true nature. It is an axiom of career progression that as one rises to higher levels of responsibility, the individual's personality becomes more public. How leaders "go public" along the way often has a great deal to do with leadership success, which can be significantly enabled by having a success profile that demystifies the language. Chapter 5 discusses the assessment of personality, and Chapter 9 examines how leaders can develop in ways that reduce the impact of their derailing personality traits.

Motivation: The Fuel for Growth

Unique from one's abilities and dispositions is motivation—the fundamental desires and aspirations that an individual brings to the workplace. Within a success profile, and particularly within an acceleration system, motivation fuels growth, which makes it curious that so many organizations ignore it.

As we have said, accelerated growth produces energy. Moments of rapid learning are consistently characterized by learners as thrilling, terrifying, or both. But thrill and terror are not the product of indifference—they are the product of vested interest and attachment to success: motivation. Motivation can be gauged broadly to determine an individual's career aspirations and desire for advancement or, specifically, to assess particular work motivations, such as the desire for collaboration, achievement, affiliation, or influence (among many others).

When applied successfully, they are coupled with behavioral measures to capture the full spectrum of indicators of the potential to lead. The next chapter looks specifically at the talent review process, including the early identification of leadership potential, and outlines the factors, process, and tools that can be leveraged to ensure that your organization is continually aware of the leaders who are most likely to benefit from accelerated development and generate a return on the organization's investment.

Making It Work

Identifying Business Drivers and a subsequent success profile that cascades from them to all levels of leadership can represent a daunting prospect—particularly for complex, global, multi-business enterprises. For many, the effort might seem too large to undertake. In truth, we believe this hesitation is well placed. We've seen many competency initiatives die under their own weight because the effort to create and socialize a new model into all HR systems has been far greater than the value gained for having done so.

> There is no greater means of garnering support and energy for a new success profile than for it to be created and used by the organization's top leadership.

A lesson we have learned, and have seen others learn, is that a success profile initiative rarely adds value when built in isolation of planned applications. This is often because the declared objectives are to define and communicate the new profile and ensure that it is available for use in all HR systems in the organization. These are the wrong initial objectives. For Business Drivers and success profiles to achieve their intended value, they must be put to use. Ideally, Business Drivers are selected and edited by top management and then used immediately as part of an important activity that involves the discussion of people. Succession management discussions (in which readiness for promotion is at issue) are prime opportunities to apply

Business Driver language to people who are well known and who can provide a platform for using new (and fewer) words to discuss talent (see Figure 3.4).

Once the language begins to take hold with senior management, application to the remainder of the organization can be staged in a way that coincides with the moments at which the language will be used, thereby avoiding the massive initiative and creating the energy and uptake that a holistic success profile deserves.

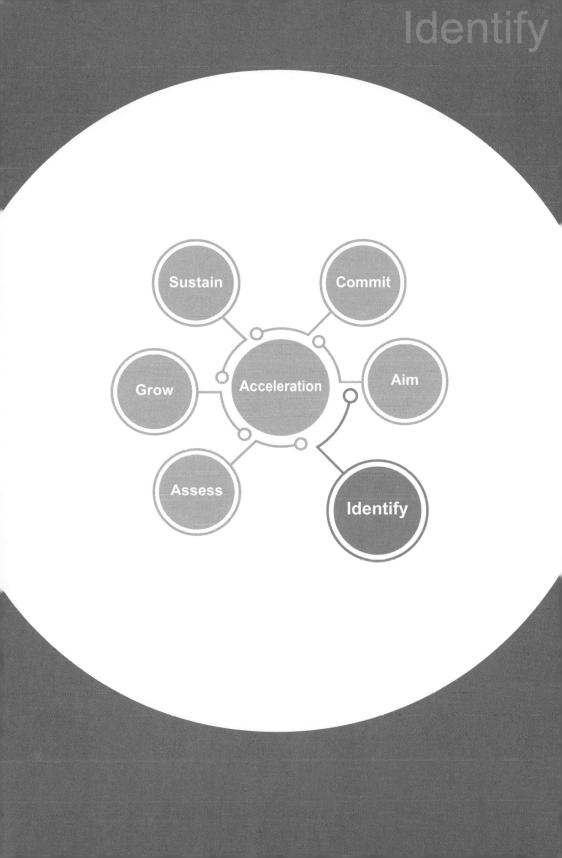

 **Identify** Make efficient, accurate decisions about whom to accelerate.

In this section…

Chapter 4 outlines how organizations become great at the IDENTIFY imperative. The practices they employ generate energy in the following ways:

- **More efficient, business-focused conversations:** An enterprise-driven, integrated talent review process with conversations that more seamlessly connect leadership talent to a range of business dialogs.

- **Less bureaucracy:** Elimination of pointless meetings to produce ratings and/or data that does not improve decision making.

- **Shrewder, more accurate judgments about people:** More well-designed talent review processes that move more quickly and teach management how to accurately identify individuals with leadership potential.

 Denotes that tools and information on this topic are available at the *Leaders Ready Now* website (www.leadersreadynow.com). Use this code to access content: LRN2016.

HAVE THE RIGHT CONVERSATIONS ABOUT THE RIGHT PEOPLE

4 | Mastering the Art and Science of the Talent Review

Your acceleration strategy and success profile are like an architect's blueprint. When you know exactly what you intend to build, the talent review is like the on-site briefing to the construction crew. The team huddle before the play. The ground control preparation before the space mission launch. It's the moment when management comes together to take stock of the organization's capacity to achieve key strategies, review the most critical leadership gaps, and discuss the individuals in whom they will invest to close those gaps. It is a conversation rife with complexity. Agendas and priorities collide as HR and senior management review the business requirements for talent, reach consensus on key people-related decisions, and determine areas of development focus for accelerated learners. Because it will have an impact on almost everything else you do to accelerate growth, the talent review is a conversation that your senior team must get right.

But amid the complexity, many talent reviews stray from the goal of acceleration.

"I didn't learn anything new." That was how the CEO of a global chemicals corporation summed up the annual talent review. After an exhausting month of presentations by business leaders across the globe, he had gained little new insight into the organization's talent and was deeply troubled by the absence of credible plans to close its urgent leadership gaps.

Ironically, this was precisely the reaction the HR team had sought to avoid. They had devoted great effort to establishing a common, business-relevant protocol for executives to use when presenting their talent summaries and plans. But the approach didn't work. For all its process discipline, the conversation was too general. While it isolated business dilemmas, it only vaguely addressed how the organization would grow leaders to solve them. Discussions about individuals were full of conjecture. No useful data was presented to confirm beliefs about leadership skills and growth needs. Ultimately, the talent review became highly bureaucratic, sacrificing any meaningful people insight, creating no spark for development, and having no way to track development progress. Despite HR's best intentions, the talent review created no change in individual or organizational readiness.

> Talent reviews that drive acceleration use structure, data, and discipline to go beyond superficial conversations.

It's not enough for the talent review to summarize the past and present. Instead, it must catalyze action that prepares leaders for the future. Talent reviews that drive acceleration use structure, data, and discipline to go beyond superficial conversations. They carefully apportion time and effort to balance discussion of organization-level talent trends with objective, data-enabled dialog about individuals. They work efficiently to establish a shared understanding of the most critical gaps, and then proceed to discuss who should be accelerated and how to make it happen.

The ideal solution for your organization won't come prepackaged. To foster the risk taking that fuels faster growth, you'll need to customize a talent review process that integrates the principles of acceleration with your organization's unique needs. With the right balance you can begin placing bigger bets on your people and create more significant growth for more leaders who have the motivation and capability to grow quickly.

What Should Your Talent Review Do?

Not all organizations have the same goals for their talent reviews, nor should they. But when the objectives are not aligned within a senior team, it creates chaos and causes influential stakeholders to (appropriately) question the purpose and utility of the process.

To create clear, direct impact on leadership readiness, the talent review needs to coordinate two levels of analysis: 1) an Organizational Review, which examines the business- or group-level supply and demand for leadership, and 2) an Acceleration Review, which zeroes in on individual-level potential, readiness, and development.

The **Organizational Review** is associated with two primary objectives:

- **Evaluate organization-, business-, or group-level leadership capability and readiness.** This includes a summary of organizational talent at both the individual and unit/group levels. It sometimes takes the form of an organization chart or other visual summary showing individuals and their levels of readiness to take on larger assignments. For some, this may intersect with workforce-planning efforts that summarize talent across the organization.

- **Evaluate critical position capability and readiness.** This typically includes analysis of select groups (e.g., levels, functions) or critical positions considered essential to strategy execution. It also may incorporate identifying critical positions (including setting criteria for what defines one) or making staffing or promotion decisions associated with open roles and/or succession candidates.

These goals are foundational to the talent review, but many organizations make the mistake of stopping here (often spending a disproportionate amount of time), rather than moving on to the higher-return efforts at the next level. The **Acceleration Review** builds on the Organizational Review and is intended to:

- **Identify the individuals who can and will grow most rapidly.** This involves determining which individuals show the greatest leadership potential and whose development will be accelerated (i.e., Acceleration Pool membership). This may include a review of leadership potential measures (discussed later in this chapter), on-the-job performance data, work experience and career history data, or other relevant inputs.

- **Evaluate readiness for placement or promotion into key assignments.** This objective aims to review current business scenarios and leadership vacancies and determine whether individuals who have been identified as high potential are ready to step up. This review should include high-quality data from individual readiness assessments (see Chapter 5), performance data, and/or development progress indicators.

- **Plan for aggressive development** (e.g., job rotations, special assignments, training). Action plans commonly include special development assignments (including "stretch" roles/promotions) and specify support requirements (e.g., mentors, training needed), while ensuring alignment of business needs and individual career interests (see Chapters 7–11).

- **Evaluate their growth progress over time.** Evaluate the impact of development actions taken by key individuals to determine a) if more or different support is needed via mentorship, training, coaching, etc., b) whether additional development actions should be taken, and/or c) if development has affected readiness for promotion or a key assignment.

Appendix 4.1 provides a more detailed look at the objectives of both reviews. We've seen organizations attempt to accomplish all six objectives in one (very long) meeting, with no tools or data to support senior management's judgments. We also have witnessed other organizations short-circuit their conversations about people and rely on a test as the sole source of insight into leadership potential and readiness. These efforts routinely fail.

A well-designed talent review accomplishes these objectives in an efficient process that is integrated into your business and operational planning cycle. One annual meeting won't be sufficient. You'll need to establish a routine. Doing so requires clarifying your objectives in both the Organizational and Acceleration Review segments.

> One annual meeting won't be sufficient. You'll need to establish a routine.

The Organizational Review

Every great talent review starts by establishing a shared understanding of the business' needs and the leadership roles most critical to making it run well, now and in the future. In the Organizational Review segment, entire business units, tiers, and groups of leaders (regions, functions) are evaluated. Leadership strengths and development needs (at the group level) are discussed in relation to business goals, and the availability (or lack) of ready-now candidates to fill anticipated openings in critical positions is summarized. Many organizations also discuss replacement plans for key positions in this forum.

The Organizational Review often takes center stage in larger organizations where management has more difficulty gaining accurate insight into talent and therefore seeks a rapid survey of organizational capability.[1] The broader focus and large volume of leaders discussed create the perception of efficiency, but also tend to result in relatively little or no time devoted to individual-level capabilities and scant data to support judgments.

---

1 Some organizations apply tests or very brief assessment measures to entire groups or business units to conduct organizationwide scans of leadership talent. With the right tools and process, these measures can add useful insight. But when used as the sole or primary indicators of potential or readiness, they can be toxic to your acceleration efforts. Later in this chapter, we discuss the appropriate use of objective assessment in the talent review process.

For that reason the Organizational Review, when applied as the sole mechanism for reviewing talent, is limited in its ability to foster acceleration. Relying on current performance, and with no in-depth measures of future leadership potential or promotional readiness, conversations about leaders often are based on subjective conclusions and unsubstantiated predictions. They also fail to increase the size or nature of the pool of leaders who are developing toward higher levels. While at first these reviews may seem as though they have been successful, after repeated attempts the process often becomes like an impersonal talent chess match that moves leaders from assignment to assignment, while yielding unimaginative development strategies, incorrect predictions of leadership success, vague accountabilities for development action, and, ultimately, failure to deliver the sought-after return.

The Acceleration Review

To catalyze the right development actions, your talent review needs to include a deeper dive into a smaller leadership population. The size of the group should be gauged to the size of your leadership gap and the resources you plan to devote to development.[i] (See Chapter 1 for guidance on how to determine whom and how many to accelerate.) In the Acceleration Review segment, management spends more time with better data about key individuals and

> With no in-depth measures of future leadership potential or promotional readiness, conversations about leaders often are based on subjective conclusions and unsubstantiated predictions.

places greater emphasis on increasing the growth rate by taking bigger risks with developmental assignments. Acceleration Reviews work in concert with Organizational Reviews, but in a way that apportions time more carefully. In businesses facing dire leadership shortages, the effort to accelerate the growth of a group of high-potential leaders (i.e., an Acceleration Pool) is an indispensable addition to the attempt to quickly evaluate a group of leaders and name replacements for emerging vacancies (i.e., replacement planning).

The defining component of the Acceleration Review is the identification of leadership potential, which creates a subset of individuals who will receive specialized (faster) development. Organizations use different names to identify these individuals (high potentials, key talent, talent pools, etc.). Some are careful not to name the group at all, in the interest of avoiding perceptions of exclusion or preferential treatment. Later in this chapter, we delve more deeply into the topic of identifying leadership potential and discuss effective process and communication strategies. However, it should be noted that the identification of potential does not need to be secret, primarily because it is a business necessity, as we have discussed. For that reason, we find the term *Acceleration Pool*® useful as a name for the group of individuals who (for some period of time, pending progress and motivation) will be given specialized development opportunities.[ii] They are not the only ones who will receive development (everyone in the organization should), and participation is no guarantee of promotion. But being clear about those individuals whose development you aim to accelerate is a fundamental outcome of the Acceleration Review.

Integrating Organizational and Acceleration Reviews

A process that effectively integrates the Organizational and Acceleration Reviews into one business-centric process needs to:

- Structure and sequence talent review sessions to build on business discussions.

- Uncover your organization's hidden leadership potential and invest in the right people.

- Use high-quality data to evaluate readiness accurately and deploy leaders strategically.

- Make bold development assignments that involve learners in key business challenges.

These are explained throughout the rest of this chapter.

Structure and sequence talent review sessions to build on business discussions.

After coming to the realization that his organization was desperately short of leaders with the skills needed for the future, the CEO of a major manufacturing corporation reflected on his own actions and disclosed that, in his routine, one-to-one updates with his business leaders, he rarely, if ever, raised questions about talent. In his most recent round of annual goal-setting discussions, only one of his direct reports came away with objectives associated with talent. Addressing his senior team in a subsequent meeting, he said, *"We've separated our talent discussions from our business discussions, and we're now a weaker company because of it."*

> One of the most consequential actions you can take as you work to accelerate leadership growth is to integrate your conversations about leadership talent into your senior management team's business discussions.

One of the most consequential actions you can take as you work to accelerate leadership growth is to integrate your conversations eabout leadership talent into your senior management team's business discussions. Figure 4.1 illustrates how some of the most successful organizations engineer their processes to make this an ongoing sequence as opposed to a single event. Most have some sort of annual event or meeting series to conduct long-range planning, after which they set business performance targets for the coming year. This leads into periodic business or operational reviews to monitor progress on short-term objectives. These operational reviews happen periodically at the group level, bringing together the entire business leadership team, as well as one-to-one between the CEO and individual business, regional, or functional leaders.

At the start of the cycle, as strategic priorities are crystallized and specific business initiatives are agreed upon, implications for talent are rigorously examined and growth targets set. This is typically the most significant and in-depth talent review session of the year. If you plan to launch a new product,

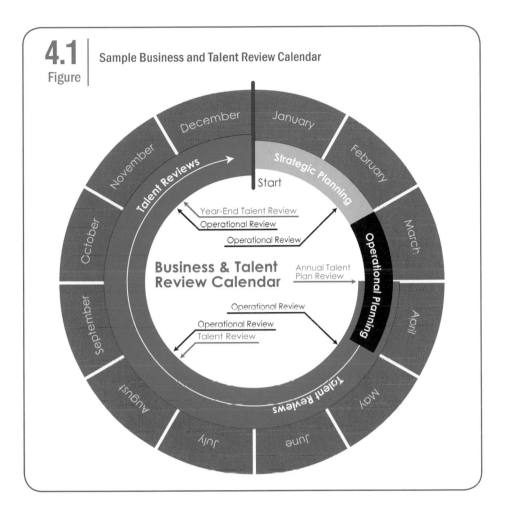

4.1
Figure

Sample Business and Talent Review Calendar

execute a shift in competitive positioning, or pivot from an efficiency focus to an innovation focus, do you have enough of the right leaders in place to make it happen? Each business decision affects the specific needs and gaps that must be addressed by your leadership-acceleration strategy (Chapter 2), so the talent review process must coincide with the moments when those determinations are being made—both for long- and short-term scenarios.

Over time, your talent review becomes the venue in which your leadership-acceleration strategy—along with the metrics of success associated with it—is updated and renewed. Subsequent review sessions throughout the year are then aimed at monitoring progress against targets and making midstream adjustments as needed.

> You also can prepare and structure your talent review discussions to make them easier and more productive and engaging for your business leaders.

While timing and sequence are important, you also can prepare and structure your talent review discussions to make them easier and more productive and engaging for your business leaders by:

- **Spotlighting critical business priorities.** All participants in the talent review should be keenly aware of, and attuned to, business priorities or initiatives that demand differential talent investment or redeployment (e.g., China focus, technology capacity). This provides tangible relevance in discussions of individuals (e.g., *"Is she ready to lead in China?"*) and helps to generate powerful, useful developmental assignments.

- **Summarizing anticipated job openings.** In advance of the talent review, HR should work with business partners to inventory all open positions and projected openings anticipated in the coming business cycle and for the longer term (two to three years). These should encompass new business priorities, structural shifts (e.g., acquisitions), transfers/promotions, retirements, etc. The inventory should include roles within the business unit along with other roles across relevant units, divisions, etc. A good template for this inventory would be the Leadership Capacity Analysis discussed in Chapter 2 (Figure 2.2).

- **Making prework a priority.** Thoughtful prework assignments for all talent review participants make a dramatic difference in the caliber of the discussion and outcomes. Arriving at the talent review having considered both business needs and key leaders in the organization enhances the quality and speed of the conversations.

Talent Review Prework

- **Critical business priorities** that the talent review is meant to address. These should be shared with talent review participants in advance— even if they are well known—to ensure focus and alignment around the intended outcomes of the review.

- **Leadership Capacity Analysis** summarizing all current and anticipated job openings in key positions (see Chapter 2).

- **Aggregate talent data** painting overall pictures of group demographics, current and expected vacancies, diversity statistics, overall performance trends, development progress, etc.

- **Individual profiles** of leaders to be discussed, including:
    - Personal information (career history, education, training, demographics).
    - Recent performance reviews/summaries.
    - Summary of interests/motivations (e.g., advancement motivation, relocation/mobility interests, retention concerns).
    - Behavioral assessment data (e.g., Acceleration Center, multirater, other).
    - Current development priorities.
    - Recent development successes.

- **Summarizing input from your informal talent network.** Talent Management (HR) has a special obligation to build deep and constant familiarity with talent. HR professionals are uniquely positioned to solicit informal views about leaders in the organization, particularly in terms of culture fit (or lack of). This can be particularly valuable in surfacing hidden talent.

- **Assigning a credible senior HR leader as the facilitator.** The sensitive, strategic nature of talent review meetings warrants capable facilitation. If you are the CEO, reinforce your expectation that HR leadership has full

> If you are the CEO, reinforce your expectation that HR leadership has full authority to steer the talent review and to guide the senior team.

authority to steer the talent review and to guide the senior team before, during, and after the meetings. In addition, strong talent review facilitation requires the following capabilities:

- Deep understanding of the organization's business context and strategy.
- Poise, credibility, and trust of senior management along with the ability to challenge and push back in a productive manner.
- Intimate knowledge of the most critical Leadership Capacity Gaps.
- An understanding of how the organization's talent review process aligns with other processes and systems.

Talent discussions often delve deeply into data, examples, stories, and personal accounts (and biases) about the capabilities of individuals and groups throughout the organization. A savvy facilitator will serve as a strong, continual beacon of business relevance, objectivity, process discipline, and integrity in discussing people. For a sample talent review meeting agenda, see Appendix 4.2.

Uncover your organization's hidden leadership potential and invest in the right people.

The second objective of the Acceleration Review is to search your organization to identify the individuals who have the greatest leadership potential.[iii] You'll need a clear definition of potential and an appropriate approach to assessing it to help your senior leaders make more accurate evaluations.[iv] What type of assessment to use is a matter of judgment and scale. We'll get to that shortly. Let's start with the definition.

Clearly define *leadership potential.* Because the goal is to identify the individuals who are most likely to grow rapidly as leaders, looking only at current performance would be dangerous and lead to mistakes. Potential is not performance, and most organizations now make that distinction. But that's not

Talent Review Meeting Ground Rules

- **Adopt an enterprisewide perspective.** During talent review meetings all participants must be strong advocates for the overall organization, not simply their particular unit. This often means they must subordinate their own interests to support promotion and rotation of key talent to other units.

- **Ensure that strategic priorities drive decisions.** Competition for scarce resources across different geographies and businesses will comprise a certain dynamic. Declaring in advance that contentious talent decisions will be ruled by strategic priorities counterbalances the risk of executives defaulting to provincial concerns.

- **Refer to behavioral data.** Executive judgment is legitimate when supported with behavioral evidence. Objectivity and behavioral evidence reduce error and bias in talent reviews, but many executives struggle to adhere to these rules as they voice their perceptions. Making executives understand that behavioral examples are simply brief descriptions of what someone said or did contributes to constructive discussions based on fact versus conjecture.

- **Scrutinize critical roles.** For roles crucial to business success, there should be no compromises on who occupies them. This may require some difficult and even unpopular decisions to both ensure the right placements into the roles and to eliminate "blockers." Critical positions are precious developmental resources that can be quickly depleted if incumbents remain in them for too long or block emerging leaders from entry.

- **Set up high-potential leaders for success.** It is a common temptation to take a high flier whose stellar performance has caught the attention of management and move that person too quickly. Take care to ensure that assignments have clear expectations, priorities, and sufficient support to achieve desired outcomes. And before reassigning leaders, ensure that they've had sufficient opportunity to achieve the desired learning and at the same time make a meaningful business contribution.

> Potential is *not* performance, and most organizations now make that distinction. But that's not all. Potential also is not *readiness*.

all. Potential also is not *readiness*. Determining how likely an individual is to learn and grow quickly as a leader is altogether different than determining if he or she is a good fit for a specific leadership role.[2] Many organizations do not make this important distinction (see Table 4.1).

4.1
Table
The Critical Distinctions Between Performance, Potential, and Readiness

	Definition	What Is Measured	How It Is Measured
Performance	How one is performing now in current role	Current performance against job objectives	The organization's performance management process
Potential	One's likelihood of long-range leadership growth (i.e., to top leadership)	Leadership Potential Factors; Motivation to lead	Inventory of potential completed by managers familiar with the individual's performance, plus management integration (self-report inventories are optional for additional insight)
Readiness	One's fit with a specific future role, job, or job family/level	Full success profile, including knowledge, experience, competencies, and personal attributes	Role-specific assessment methods, such as assessment centers, interviews, simulations, and tests

---

2 Readiness assessment requires careful consideration of the entire success profile of a target position or level. The evaluation of potential is a more preliminary judgment—one that can be made relatively quickly, without having to do a full-blown readiness assessment. Readiness assessments are appropriate when individuals are being considered for placement or promotion into key positions. In the next chapter we discuss this in greater detail.

In a talent review senior leaders must understand that the identification of potential is a decision to invest in growth, not a determination of readiness for promotion. The factors to be considered in the evaluation of potential are fewer and more general than those

> In a talent review senior leaders must understand that the identification of potential is a decision to invest in growth, not a determination of readiness for promotion.

in a readiness assessment. The sidebar on the next page lists the factors that we've applied across hundreds of organizations and found to predict leadership success over time.[v] These factors can be incorporated into the talent review conversation using a variety of different methods, which we turn to next.

When assessing potential, apply methods appropriate to the level of leadership. Across the pipeline there are options for how to assess for leadership potential. Applying the most basic approach, you may elect to supply management with a definition (e.g., like the factors included in the sidebar) and rely on available performance data and the judgments of your senior leaders to determine who has the greatest potential. In our experience this approach yields high rates of false positives, low rates of uncovering hidden talent, and propagation of knowledge and experience over true leadership skill. Adding some level of objective assessment improves accuracy and addresses these problems.

Factors of Potential That Predict Leadership Growth and Future Performance

LEADERSHIP POTENTIAL FACTORS

Leadership Promise: Describes individuals who readily step up to take on leadership roles (either formally or informally) when challenges emerge and bring out the best in others when doing so. These individuals operate with authenticity and an unselfish interest in achieving outcomes that help the organization and their colleagues.

Development Orientation: Describes individuals who value new experiences and seek to grow from them by leveraging feedback and new learning. They show positive responses to others' suggestions for improvement and actively seek constructive feedback. They continually adjust their approaches to incorporate new learning.

Mastery of Complexity: Describes individuals who navigate effectively through complex challenges by focusing on the few highest priorities and adapting quickly to obstacles. They demonstrate the ability to think conceptually and navigate the ambiguity associated with difficult assignments. They also adapt their personal approaches as situations around them change.

Balance of Values and Results: Describes individuals who consistently achieve positive results in a way that fits with the organization's unique culture. They are pillars of the organization's values and demonstrate a passion for seeing assignments through to completion and achieving tangible outcomes.

OTHER FOUNDATIONAL CONSIDERATIONS

Sustained Performance in Current Role: It is essential that leaders not be nominated for accelerated development until they have demonstrated sustained, positive performance in their current role.

Motivation for Leadership: Not everyone wants to lead, and some who say they don't want leadership find they actually enjoy it after trying it. Having in-depth conversations with individuals about their motivation for leadership is essential. This includes aspirations, work motivators, stressors, personal circumstances, etc.

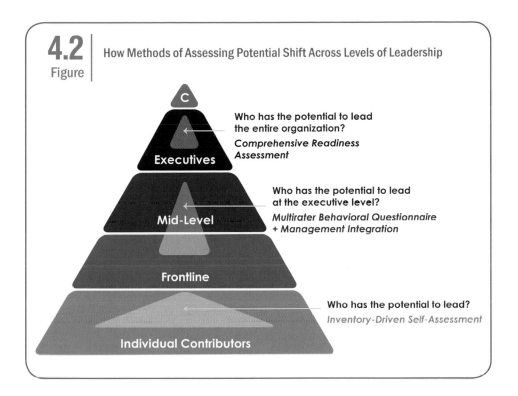

4.2 Figure | How Methods of Assessing Potential Shift Across Levels of Leadership

Who has the potential to lead the entire organization?
Comprehensive Readiness Assessment

Executives

Who has the potential to lead at the executive level?
Multirater Behavioral Questionnaire + Management Integration

Mid-Level

Frontline

Who has the potential to lead?
Inventory-Driven Self-Assessment

Individual Contributors

But, of course, conducting full-scale readiness assessments of every leader in the organization would not be practical. If your organization is midsize or large and you seek to identify individuals with leadership potential very early in their

> If your organization is midsize or large and you seek to identify individuals with leadership potential very early in their careers, it will be essential to scale your assessment of potential to the level and size of the audience you're considering.

careers, it will be essentiuyal to scale your assessment of potential to the level and size of the audience you're considering. Figure 4.2 illustrates an effective approach.

The key is to not over- or under-assess for potential. At the lowest levels of leadership and with individual contributors, the question is *who has the potential to lead* (the lowest triangle in Figure 4.2). At this level volume is typically much higher, and senior management has very little insight into people's performance. A well-validated self-assessment of potential can be useful in this situation, but use caution: This approach runs the risk of creating a perception that management has reduced the judgment of an individual's future career possibilities to a test. To avoid that outcome, any self-assessment of potential must be applied as a developmental tool for those taking it as well as a valuable source of insight for management. Communications about how results will be used must be clear and transparent, and meaningful feedback and development for participants must be coupled with the assessment.

At higher levels of leadership, the assessment of potential carries more risk. Determining *who has the potential to lead at the executive level* (the center triangle in Figure 4.2) warrants more senior management involvement and discussion. Behavioral questionnaires (completed by management, not the individual) are useful as prework to the talent review discussion. In the meeting, results can be used to structure conversations, anchoring them to observations of individual performance in relation to the potential factors.

At the top of the organization, the question is whether an already-successful leader has the capability to *lead the entire organization* (the upper triangle in Figure 4.2). This refers primarily, but not strictly, to the CEO role. To make these judgments, the most comprehensive readiness assessment is warranted, and under no circumstances should it be compromised (Chapter 5 outlines specific approaches).

Use an efficient process to discuss and finalize ratings of potential. Evaluations of potential come together with evaluations of performance, which the senior team uses to arrive at final judgments about how to differentiate investments in accelerated development. You may have gathered ratings of potential (via behavioral questionnaires) from the senior management participants in the talent review. You also may have self-report inventory results in hand. The question is how to process this assessment data in an efficient way that yields the correct judgments. We find, as many organizations have, that a performance-by-potential grid (typically a 9-box grid) is a reliable approach.

While there are different ways to facilitate a 9-box discussion, we prefer to leverage technology to do so. For example, Figure 4.3 visually depicts performance and potential ratings and presents the findings in a dynamic 9-box grid that can be manipulated in real time during the review discussion. Discussion participants have access to both individual and group reports of potential to further probe, debate, and calibrate each person's performance and potential and ultimately reach consensus on which box on the grid is most appropriate for each individual.

The combined judgments of performance and potential facilitate planning for the development of everyone in each box. The descriptors in Figure 4.4 help to make

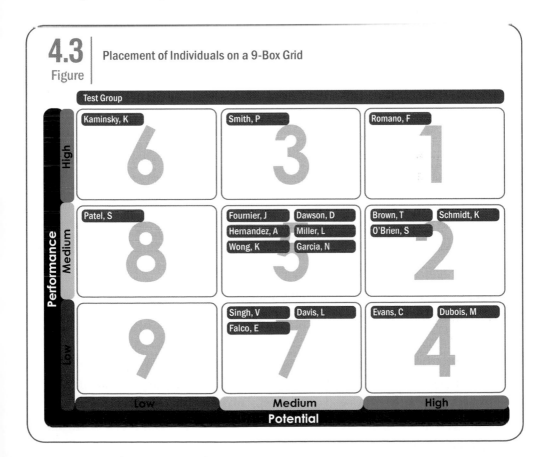

4.3 Figure | Placement of Individuals on a 9-Box Grid

Test Group

	Low	Medium	High
High	Kaminsky, K — 6	Smith, P — 3	Romano, F — 1
Medium	Patel, S — 8	Fournier, J; Hernandez, A; Wong, K; Dawson, D; Miller, L; Garcia, N — 5	Brown, T; O'Brien, S; Schmidt, K — 2
Low	9	Singh, V; Falco, E; Davis, L — 7	Evans, C; Dubois, M — 4

Performance / Potential

these distinctions (recall that all those in the box are currently high performers in their current roles, but may have been placed in the "low" performance box because of their position relative to the others being considered).

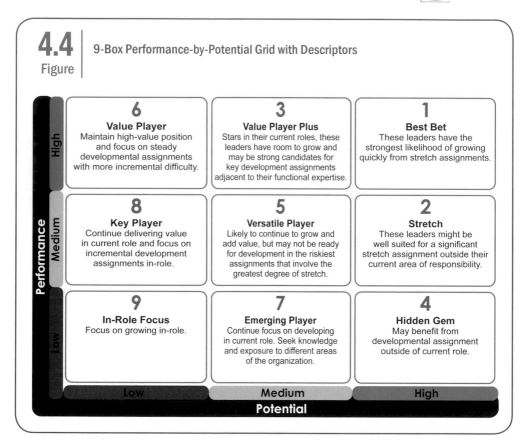

4.4 Figure | 9-Box Performance-by-Potential Grid with Descriptors

Performance — High

6
Value Player
Maintain high-value position and focus on steady developmental assignments with more incremental difficulty.

3
Value Player Plus
Stars in their current roles, these leaders have room to grow and may be strong candidates for key development assignments adjacent to their functional expertise.

1
Best Bet
These leaders have the strongest likelihood of growing quickly from stretch assignments.

Performance — Medium

8
Key Player
Continue delivering value in current role and focus on incremental development assignments in-role.

5
Versatile Player
Likely to continue to grow and add value, but may not be ready for development in the riskiest assignments that involve the greatest degree of stretch.

2
Stretch
These leaders might be well suited for a significant stretch assignment outside their current area of responsibility.

Performance — Low

9
In-Role Focus
Focus on growing in-role.

7
Emerging Player
Continue focus on developing in current role. Seek knowledge and exposure to different areas of the organization.

4
Hidden Gem
May benefit from developmental assignment outside of current role.

Potential: Low · Medium · High

Use high-quality data to evaluate readiness accurately and deploy leaders strategically.

As the talent review transitions from the Organizational segment to the Acceleration segment, conversations become more targeted and dig further into individuals, positions, and business scenarios. Questions move beyond determining who has potential and become increasingly specific to individual readiness. At this point, two fundamental questions become central to the conversation:

- **Transition readiness**—For example: Can she make the jump to the next level? How far/high do we believe she can jump, and how soon?

- **Role readiness and fit**—For example: Is he ready to lead *in this specific role and business context* (e.g., general manager of operations in Brazil)? Do his capabilities and personal attributes fit with the culture and team he would be leading? Are there any expected shifts/changes that could alter his fit?

As we signaled in the previous section, to answer these questions you will need insight into individuals' capabilities as they relate to the full success profile of the positions in question. Insight from your ratings and discussions of potential will accurately identify the people you should accelerate, but won't answer all the questions you will have about their readiness (see Table 4.2).

4.2
Table

Common Scenarios and Readiness Questions Encountered in the Talent Review

What If...	Then...
New Product: We are introducing a "blockbuster" drug that requires us to double our sales force in the next eight months?	Who should we assign to lead the product launch? Do we have sales leaders who can attract and develop sales reps who will take a more consultative approach with physicians?
Regional Growth Strategy: We want to strengthen our presence in Latin America and China, but recently have lost both regional vice presidents in those geographies to retirement?	Who is best suited to grow our existing base in each of these high-growth regions? Who will best fit the culture and understand implications for positioning current and future products in these markets?
Consolidation: We have acquired one of our largest competitors and now have redundant talent?	What is the right management team for our new company? Who will be best suited to oversee the integration? Who should drive our quality and cost-containment imperatives?
Need for Change: The next business unit leader needs to drive horizontal integration of core processes to maximize efficiencies and our ability to serve global customers?	Who has the change leadership orientation, influence, and discipline to lead our new global supply chain initiative across our heavily matrixed organization?

A Real-Life Example of How Data Enhances Readiness Decisions in the Talent Review

Jorge is a senior director in the generics distribution division of a pharmaceutical company. He is a high-potential leader, under consideration for two new roles. One is a regional vice president for the high-growth Latin America division; the other is business unit head for a new, ventures-focused group. A review of Jorge's experience shows that he has held numerous positions over a relatively short time with the organization (director, risk management; operations director for med-surgical; and senior analyst in corporate finance for Asia). He has been highly effective in each of these roles. His education includes a bachelor's degree in engineering, an M.B.A., and a supply-chain black belt certification. Among his key accomplishments is helping to negotiate a successful $200 million acquisition.

During a talent review discussion, the senior team discussed Jorge's knowledge and experience alongside data and insights gathered from an Acceleration Center, including simulations, interviews, and personality inventories. Jorge's assessment profile shows that he is proficient (i.e., effective) in 11 of the 13 target competencies and is quite strong in 2— Empowerment/Delegation and Driving Execution. This *snapshot* view also demonstrates both his positive personal attributes (Ambition) and potential executive derailers that could lead to failure (e.g., Risk Averse).

Finally, the report summarizes performance implications, including readiness to lead effectively in different business contexts (Readiness: Business Driver ratings—see diagram). Business Driver ratings suggest he will excel in pushing process efficiency and cross-functional partnerships. As a result of this review and discussion of Jorge's profile, it is determined that he is better suited for the Latin America role. In this assignment his operational focus, relationship, and cross-cultural competence will serve him well.

[continued on the next page]

[continued from previous page]

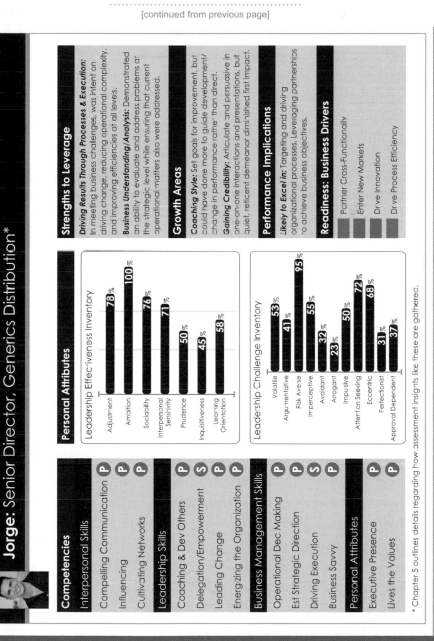

Jorge: Senior Director, Generics Distribution*

Competencies

Interpersonal Skills

Compelling Communication (P)
Influencing (P)
Cultivating Networks (P)

Leadership Skills

Coaching & Dev Others (P)
Delegation/Empowerment (S)
Leading Change (P)
Energizing the Organization (P)

Business Management Skills

Operational Dec Making (P)
Est Strategic Direction (P)
Driving Execution (S)
Business Savvy (P)

Personal Attributes

Executive Presence (P)
Lives the Values (P)

Personal Attributes

Leadership Effectiveness Inventory

Adjustment 78%
Ambition 100%
Sociability 76%
Interpersonal Sensitivity 71%
Prudence 50%
Inquisitiveness 45%
Learning Orientation 58%

Leadership Challenge Inventory

Volatile 53%
Argumentative 41%
Risk Averse 95%
Imperceptive 55%
Avoidant 32%
Arrogant 23%
Impulsive 50%
Attention Seeking 72%
Eccentric 68%
Perfectionist 31%
Approval Dependent 37%

Strengths to Leverage

Driving Results Through Processes & Execution: In meeting business challenges, was intent on driving change, reducing operational complexity, and improving efficiencies at all levels.

Business Understanding/Analysis: Demonstrated an ability to evaluate and address problems at the strategic level while ensuring that current operational matters also were addressed.

Growth Areas

Coaching Style: Set goals for improvement, but could have done more to guide development/change in performance rather than direct.

Gaining Credibility: Articulate and persuasive in one-on-one interactions and presentations, but quiet, reticent demeanor diminished first impact.

Performance Implications

Likely to Excel in: Targeting and driving organizational processes. Leveraging partnerships to achieve business objectives.

Readiness: Business Drivers

Partner Cross-Functionally
Enter New Markets
Drive Innovation
Drive Process Efficiency

* Chapter 5 outlines details regarding how assessment insights like these are gathered.

Having the right data to support your judgments of readiness not only mitigates the risk of bad decisions, but also dramatically heightens creativity and ingenuity in making development assignments that will help individuals prepare more quickly. Senior leaders soon learn the value of these data-enabled discussions, which further fuels the energy in your talent review process.

Because readiness assessment is so crucial to the success of your acceleration efforts and your business, the next chapter is devoted entirely to that topic. In it we outline how you can efficiently generate unique, powerful insight into your leaders' capabilities and teach your senior executives to use it consistently and accurately as they make key decisions regarding leadership deployment.

> Organizations report that the most valuable outcomes of the talent review are the new—and often surprising—insights gained from holistic readiness assessments.

Time and again we hear organizations report that the most valuable outcomes of the talent review are the new—and often surprising—insights gained from holistic readiness assessments. When leaders are viewed through the lens of in-depth, objective evaluation and benchmarked against high leadership standards, judgments are often altered—and even reversed—from past assumptions. And research convincingly demonstrates that more accurate talent decisions are made.[vi]

Make bold development assignments that involve learners in key business challenges.

After all the analysis, discussion, and debate, the time will come to make development assignments for key people. You probably won't be finalizing the specifics in the talent review meeting, but at a minimum, recommendations will be made. Job moves, special assignments, training, and coaching all are among the prescriptions. And in these moments, you, as a leader and champion of acceleration, face one of your most important roles: to aggressively challenge your team. Remember, to get more leaders ready to lead your business, you must find ways to get them in the game sooner. You and your team are now on the sidelines, pushing less-experienced players onto the field. It will (and should) feel risky.

It pays to be ready for these moments. Work with your business leaders in advance of the talent review to build a bank or list of business concerns that can be converted into development assignments (not formal positions) and offered to accelerated learners. Start by asking, *"What important problems or opportunities exist in our business right now that are not being addressed by our current strategic initiatives or operational plans?"* It is worth discussing this question as a senior team. The answers you reach will create more opportunities for accelerated learners to become part of your business and get in the game. The developmental assignments you generate will matter to the business. Individuals who take responsibility for addressing them will feel the energy and tension associated with rapid learning. Examples from various organizations include:

> Remember, to get more leaders ready to lead your business, you must find ways to get them in the game sooner. It will (and should) feel risky.

- Research and recommend an approach to align pricing approaches across product lines.

- Participate in a product launch to recommend improvements to the launch process.

- Become an expert about one or more key competitors and recommend enhancements for educating associates about the competition.

- Generate a business plan for a highly futuristic (but potentially viable) business concept.

- For individual experts or functionally trained professionals such as physicians or engineers, take leadership responsibility for a key initiative in a new or unfamiliar functional area.

- Participate in key meetings with alliance partners and develop recommendations for enhancing and expanding the strength of the organization's alliance network.

- Analyze the impact of the organization's safety awareness campaign.

It also is useful to have a more general list of potential development assignments in hand. These may include both short- and long-term assignments or assignments to help leaders prepare for a particular role or position (see Appendix 4.3 for a sample list). As you make assignments, several additional considerations are important:[vii]

- **Tap into motivation.** Recognize and factor in accelerated learners' career aspirations and personal concerns. These drivers often are ignored or treated as an afterthought in talent reviews. While participation in acceleration is certainly elective, it also should be attractive in its flexibility to meet individuals' unique needs and goals.

- **Address mobility constraints creatively.** Many organizations have traditionally—and rigidly—viewed mobility as a minimum requirement for participation in accelerated learning. That thinking has become antiquated, given shifting demographics and a scarcity of talent as baby boomers retire. Instead, more organizations are offering alternatives that enable highfliers to take developmental

> Many organizations have traditionally viewed mobility as a minimum requirement for participation in accelerated learning. That thinking has become antiquated.

assignments that optimize the interests of their partners and children. This can include, for example, short-term assignments that allow them to avoid uprooting school-age children. Assignments also can be purposefully chosen that serve a spouse's career or the educational needs for teens/young adults (e.g., ideal university options). Others are developing commuter options for roles that had previously been viewed as requiring a full-time local presence (e.g., managing director of India, corporate sales leadership role). Even distant international assignments are more frequently filled by leaders who spend dedicated time in their office locale, returning to family and home every four to six weeks.

- **Encourage experiences outside of one's core profession.** The issue of professional affiliation can present a significant barrier for some individuals. Many have spent years completing advanced degrees and are established thought leaders in their occupational niches (e.g., engineering, medicine, finance, technology). For some of these individuals, their sense of identity is closely tied to their scientific or professional origins. From a business perspective, it is essential to ask people to set aside their technical affiliations and step out of their niche to build their cross-business exposure and broader general management skills. However, equal consideration must be given to fueling the preferences of those specialized individuals who may be most attractive to the competition. The goal is to ensure that a balanced case is made, articulating clear benefits for the individual and the organization.

> From a business perspective, it is essential to ask people to set aside their technical affiliations and step out of their niche to build their cross-business exposure and broader general management skills.

At this point, we have only scratched the surface of the topic of making assignments that create faster and more significant growth. In Chapter 9 we address this topic fully in the complete context of the accelerated learner's pathway to greater capability.

Understanding the Various Objectives of Talent Reviews

	Review Organizational Capability	Review Key Talent Capability	TALENT REVIEW OBJECTIVES[3] — Identify Leadership Potential	Evaluate Leadership Readiness	Make Development Assignments	Evaluate Development Progress
Scope (who or what is to be reviewed)	Entire organization, business unit, or region	Critical positions or groups of positions (e.g., C-suite, general managers, country managers)	Select group(s) of nominees	Individuals being considered for promotion or key assignments	Individuals targeted for accelerated development (e.g., Acceleration Pool members)	Individuals targeted for accelerated development (e.g., Acceleration Pool members)
Key questions to be answered	*Do we have the talent we need to achieve our business and cultural priorities?*	*Is this particular group ready to conquer the leadership challenges that it soon will face?*	*Who are the individuals with the greatest potential for leadership, and who should receive our best development assignments?*	*Are these key leaders ready for promotion to the next level or to take on critical roles, jobs, or assignments?*	*How can we develop these key leaders as rapidly and effectively as possible?*	*Have adequate growth and development taken place, and what, if anything, needs to change to ensure that they do?*
Recommended tools, approaches, assessment methods (to support review sessions)	• Leadership Capacity Analysis (see Chapter 2)	• Leadership Capacity Analysis (see Chapter 2) • Readiness assessment for critical positions (see Chapter 5)	• Test of leadership potential with facilitated management integration (see Chapter 4) • Performance data	• Readiness assessment (see Chapter 5)	• Readiness assessment (see Chapter 5) • Strategies for making acceleration happen faster (see Chapters 7–11)	• Readiness assessment (see Chapters 6–7) • Strategies for making acceleration happen faster (see Chapters 7–11)
Desired outcomes	• Calibration between executives and HR on talent readiness and critical gaps • High-level understanding of leadership capability and business vulnerabilities • Business case for accelerated leadership growth	• Specific understanding of readiness and critical gaps in key areas • Strategies/Plans for closing gaps in key areas or in key units, teams, regions, etc.	• Accurately identify leaders with the ability to grow quickly • Retain top talent • Find hidden talent • Enhanced ability among top leaders to spot potential • Greater diversity in Acceleration Pools	• Succession plans for critical positions/roles • Better performance among successors to key positions • Fewer executive failures • Better analytics for evaluating both individual and group readiness	• Generate high-impact, creative development assignments that work • Identify group development needs and prescribe solutions • More growth, faster • More leaders ready now	• Sustain positive growth tension • Reenergize stalled development efforts • Clarify accountabilities and ensure progress

3 Talent reviews are routinely designed to achieve more than one of these objectives. Often, a single (annual) review meeting is aimed at achieving all of them at once—a practice that nearly always fails to achieve the desired outcomes (i.e., more ready-now leaders).

Appendix 4.2
Sample Talent Review Agenda

Organizational Review Segment (Part 1)

1. Review and reaffirm Business Drivers (leadership priorities):
   - What are the key challenges our leaders must face to execute critical business objectives?
   - What are our highest-priority leadership needs, and what outcomes are we seeking?

2. Review Leadership Capacity Analysis (see Chapter 2):
   - Determine immediate needs and emerging needs (2–3 years out).
   - Clarify areas of differential focus and investment (e.g., new service launch, key unit, region).

3. Review openings in key/critical positions:
   - Review current and projected job openings.
   - Highlight critical positions for which unique talent is required or that offer special development opportunity.

Acceleration Review Segment (Part 2)

4. Review individuals to be discussed:
   - Consider new nominations for pool membership (high potentials):
     - Position on existing pool 9-box grid.
   - Prioritize discussion of existing pool members by:
     - Unit or targeted talent pool (e.g., China Acceleration Pool).
     - Position on 9-box grid.
     - Likelihood that individuals will be ready to move now (versus a new member or those viewed as well placed in current role).

5. Review status and possible actions for current high-potential leaders/pool members/key leaders:
   - What are their current development priorities?
   - How are they performing relative to job responsibilities? Behavioral examples?
   - How are they progressing against development priorities? Behavioral examples?
   - Are they a fit for a potential opening?
   - Will they benefit from additional development (training, coaching, assignments)?
   - Are they a retention challenge? Why?
   - Should they remain in the pool? Why or why not?

6. Review openings and tentative decisions made during discussion of pool members:
   - Consider diversity targets and opportunities.
   - Consider filling roles from outside the pool when there is no good fit within.
   - Document decisions, contingencies, and "caveats" (e.g., this person will be placed in an important developmental role "if" we determine his or her willingness to move for the next assignment).

7. Review aggregate trends and implications for action.
   - Determine group-level or cadre development goals.
   - Ask: Do trends surface a need for consideration of targeted programs or development events?
   - Other.

8. Ask: Should anyone be dropped from the Acceleration Pool?

9. Ask: Should anyone be added to the pool?

10. Reaffirm accountabilities and communication plans.

4.3
Appendix

Sample List of Development Assignment Ideas

Short-Term Assignments	Longer-Term Assignments	Preparation for Senior Role
• 6 weeks to 6 months • Task or project oriented • Address some challenge—low risk • Early testing in a variety of circumstances	• 6 months to 1 year • Set specific objectives/clear measures • Opportunity to test/develop competencies • International assignment	• 1- to 2-year assignment • Exposure to "tough-call" decisions, unplanned crisis; demonstrate executive judgment/wisdom
1. Serve as a temporary member of a pricing team. 2. Work with the new customer analysis team. 3. Lead a short-term research project exploring talent trends in an emerging country and tie that to our solutions. 4. Participate in a midyear review presentation. 5. Participate in writing/presenting business plan at Business Planning. 6. Become an expert on one of our competitors. 7. Practice making a case for (client need) using job/industry situations in preparation for client discussion (Business Acumen).	1. Play a role on a product launch team. 2. Play a role on a product development team. 3. Work on a global project. 4. Follow an entire client engagement cycle with a customer. 5. Get closer to the strategic partnership approach/business through a rotational assignment. 6. Become an expert rainmaker for significant, strategic sales situations.	1. Take on an international assignment. 2. Assume the role of general manager. 3. Work as head of sales/consulting

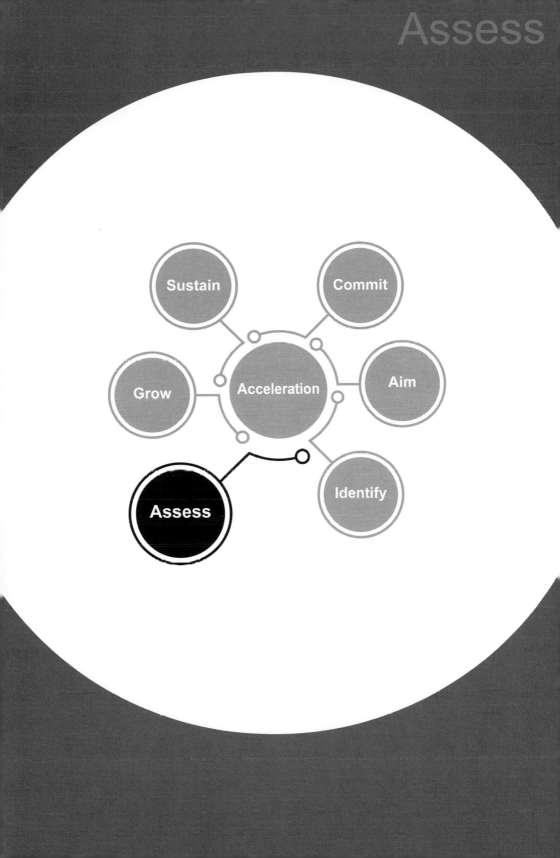

Assess

Accurately assess readiness gaps and give great feedback.

In this section…

Chapters 5 and 6 outline how organizations become great at the ASSESS imperative. The practices they employ generate energy in the following ways:

- **Better data that sparks bolder development:** Acceleration Center intelligence provides a more accurate window into what will happen in future leadership scenarios, enabling better, bolder development.

- **More in-depth insights that increase self-awareness:** More personalized, experiential assessment approaches provide far deeper insight into how one's own tendencies will play out in future situations.

- **More accurate data that reduces the rate of failure:** Data aligned to the organization's context facilitates better decision making about whom to place into key roles, dramatically reducing failure rates.

- **A different approach to feedback that inspires bold developmental action:** This approach puts the individual learner in charge of his or her own development and provides an inspiring platform for growth.

- **More use of feedback:** Leaders who receive feedback from acceleration centers are more likely to seek and use feedback from others back in the workplace.

 Denotes that tools and information on this topic are available at the *Leaders Ready Now* website (www.leadersreadynow.com). Use this code to access content: LRN2016.

GATHER GREAT DATA ABOUT YOUR PEOPLE

5 | Assessing Readiness for Big Leadership Jumps

So far, we have dealt entirely with the elements of acceleration that pertain to top management and Human Resources (aka Talent Management). We have helped you craft an acceleration strategy (Chapter 2), build a robust success profile (Chapter 3), and structure your talent review process to identify high-potential leaders (Chapter 4). We have yet to delve into the details of engaging the people you are seeking to accelerate. That shift in focus happens here, and it raises a central challenge in the journey of acceleration: the risk of accelerated growth.

It's relatively easy to design an acceleration system. But creating the energy and tension that fuel growth doesn't happen in the design process. It happens as you make decisions about people—how to develop and deploy them into jobs, assignments, and experiences that stretch them as far as possible, as early as possible, without creating too much risk (i.e., failure), all while sustaining business performance. For the remainder of this book, we turn to the components of acceleration that directly involve the individuals whose growth you are targeting. We begin with assessing readiness, the most fundamental way to mitigate risk as you make decisions that maximize the speed of growth.

What is *readiness* assessment?

Assessment guides decision making, and it can be used to improve decisions about selection, development, or placement into jobs—or for succession when the purpose is initially development and eventually selection. *Readiness* assessment refers to any assessment used to gauge how prepared a leader is to make the jump to a different role and to specify the skill gaps that must be closed for that person to become fully ready. In the context of acceleration, readiness assessments are built to measure capabilities that are well beyond the current experience levels of those being assessed. They typically evaluate individuals against roles two or more levels above their current level of leadership. Assessments that are used solely for in-role development are **not** readiness assessments (although they *are* very important)..

How Assessment Increases the Velocity of Growth

> Assessment gives you control over the *velocity* (direction and speed) of growth.

Setting out on the journey of acceleration without a good system for assessing readiness is like attempting to drive your car without a steering wheel or gas pedal. The engine runs and the car moves, but your course and speed are haphazard. In other words, assessment gives you control over the *velocity* (direction and speed) of growth. We now know from extensive research that when built and applied effectively, the right assessment achieves outcomes that are crucial to acceleration.

A 2014 research summary, spanning more than 10 years and 142 large organizations, showed that: [i]

- **Assessment makes growth happen faster and reduces the risk of failure that comes with accelerating the speed of development.** Well-designed assessment (not just any assessment) leads to better decisions about how to deploy and develop leaders. More accurate, predictive data not only reduces your error rate in promotion decisions, but it also leads to significantly higher levels of leader performance, more significant performance *improvement* over time, and more rapid career progression.

- **Assessment teaches leaders how to use feedback and makes them more receptive to it as they take on bigger assignments.** Across organizations, more than 90 percent of participants became more interested in feedback after participating in a future-focused assessment process (read on for more details). By enhancing self-insight and equipping individuals with a more precise lexicon for leadership effectiveness, assessment increases leaders' ability to gather and use feedback more productively. This, in turn, heightens the value and frequency of feedback and optimizes its use when leaders receive it.

You might ask why, given these predictable gains, assessment is not used universally. But what is not widely known is how assessment has evolved:

- **Assessment has become significantly more efficient and less expensive, and it provides far more useful insight than ever before.** The investment needed to assess 10 leaders a decade ago could now assess 50 or more, and the outputs produce more in-depth insights and more useful analytics to support business decision making. Advanced methods of assessment that leverage new technologies and evaluation techniques have produced approaches that enrich the experience for participants, while reducing time and resource requirements (by as much as 50 percent or more).

Assessment is fundamental to acceleration, and it is more scalable than ever. But not all assessment systems achieve these outcomes.

What You Should Insist Your Assessments Do

Before we leap to specific assessment approaches, it's important to articulate two essential outcomes you will need from your readiness assessments in order to fuel acceleration. Assessment that drives acceleration *must:*

- **Generate clear, new insights that spark bolder, more aggressive development plans with lower risk of failure.** If you plan to ratchet up the rate at which your leaders grow, you will face difficult choices about how much risk to take on when determining job rotations, making assignments, etc. And without deep insight into your people, your senior leaders will (rightly) be wary of costly mistakes and default to a more conservative stance. This occurs often and causes development to be incremental, rather than transformational. Readiness assessment must enable you to see beyond your people's known strengths and weaknesses and project how they will operate in situations they have yet to encounter. This level of clarity promotes innovative ideas for development while mitigating risk to the business.

> Without deep insight into your people, your senior leaders will (rightly) be wary of costly mistakes and default to a more conservative stance.

- **Assess readiness for your business context.** Assessment will not accurately gauge readiness if it is simply an attempt to profile the leader. It should enable you to match individuals' capabilities with the specific demands of your business environment. This won't happen by changing the names of competencies to sound more like your organization's language. Your readiness assessment must take objective account of your business and cultural challenges to ensure that it measures and reports on how leaders' skills and personalities stack up against the challenges they will face at higher levels. In Chapter 3 we introduced Business Drivers, which are an objective means for characterizing context and represent a central element to a successful assessment system.

You're likely aware that assessment validity improves as multiple, valid methods are brought together to assess leaders from varying angles. Beware the "magic" test or simple online tool that produces a single, final leadership score or stack-ranks your leaders top to bottom, best to worst.

People are never that simple: The full profile of a leader cannot be measured with one tool or method. Your people have varied capabilities and characteristics that make them good fits for some contexts and poor fits for others. Like a mosaic, creating a picture of a person's capabilities requires more than one color and shape. The more complex and high-risk the situation, the more colors and shapes are required to create a vivid image. It is essential to bear in mind that your goal is not simply to accurately describe each individual, but to do so in a way that enables specific, objective conversation among your senior leaders and increases your creativity and certainty about the risks you can safely take with each person's development.

> Your goal is not simply to accurately describe each individual, but to do so in a way that enables specific, objective conversation among your senior leaders.

The Assessment Game Plan

To help navigate a very crowded and at times complex field of practice, you have three choices when you select an approach to readiness assessment:

- **Multi-perspective (360°-driven) assessments:** This approach relies primarily on coworker input to gather data and can take the form of surveys or interviews. For lower-level leadership roles, survey-only methods are common. At senior executive levels, multiple coworkers may be interviewed by a professional assessor or coach who creates a report summarizing results. Survey and/or interview data may be combined with other measures, such as personality inventories, to add insight and developmental value to the feedback. *Because they are primarily based on perceptions of current and past performance, 360°-driven assessments are more useful for development than for projecting readiness for future roles.*

- **Interview-driven assessments:** This approach relies mainly on behavior-based interviews to gather insight on how leaders have approached challenges in the past. It also may be combined with other measures, including personality and cognitive testing or multi-perspective (360°) surveys. The most predictive methods, such as DDI's Targeted Selection®, apply rigor, consistency, and precision in evaluating past behaviors against potential future challenges and integrate the inputs of several interviewers to achieve reliability of judgment. *Interview-driven assessments are useful for assessing readiness for more incremental transitions, for which behavior in one's current role is relevant to requirements in the target role.*

- **Acceleration Centers:**[1] The term "center" implies a location but is actually meant to convey a combination of approaches into one holistic experience. It uses highly realistic and immersive leadership simulations as the foundational method and combines other methods, such as behavior-based interviews, personality inventories, and cognitive tests, to provide comparative insights pertaining to all aspects of the success profile. Trained assessors—often aided by scientifically derived algorithms—integrate findings from all sources. (**Note:** At higher levels of leadership, Acceleration Centers employ more in-depth methods and tools to achieve a more comprehensive understanding of leaders' skills and personal attributes. At lower levels, more scalable approaches with fewer tools and methods are more common.) Behavior patterns in the simulation then are compared to behaviors demonstrated in the workplace and dispositions inherent to the individual. Acceleration Centers are particularly useful for assessing readiness for multilevel leadership jumps, because they are highly comprehensive and enable precise observation in leadership challenges and dilemmas (simulations) that participants have yet to experience.

As you evaluate alternatives, we advise caution. There are many assessment methods and tools that provide insight, but there are few that catalyze

---

1 The term "Acceleration Center" is our preferred label for assessment center. We explain why on the following pages.

acceleration. We have seen some of the most respected organizations in the world make huge investments in assessments that were soon—but not soon enough—deemed to have no benefit to the accelerated growth of leaders.

Because not all transitions (jumps) are created equal, assessment must be aligned to the scope and risk inherent to it. Generally, more risk warrants more in-depth assessment. We also recognize that there are many other available

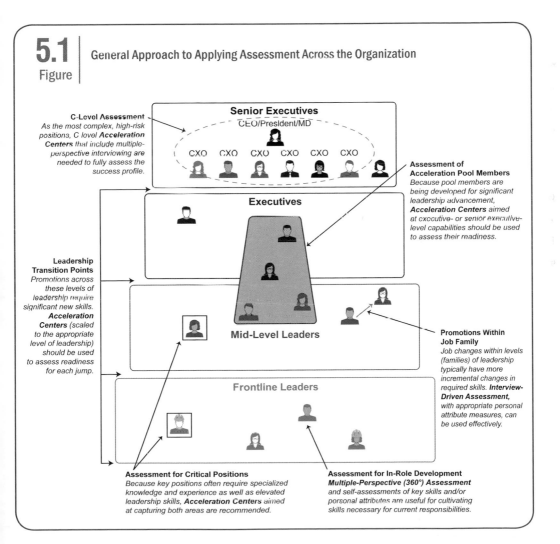

5.1
Figure

General Approach to Applying Assessment Across the Organization

C-Level Assessment
*As the most complex, high-risk positions, C-level **Acceleration Centers** that include multiple-perspective interviewing are needed to fully assess the success profile.*

Senior Executives
CEO/President/MD
CXO CXO CXO CXO CXO CXO

Assessment of Acceleration Pool Members
*Because pool members are being developed for significant leadership advancement, **Acceleration Centers** aimed at executive- or senior executive-level capabilities should be used to assess their readiness.*

Executives

Leadership Transition Points
*Promotions across these levels of leadership require significant new skills. **Acceleration Centers** (scaled to the appropriate level of leadership) should be used to assess readiness for each jump.*

Mid-Level Leaders

Promotions Within Job Family
*Job changes within levels (families) of leadership typically have more incremental changes in required skills. **Interview-Driven Assessment**, with appropriate personal attribute measures, can be used effectively.*

Frontline Leaders

Assessment for Critical Positions
*Because key positions often require specialized knowledge and experience as well as elevated leadership skills, **Acceleration Centers** aimed at capturing both areas are recommended.*

Assessment for In-Role Development
Multiple-Perspective (360°) Assessment *and self-assessments of key skills and/or personal attributes are useful for cultivating skills necessary for current responsibilities.*

forms of assessment, such as test-driven assessments, motivational assessments, judgment inventories, and so on. Most often, however, these tools are used as components of one of the three primary approaches and reflect measurement of a segment of the success profile. As you consider the many tools, methods, and applications you will encounter across your organization, refer to Figure 5.1 for illustrations of a general approach to deploying assessment to meet the needs of acceleration.

Acceleration Centers

> **Insight isn't enough. To drive acceleration, you will have to convey that insight in a way that equips management and accelerated learners with the clarity and confidence to adopt more risk.**

Any of the three primary assessment methods can gain insight into what individuals might need to grow faster. But the insight isn't enough. To drive acceleration, you will have to convey that insight in a way that equips management and accelerated learners with the clarity and confidence to adopt more risk in making developmental assignments. And because interview-driven and 360°-driven approaches are rooted in past events and behaviors, they are less effective at sizing up risks about future scenarios.

Acceleration Centers are uniquely valuable to acceleration for the same reasons that auditions are important when casting actors (even the most famous and well-known) and that athletic tryouts are essential to make final evaluations of players. You might be able to imagine an actor playing a specific role in a play or movie, but until you see that person in character reading for the part, you can't make a full assessment of fit. In many cases, hours of recorded (past) performances or game films are available to inform judgments, but they aren't enough. Because the future is dynamic, and because actors and players evolve, the audition or tryout is vital to make a final assessment of readiness and to determine what coaching or skill enhancement might be required to ensure success.

A Case in Point

To bring this into focus, let's look at two parts of a conversation among senior management about the strategic-thinking capability of a high-potential leader. We'll call her Kat Smith.

- Referencing interview and 360° data: *People see Kat as a smart, strategic thinker. She did a great job on the previous year's business analysis and impressed senior management in her presentation of the results. Kat has a deep understanding of our operation and has built a strong network among our customers and alliance partners.*

- Adding the results of a strategic business-planning simulation: *In her strategic plan for the business unit, she relied heavily on financial analysis to isolate the cost and margin problems the business was facing. She devised a plan to address those problems, but it didn't include any customer-facing initiatives to generate top-line growth or penetrate new markets. Her plan was almost entirely focused internally and lacked consideration of the business environment. Her strategy might have fixed the cost and efficiency problems, but it wouldn't have grown the business.*

Placing yourself in the position of determining the right next step for Kat, you likely would make very different judgments if using only interview and 360° data. Because the simulation placed her in a more complex planning environment, we are able to pinpoint how her current tendencies would play out in a realistic future scenario. Combining these observations with other essential ingredients—such as personality data that indicates how naturally conceptual her thinking is or how inclined she is toward learning and self-insight—would further strengthen the understanding of her ability to think strategically. While Kat might be less ready than anticipated for a role requiring heavy strategic planning, her development can be targeted to cultivate that capability. Or, if necessary, to avoid roles requiring it if the risk is too great. This is risk mitigation through behavioral specificity, and our experience shows unequivocally that your senior leaders will be far more risk-averse without it.

Figure 5.2 provides a window into this specificity. It shows a dashboard of Kat's results from her Acceleration Center experience that included simulations, a behavioral interview, and personality inventories. (Note that Figure 5.2 is a *management* summary, and that Kat would have received far more detailed results.) Included on this one-page summary are results pertaining to the Interaction Essentials, competencies (behaviors), personality enablers and derailers, and readiness to lead in the specific context (Business Drivers) that the organization has identified.

Competency patterns obtained from simulations and interviews can be better understood by examining personality patterns that help to explain why some behaviors were more prevalent than others. Ultimately, each additional angle (method) adds to our understanding of the leadership performance areas that will be more or less difficult for Kat to master. As participants and their managers discuss these unique inputs and integrate them with what they know of Kat's performance on the job, valuable insight is gained into a) which Business Drivers she is ready to conquer (or not), and b) how best to craft development that will exploit strengths and cultivate capability where growth is needed.

The other aspect that must be managed is the degree of risk that Kat must assume. She will be far less inclined to sign up for bold development assignments if her experience in the assessment process feels evaluative and if she doesn't believe in the data and its importance.

> Because of its realism and immersive nature, the Acceleration Center approach provides a deeper, more personalized learning experience, which unfreezes thinking.

Because of its realism and immersive nature, the Acceleration Center approach provides a deeper, more personalized learning experience, which unfreezes thinking about the best leadership tactics and opens participants to new alternatives. How? In a typical application, after being invited and oriented to the process, Kat would have completed personality inventories in advance of a simulation experience. This is not a simulation exercise, but an *experience* in which Kat carves her own path through a leadership role that requires analysis, decision making,

5.2 Figure | Dashboard of Acceleration Center Results—Management Report

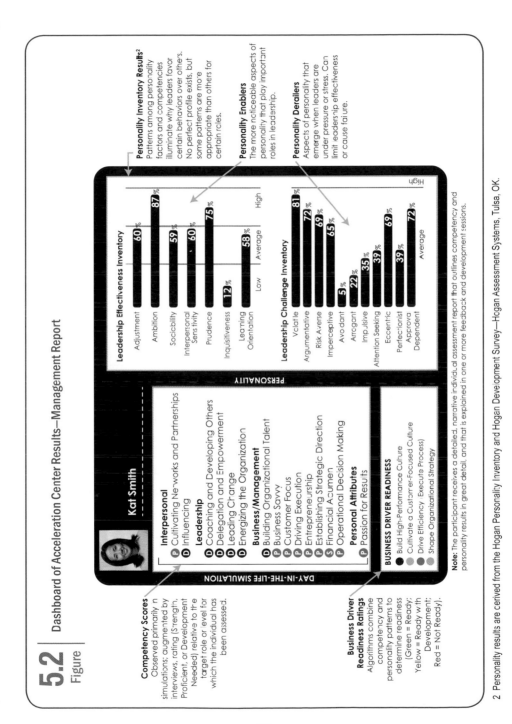

Competency Scores
Observed primarily in simulations; augmented by interviews, rating (Strength, Proficient, or Development Needed) relative to the target role or level for which the individual has been assessed.

Personality Inventory Results[2]
Patterns among personality factors and competencies illuminate why leaders favor certain behaviors over others. No perfect profile exists, but some patterns are more appropriate than others for certain roles.

Personality Enablers
The more noticeable aspects of personality that play important roles in leadership.

Personality Derailers
Aspects of personality that emerge when leaders are under pressure or stress. Can limit leadership effectiveness or cause failure.

Business Driver Readiness Ratings
Algorithms combine competency and personality patterns to determine readiness (Green = Ready; Yellow = Ready with Development; Red = Not Ready).

Kat Smith

Interpersonal
- (P) Cultivating Networks and Partnerships
- (D) Influencing

Leadership
- (D) Coaching and Developing Others
- (D) Delegation and Empowerment
- (D) Leading Change
- (D) Energizing the Organization

Business/Management
- (D) Building Organizational Talent
- (P) Business Savvy
- (P) Customer Focus
- (P) Driving Execution
- (P) Entrepreneurship
- (P) Establishing Strategic Direction
- (S) Financial Acumen
- (P) Operational Decision Making

Personal Attributes
- (P) Passion for Results

BUSINESS DRIVER READINESS
- ● Build High-Performance Culture
- ◐ Cultivate a Customer-Focused Culture
- ◐● Drive Efficiency (Execute Process)
- ● Shape Organizational Strategy

DAY-IN-THE-LIFE SIMULATION

PERSONALITY

Leadership Effectiveness Inventory

- Adjustment — 60%
- Ambition — 87%
- Sociability — 59%
- Interpersonal Sensitivity — 60%
- Prudence — 75%
- Inquisitiveness — 12%
- Learning Orientation — 58%

Low — Average — High

Leadership Challenge Inventory

- Volatile — 81%
- Argumentative — 72%
- Risk Averse — 69%
- Imperceptive — 65%
- Avoidant — 5%
- Arrogant — 22%
- Impulsive — 35%
- Attention Seeking — 39%
- Eccentric — 69%
- Perfectionist — 39%
- Approva[l] Dependent — 72%

Average — High

Note: The participant receives a detailed, narrative individual assessment report that outlines competency and personality results in great detail, and that is explained in one or more feedback and development sessions.

2 Personality results are derived from the Hogan Personality Inventory and Hogan Development Survey—Hogan Assessment Systems, Tulsa, OK.

planning, coaching, communicating, influencing, and other skills required to lead a team, function, business, or organization through its challenges and opportunities. Her experience in the Acceleration Center might have been as a supervisor, mid-level manager, executive, or CEO. It may have been live or virtual. But it certainly would not have been uninteresting. (See the sidebar on the following pages for details on how Acceleration Centers have changed in recent years.)

The holistic nature of an Acceleration Center matters because leadership is not a task—it is a *role*. And to simulate it, the entire role must be represented.

> Leadership is not a task—it is a *role*. And to simulate it, the entire role must be represented.

Kat's simulation experience would have taken her first through the history and evolution of a large corporation, its products and services, structure, customers, competitors, and leaders, and then assigned her to a role with responsibilities well beyond her current duties. On simulation day she would have faced myriad challenges, including difficult operational decisions, planning for her unit (be it a plan for a production team or the entire corporation), tough meetings, and presentations with partners, direct reports, and customers—all in the same fluid (and at times hectic) manner in which a leader's work life happens.

After trained assessors integrated Kat's responses, a report like the one shown in Figure 5.3 would have been created. Published as a web page rather than on paper, it is actually less of a report and more like a discovery tool. Not only can Kat scan the observations of her performance in any way she prefers, but she also can manipulate them to structure her own thinking and development planning. She can sort data to imagine varying career scenarios, prioritize her next steps to capitalize on her strengths, and steer her own development.

5.3 Figure

Sample Individual Assessment Report Portal

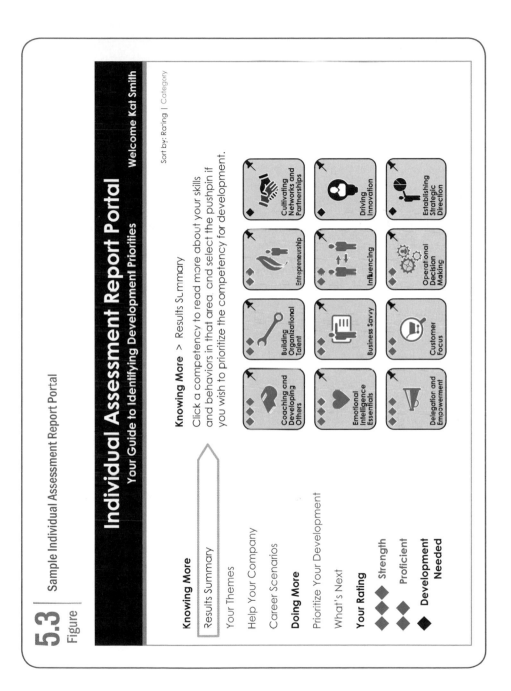

Individual Assessment Report Portal
Your Guide to Identifying Development Priorities

Welcome Kat Smith

Knowing More

Results Summary

Your Themes

Help Your Company

Career Scenarios

Doing More

Prioritize Your Development

What's Next

Your Rating

◆ Strength

◆ Proficient

◆ **Development Needed**

Knowing More > Results Summary

Click a competency to read more about your skills and behaviors in that area and select the pushpin if you wish to prioritize the competency for development.

Sort by: Rating | Category

Coaching and Developing Others

Building Organizational Talent

Entrepreneurship

Cultivating Networks and Partnerships

Emotional Intelligence Essentials

Business Savvy

Influencing

Driving Innovation

Delegation and Empowerment

Customer Focus

Operational Decision Making

Establishing Strategic Direction

Acceleration Center Innovations Across the Pipeline

New assessment technologies and methods have fundamentally changed the way traditional assessment centers are administered, scored, and reported. This has given rise to a new generation of more scalable *Acceleration Centers* that simulate the most difficult transitions leaders face across their careers and provide the feedback needed to conquer them—at a fraction of the time and investment. Three primary innovations have driven these changes:

- **Virtual immersion**—Video and e-communication methods create highly realistic, yet virtual, environments in which participants encounter leadership challenges just as they would in a live scenario.

- **Digitally enabled response and evaluation**—All participant responses are gathered digitally and made available instantly to evaluation teams who leverage sharing technology to review and combine responses guided by evaluation criteria and scoring algorithms that heighten reliability and validity.

- **Feedback and development portals**—Assessment results are made available via interactive web portals that allow participants and managers to review and organize data and to directly access and connect development tactics to them.

The following new approaches from DDI have made Acceleration Centers practical for much larger audiences, at all levels of leadership.

Manager Ready®: The frontline leader transition experience—Manager Ready®—leverages video and electronic communication methods in a completely virtual environment to present the major challenges facing frontline leaders. Fast-paced and interactive within a job-relevant scenario, Manager Ready requires participants to speak or type responses after which a team of specialized assessors (each trained to observe specific types of behaviors) catalogs them to quickly and accurately summarize performance against competencies and Key Actions. Feedback is highly specific at the Key Action level (see Chapter 3) and points out actionable growth opportunities.

[continued at top of next page]

124

[continued from previous page]

Leader3 Ready® (for the mid-level leader transition): Successful frontline leaders often are promoted, but if they are promoted again into mid-level (operational) leadership, they typically face very different challenges in the realms of analysis, influence, leading change, and decision making. Leader3 Ready®, named for this third leadership jump, introduces the participant to a far more dynamic and complex leadership environment, but does so in a way that feels more like being part of a movie than an assessment. Coupling live interaction with video and e-enabled decision challenges, leadership dilemmas, and people problems, participants carve their own path through scenarios in a game-like environment, all done virtually. Assessment evaluations adhere to the same behavioral methods as Manager Ready, but incorporate motivational and personality assessments, as well as relevant knowledge and experience measures. Results are made available via an interactive web portal that allows participants and managers to navigate and view feedback in any manner that suits their preferences and to dynamically link assessment results to development recommendations in constructing development plans.

Executive Acceleration Centers® (for executive and C suite transitions): All leadership roles are complex, but none more than those at the top of the organization. Executive, C-suite and CEO Acceleration Centers are designed to immerse the most accomplished leaders into deep business and cultural dilemmas they have yet to encounter. These situations challenge their ability to integrate, strategize, influence, and lead in a context similar to that of their own organization but at a new, higher level. Participants are granted the autonomy to lead as they see fit and to shape a future that they deem most fruitful for the organization. Their leadership actions in the simulation converge with their actual leadership experiences (via interviews as part of the process) and integrate with personal attributes (personality, cognitive ability, etc.). The results are used in a series of feedback discussions with the participant, management, and, if appropriate, the board of directors to determine fit with potential future roles and to construct the highest-value development action plans.

Acceleration Centers Produce Insights for Groups Too

These types of insights can be achieved for groups as well as individuals. Having gained the perspective that enables Business Driver readiness judgments, observations like the ones shown in Figure 5.4 are possible. This figure represents an aggregation of data from assessments of the senior team at a large corporation (competency and personality data were linked to yield Business Driver readiness ratings). In the midst of a significant strategic shift, this team became aware (somewhat painfully) that they were far more equipped to generate strategies for the future than they were to execute them. Across nearly all members of the team, behavior patterns in the Acceleration Center showed highly creative business planning and strategic thinking. But it also revealed far less effective behaviors in cultivating clear performance expectations, processes, and relationships that would be needed to promote receptivity and clarity for ensuring sound strategic execution.

> In the midst of a significant strategic shift, this team became aware (somewhat painfully) that they were far more equipped to generate strategies for the future than they were to execute them.

And this pattern of results was not simply a matter of competencies; there were dispositional origins as well. Figure 5.5 shows that every team member was exceptionally driven and competitive (high Ambition); but simultaneously, most were lacking in their tendency to provide clear guidance and direction to the organization (high in Attention Seeking and Eccentric, which often translates to not leading through others as well as giving unclear guidance).

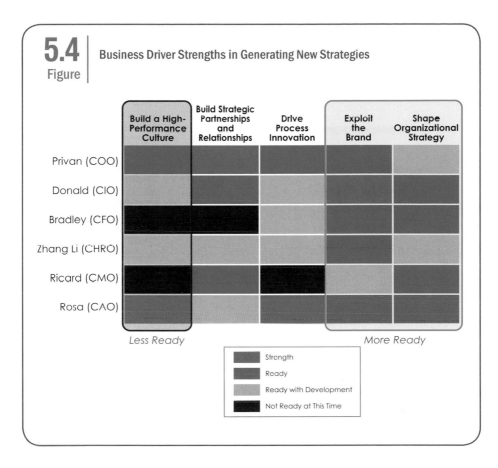

5.4 Figure | Business Driver Strengths in Generating New Strategies

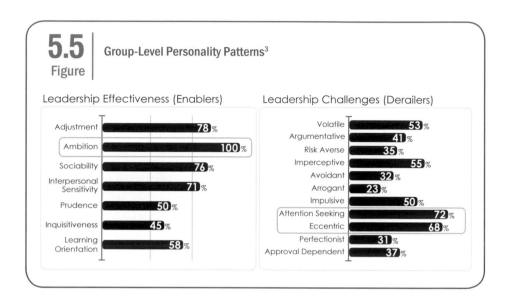

5.5 Figure | Group-Level Personality Patterns[3]

Leadership Effectiveness (Enablers)

Adjustment	78%
Ambition	100%
Sociability	76%
Interpersonal Sensitivity	71%
Prudence	50%
Inquisitiveness	45%
Learning Orientation	58%

Leadership Challenges (Derailers)

Volatile	53%
Argumentative	41%
Risk Averse	35%
Imperceptive	55%
Avoidant	32%
Arrogant	23%
Impulsive	50%
Attention Seeking	72%
Eccentric	68%
Perfectionist	31%
Approval Dependent	37%

This organization also sought to examine the level of readiness of entire business units. Figure 5.6 shows the organization chart of the unit, with each position color-coded to the Business Driver readiness of the incumbent. In this example, assessment data is aggregated to examine readiness against the Business Driver: Drive Process Innovation. Multiple competencies and personality patterns underlie the readiness ratings, but the color-coded organization chart enables a level of insight that helps senior leaders set priorities for talent development at the business unit level.

With respect to this large corporation, the Acceleration Center data and feedback process illuminated a leadership team that was poised to launch a series of sweeping new strategies, yet was unprepared to sufficiently guide the organization to ensure that they worked. This insight naturally sparked both individual and group development responses that provided this senior management team with guidance around the more thoughtful execution of strategies, enabling a very different (and more successful) method of preparing

---

3 Results are derived from the Hogan Personality Inventory and Hogan Development Survey—Hogan Assessment Systems, Tulsa, OK.

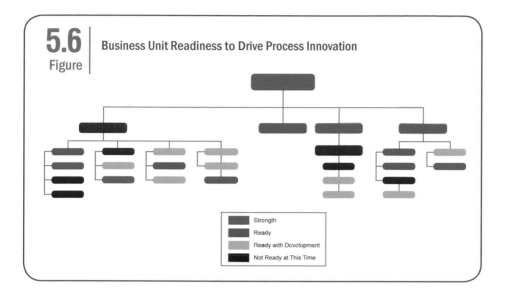

5.6 Figure | Business Unit Readiness to Drive Process Innovation

Strength
Ready
Ready with Development
Not Ready at This Time

for their emerging business situation. It is important to note, however, that this level of insight could not have been attained by simply conducting 360° feedback or interviewing each senior team member. Multiple perspectives, particularly those from the Acceleration Center simulations and personality inventories, enabled the team to see specifically how they tended to handle complex strategic challenges and the underlying dispositions that led them to repeat their habits time and again.

Should Cognitive Tests Be Included in Readiness Assessments?

Cognitive ability (intelligence) has been shown through many years of research to be one of the strongest predictors of leadership.[ii] It is commonly stated that as jobs become more complex, cognitive ability, like personality, becomes more important. We would concur, but with some important caveats that have special pertinence to acceleration.

First, while there can be no question that as roles become more complex, their cognitive demands increase substantially, it is not necessarily true that cognitive ability accounts for a larger *proportion* of the success profile.[iii] In more advanced leadership roles, cognitive demands are not the only ones that increase. One could easily make the argument (and we do) that other demands—such as interpersonal dynamics, leadership challenges, and business management tasks—together amount to the larger proportion of what accounts for success in

> Because cognitive ability is the success profile component individuals can least develop, it must be considered carefully when your organization is seeking to accelerate growth.

more advanced leadership assignments (senior leaders, executives). In other words, cognitive ability is a reliable predictor of leadership success, but not because it is the greatest determinant of success. In addition, because cognitive ability is the success profile component individuals can least develop, it must be considered carefully when your organization is seeking to accelerate growth.

When determining leadership readiness, cognitive ability is most useful as one component of a more comprehensive assessment. For lower levels of leadership, more focused assessments of cognitive ability may take the form of situational judgment tests, while more comprehensive measures of critical thinking or complex reasoning can be applied at advanced leader levels. Also at lower levels, where the volume of leaders is higher and external screening is more commonly needed, cognitive ability is often applied as a component (along with other behavioral measures) of a selection system to screen for foundational capabilities or to determine which candidates may advance to more in-depth screening. For leaders being considered by management for executive-level assignments, cognitive ability is an essential part of the overall picture when making promotion decisions. However, when using assessment data to create accelerated development plans, interpretation and communication of results must be positioned thoughtfully. There are many stories of highly intelligent leaders who have failed and of less-intelligent leaders who have achieved great success. Cognitive ability must be interpreted in light of the overall profile of skills and attributes and be recognized as a stable characteristic that should be understood for its role in each leader's unique strengths and growth needs.

Leaders seeking to accelerate growth would do well to understand that in leadership, the *application* of intelligence is as important as intelligence itself.

How Much Assessment Is Enough?

For assessment to work for your acceleration efforts, it must be administered in the correct amount. Apply too little, and the data will fail to improve decision making; apply too much, and the investment required to collect and digest the information will be so large that it will outweigh the value gained. So how, exactly, do you determine how much assessment is enough? *Focus* is the key. Watch a cat—any cat, domestic or wild, big or small—and its eyes teach an important lesson about focus—and about assessment. At rest, the cat's pupils are thin, black vertical slits. In this mode, vision is broad and wide, including focus on many different objects and depths. In hunting mode, the focus becomes much sharper, as the pupils dilate fully to let in maximum light so that a target can be seen in as much detail as possible. In this mode everything in the environment becomes blurred *except* the target. Through a beautiful and complex natural phenomenon, the cat adjusts its vision to the nature of the task.

Assessment tools can be deployed to operate like a cat's eyes. For jobs with more narrow focus, such as customer service rep, maintenance technician, or software engineer, we may elect to isolate key elements of the

> Assessment tools can be deployed to operate like a cat's eyes.

success profile (i.e., sharp focus) that have proven to be most crucial to job performance (e.g., service orientation, work standards, technical knowledge) and assess for those. This approach would be appropriate because overall job performance is determined by a smaller set of skills and attributes. As roles become more complex and require more varied skill sets, including leadership capabilities (e.g., supervisor, manager), it becomes important to assess the success profile more comprehensively (i.e., with a wide focus) to not only ensure minimal capability for leadership tasks, but to fully inform growth needs so that development can be aimed in the most fruitful directions.

131

For the most complex, high-risk positions, such as vice president, general manager, or chief officer, a combination of both approaches (i.e., wide and sharp focus) must be adopted to understand the entire success profile at a level of precision that meets the complexity of the particular role. Because these roles have such varied and complex challenges and so many determinants of success, to isolate a subset of success factors would result in an overly narrow field of view and would likely miss crucial insights. At this highest level of job complexity, assessment also must account for the context in which the leader will operate. As we discussed in Chapter 3, Business Drivers are incorporated into the assessment to enable an analysis of not only the leader's capabilities and characteristics, but also an overlay of these capabilities onto the specific environment in which they will be applied.

Most organizations have multiple acceleration needs amid many competing business demands and therefore must scale assessments in ways that align with these priorities and allocate limited resources. A business might simultaneously face the need to rapidly develop a stronger stable of global project leaders, to prepare high-potential senior managers for key corporate executive roles, and to implement a senior executive team development process. All of these initiatives would be similar in their aim to accelerate leadership growth, but their specific assessment needs are very different. Table 5.1 provides a useful means for evaluating competing needs for assessment and helps users to arrive at the appropriate balance between scalability and comprehensiveness.

Assessment scenarios with greater decision risk and more significant growth imperatives call for more comprehensive assessment; those with large execution challenges and large volume and scale, by contrast, call for more scalable, focused solutions. Obviously, there is no simple equation that will yield the perfect answer for each instance. These factors enhance understanding of assessment needs so that better judgments can be made about how to allocate limited resources.

5.1 Table	Four Factors to Consider in Determining How to Scale Assessments		
Factor	**Low**	**Moderate**	**High**
Decision Risk What types of management decisions will the assessment data support?	Development only, Lower-level position(s)	Development first, eventually for promotion	Immediate promotion or selection; higher-level position(s)
Growth Imperative How much growth (development) is needed as an outcome of the assessment process?	Build a skill	Increase readiness for a role or business challenge	Transform organizational capability
Execution Challenge How difficult will it be to implement the system, and are we ready as an organization to do so?	Ready to execute now	Somewhat ready for near-term need	Significant obstacles, urgent need
Volume & Scale How large and geographically dispersed is the audience for assessment?	Low volume, local need	Moderate volume and spread	High volume, widely dispersed

With the Right Assessment Data, Feedback Is Radically Different and Better

Assessment data—particularly the kind of data we have outlined here—is powerful. And its unique power enables dramatically better feedback that fundamentally improves the prospects for accelerated growth. In the next chapter we outline a different approach to feedback—one that leverages assessment in ways that inspire individuals to seek out and maximize developmental opportunities and guide them toward success as they make big leadership jumps.

RETHINK FEEDBACK

6 | Providing Feedback That Inspires Rapid Growth

"I have some feedback for you."

This is not a statement that typically inspires enthusiasm for what's coming next. Unfortunately, when feedback *should* generate surges of energy in the growth process, it often drains it instead. Why? Because to create the energy needed to accelerate growth, feedback must do much more than simply deliver a message. No matter how true a feedback message may be or how convinced one might be that it will improve another person's performance, to inspire a talented individual to embrace a risky challenge or adopt a new mind-set, feedback must create *insight*. Growth needs energy, and *feedback energizes growth by creating insight* in an accelerated learner's mind.

Delivering feedback for accelerated growth requires skillful dialog, based on the right inputs and preparation, that reframes the way accelerated learners regard their own skills and tendencies relative to future leadership transitions.

By creating insight, feedback builds value for growth *before* leadership challenges arise, and your acceleration system will run much more efficiently if you can make that happen consistently.

The Important Difference Between Feedback and Coaching

In the context of an acceleration process, the distinction between feedback and coaching is significant, because each serves a different and essential purpose. Feedback clarifies leadership strengths and growth needs, while coaching supports the actual growth process. Feedback helps an individual understand the aspects of the success profile that he or she must improve or leverage to be successful in the future. And it builds value for making personal change happen. Feedback also serves the critical function of helping individuals prepare to discuss their development priorities with other key players (e.g., managers, mentors).

Coaching is the dialog, insight, advice, and guidance that steers the individual's efforts during the process of change. Because feedback can be considered a part of coaching, we use the term *feedback coach*. Bear in mind, however, that one can be a strong feedback provider without being a strong coach, and vice versa.

How Does Feedback Energize an Acceleration Process?

Typical feedback is characterized by that uncomfortable moment when your boss leaves you feeling like a failure because of something you did, did poorly, or didn't do at all. But feedback for acceleration is quite different. It is thought provoking, illuminating, sometimes surprising, and most importantly, inspiring. In the context of an acceleration process, feedback is when a coach (feedback provider) helps a learner take stock of himself in relation to the future. It is an accurate,

> Feedback for acceleration is quite different. It is thoughtful, comprehensive, and most importantly, inspiring.

holistic reflection of a person's capabilities against roles and challenges not yet encountered. And that means the feedback must be enabled by an assessment[1] that fully illuminates strengths and growth needs against a higher-level success profile.

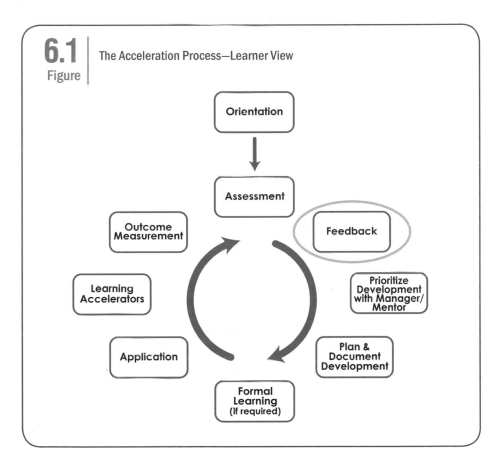

6.1 Figure | The Acceleration Process—Learner View

Orientation

Assessment

Outcome Measurement

Feedback

Learning Accelerators

Prioritize Development with Manager/ Mentor

Application

Plan & Document Development

Formal Learning (if required)

---

1 Because the outputs from Acceleration Centers are highly behaviorally specific and oriented toward future leadership levels, receiving feedback from them garners more positive reactions and generates more development action than feedback from other methods. DDI research shows that receptivity to feedback from Acceleration Centers is exceptionally high. Executive sponsors observe more than 90 percent of participants (learners) as more receptive to feedback following an Acceleration Center experience. Learners also engage in meetings with managers and mentors and have high-impact development plans more than 90 percent of the time.

With feedback, assessment results are processed collaboratively with the assistance of a feedback coach.[2] But the process view in Figure 6.1 is just that: a process. It does not adequately convey the true heart of feedback. A strong feedback coach is not simply one who is credible or persuasive. Compelling insight can produce a transformational moment in a leader's career, but doing so demands a more thoughtful approach than sharing knowledge or following a feedback outline.

A strong acceleration process demands that leaders receive high-impact feedback. Skillful, prepared feedback coaches need to capitalize on assessment insights to anticipate reactions, build on enthusiasm, confront risks, and generate energy for change—the *right* change that awakens the leader's heart and mind and then catalyzes action in ways that help the business. This requires feedback discussions that are structured correctly and conversations that are less about reporting information and more about guided self-discovery. Let's examine how to make that happen so that, as you design and build processes, you can ensure that feedback produces the energy your system needs.

Preparing Learners for Feedback

The communications shared with leaders in advance of an acceleration process will have a great deal to do with the energy they get from feedback. And if you have struggled with these communications in the past, you're in good company. Many organizations have inadvertently sent the wrong messages to learners about the purpose and intent of assessment and feedback. As a result, they have lost their

> It will be impossible to achieve faster growth for leaders who are not aware that acceleration is the goal.

learners' engagement. Words matter, particularly to ambitious, hard-working high potentials seeking to have greater impact on the business.

---

2 A "feedback coach" may or may not be a professional leadership or executive coach, but it is essential to have an impartial, objective individual who is: a) knowledgeable about the leadership level toward which the learner aspires, and b) skilled at leveraging assessment data to provide high-impact feedback. This ensures far greater receptivity, clarity, and actionable outcomes that can easily be converted into development plans.

But regardless of your overall communication plan, one thing is true: It will be impossible to achieve faster growth for leaders who are not aware that acceleration is the goal. Acceleration is risk, as we have said, and must be shared between the individual and senior management. This means the entire process—and particularly feedback—must be framed around that shared risk. Leaders must be oriented not only to a process, but also to the objective of faster learning for the purpose of making the business more competitive and its leaders more engaged and fulfilled. Thoughtful orientation increases the likelihood that individuals will embrace the prospect of bold development by clarifying business purpose, personal benefits, expectations, how to prepare, and what will happen in terms of feedback and development planning. Clear messaging at the outset creates trust and openness to new insights.

When the process begins for a learner, the first taste of feedback occurs prior to the receipt of any report or discussion. The simple act of participating in the right kind of assessment—simulations, personality inventories, etc.—will trigger self-reflection. For example, it's common to hear participants in Acceleration Centers report that they began having new insights about their readiness for higher-level leadership as early as their drive home from the assessment day.

As a general rule, learners should receive assessment reports in advance of a feedback discussion, but not too far in advance. Several days generally is sufficient to review and develop initial reactions in preparation for a discussion with a coach. This time allows the learner to absorb the highlights, identify questions, and begin to process any emotions or concerns. Many devour their report and ruminate on implications prior to feedback; others skim it to size their immediate reaction. Some have their predictions confirmed, while others become surprised and even defensive if results contradict self-perceived strengths or reflect poorly on desirable skills for their role. In any case, participants arrive at feedback sessions with a point of view on what they have read—fair, unfair, expected, surprised, reinforced, uncomfortable, and so on. Being prepared to productively process these reactions is part of what it takes to convert these results into insights and energy for growth.

Who Should Give Feedback for Acceleration?

As one responsible for driving acceleration in your organization, you may find yourself in the position of being a feedback coach, and you will need to engage other coaches, either internally or from outside the organization. You and your team together will have responsibility for honing what is often regarded as one of the most important and memorable moments in a leader's career. No pressure!

> You and your team together will have responsibility for honing what is often regarded as one of the most important and memorable moments in a leader's career.

Providing feedback can be intimidating. People can become defensive—especially successful leaders who are accustomed to receiving positive reinforcement. They may be some of the most respected people in your organization, perhaps in your industry. They also may have received little or no leadership-related feedback on anything other than quarterly results. Who will have the credibility to help them grow? And how exactly will feedback coaches add value to such accomplished professionals?

The answer is that feedback providers don't need to advise leaders on how to do their jobs. The feedback coach's role in an acceleration process is to help the learner anticipate what could make or break success in the next role and prepare for further discussions with others. Feedback for acceleration often represents the first time a leader stops to consider the standards for leadership behavior, and particularly how he or she might change in future assignments. The high rates of leadership failure are stark reminders that a track record of good performance is no guarantee of survival through the big leadership transitions. So, feedback adds value when it creates a clear picture in the learner's mind of precisely how to adapt behaviors to prepare for situations he or she has yet to encounter.

Feedback coaches can help emerging leaders see around corners and dodge the disasters that befall so many. To do so, they need to be prepared for discussions to take many different directions. Being purposeful about styles and approaches with different types of individuals will be critical, as will recognizing that some feedback messages are harder to hear than others, especially when poor performance shows up in competencies seen as central to an individual's current role. A sales leader, for example, may find it difficult to accept a development need in *Strategic Influence,* while an R&D-focused director could be embarrassed by a low rating in *Driving Innovation.* Participants who generally are apprehensive may need a balanced approach to hearing strengths and development needs, while those who project overconfidence or arrogance may need a more direct approach that ensures they hear critical feedback.

You may employ feedback coaches from within Talent Management or have access to line executives who have volunteered or been designated as mentors. Some organizations leverage internal professionals, particularly if they have acquired the knowledge and skill to provide feedback on assessment results. Alternatively, many organizations tap external consultancies that offer pools of highly trained, expert coaches. As you select and develop a cadre of coaches, however large or small, adhering to some minimum expectations will help to maintain excellence. Expect your feedback coaches to have *credibility, business acumen,* and *leadership expertise* along with the ability to:

- Understand and synthesize results from different assessment tools (e.g., Acceleration Centers, multiple-perspective [360°] feedback, personality inventories, motivational inventories).

- Capably explore the business context in which the leader operates and generate relevant implications of behavioral trends to likely leadership situations (e.g., *"If you tend to overlook helping others manage their reactions to change, how will that affect your ability to create the efficiency you've said is so important?"*).

- Anticipate and overcome objections while representing important developmental themes and trends.

- Recognize and embrace opportunities to positively influence leaders by packaging insights in a manner that catapults their perceived value from *"That's interesting"* to *"Wow, I never thought about it that way!"*

The Talent Management function also should take a purposeful approach to matching coaches to participants. Some key considerations for the would-be coach include:

- Seniority, business acumen, and experience relative to participant level.

- Experience in the participant's industry, function, culture, or region.

- Match to the participant's personality and style.

- Sensitivity to diversity nuances and issues (culture, gender, race).

- Predicted credibility with the participant's manager.

- Experience with known development needs or specific skill challenges.

Preparing Learners to Meet with Their Managers or Mentors

As the feedback session closes, the learner should hone in on preliminary development priorities. Feedback coaches should support this effort, reflecting themes from the discussion to help focus the learner's ideas about where to place emphasis. The coach also should help the participant package a message, including how to share his or her developmental profile (and priorities) with a manager or mentor. Last but not least, the coach needs to help preserve time at the end of the session to complete this preparation phase. Chapter 7 provides further details on how participants and their managers can clarify and refine development priorities in the follow-up meeting.

Feedback Tactics

As a leader of acceleration, it's unlikely that you will be delivering feedback to accelerated learners (at least not to all of them). However, you'll want to ensure that your feedback coaches are consistent and successful in inspiring growth. If you wish to gain more insight into specific tactics that feedback providers can use to catalyze growth, we've provided additional information in the appendices at the end of this chapter. There, you'll find a variety of topics, including:

- Appendix 6.1—How feedback providers help learners generate their own insights and catalyze more significant growth.

- Appendix 6.2—Guidelines and tips for conducting feedback discussions that build energy for growth.

- Appendix 6.3—How to handle difficult challenges that often emerge in feedback discussions.

- Appendix 6.4—A sample format for a development plan that helps to translate feedback insights into actionable, high-impact growth plans.

Why Not Simply Capitalize on Strengths?

Publications such as "Now, Discover Your Strengths"[ii] have popularized the notion that it is sufficient to exploit one's strengths and accept the fact that not everyone can be good at all things. Buckingham's proposition around wanting to start a "Strengths Revolution" is understandably appealing, as people are drawn to doing more of what they are good at or enjoy doing.

However, research on executive derailment[iii] shows that "overused" strengths are a common trigger for derailment. For example, someone who has been valued for operational excellence and tenacious focus on execution may hold onto old approaches to success even as customer expectations and organizational complexity demand more fluidity and associate engagement in process innovation. As a leader, the person might need to learn how to balance results orientation and perfectionistic tendencies with openness to the time and empathy requirements in times of change.

In certain non-leadership positions, it might be possible for people to change job responsibilities to utilize their strengths and avoid areas in which they need to develop. For example, if you are good at selling to customers but poor at sales analysis, you possibly could get someone else to handle your analysis duties so that you can concentrate on selling.

But as one moves into leadership, especially senior manager or executive positions, such a "role avoidance" strategy becomes impossible. Many leadership and management competencies are difficult to delegate, and effective leaders need to use all the required competencies at one time or another. For example, you can't avoid coaching others for success, as part of your legacy is to build leadership capacity; and, your ability to "see the big picture" and think strategically will prove important if you are to help your organization execute against business priorities. Organizations want people in leadership roles who can operate at least at a minimal proficiency in all the leadership and management competencies and who can demonstrate as many strengths as possible. This means you will need to target a combination of your significant growth opportunities and strengths.

Appendix 6.1

How Feedback Providers Help Learners
Generate Powerful Insights

Once they reach mid to senior levels, most leaders have developed a fairly entrenched self-image, at which point it becomes more difficult to offer them new perspectives on how to be successful. So, strong coaches help participants come up with their own epiphanies. And these won't occur without the coach's preparation, which we call *planning for insight*.

A typical method has the coach poring over all the available information regarding the leader—career history, declared aspirations/motivations, multiple-perspective (360°) data, Acceleration Center results, etc.—to achieve the most accurate understanding possible, calling out dominant trends and themes from the data. Then, the coach would choose the best language to express these observations to the leader. An example:

> *Nigel is an active listener and very empathetic. He builds and sustains relationships that last, even in the midst of conflict. His influence skills are outstanding—sensitive and responsive to others, yet firm in his convictions. However, Nigel struggles to make change happen. His desire for strong relationships seems to prevent him from questioning established practices or pushing for improvements in anticipation of future challenges. Nigel would likely benefit from some development in change leadership.*

Coming from reliable assessment sources, these are well-reasoned conclusions about Nigel, and most coaches would seek ways to explain them, illustrating how the data supports each one. In all likelihood, Nigel would agree. And what choice would he have, given the amount and depth of the data from which the conclusions came? He would need to mount a compelling counterargument to refute the coach's case.

Tactics for Generating Insight Hypotheses

Compare and contrast behavioral data with personality data. Discrepancies between what we can see and what the data says about what lies underneath are excellent sources of insight because they point to why people do what they do. For example, imagine an individual whose personality is volatile, but who is described by others as even-keeled. Your hypothesis might center on the possibility that the anxiety is internalized and taking a secret toll (e.g., the young country manager who appeared resilient and calm to others but needed dental work from repeatedly grinding his teeth while sleeping). You might hypothesize that the volatility could represent a derailer that has not yet emerged as a risk factor. Inviting the learner to reflect on this possibility would help to clarify how volatility might play a role in future assignments.

Look for discrepancies in 360 data. Who offers the most accurate perception of current skill for target competencies—the manager, peer, direct report, or self? Obviously, the answer differs by competency; for example, a participant's effectiveness in coaching or driving innovation is probably best evaluated by direct reports. However, extreme discrepancies between rater sources on these same competencies might reflect new, underlying insight hypotheses; that is, poor ratings from a manager on innovation versus excellent ratings from direct reports might imply a need for stronger upward communication, personal branding, and/or self-promotion.

Play out scenarios with known career aspirations or desired roles. Individuals with strong advancement motivation (evidenced in background or personality data) may benefit from a deeper discussion about the challenges of future transition. The coach may develop insight hypotheses associated with issues the participant is likely to face during "key turns" given his or her assessment profile. For example, someone who struggles with delegation will have difficulty sustaining direct involvement in everything as the scope, strategic implications, and visibility of responsibilities expand.

But when seeking access to Nigel's real energy for growth, agreement is not the goal. It's *insight* we're after—Nigel's insight. His acceptance of the coach's well-reasoned, data-driven conclusions might feel like success in the moment, particularly if he hasn't become combative and rejected the feedback entirely; but acceptance falls far short of catalyzing action. What's needed is a

> Agreement is
> not the goal.
> It's *insight* we're after.

different way to discuss the coach's conclusions and a more intentional method of involving Nigel in shaping them. This means bringing business-relevant perspective and being prepared for Nigel to amend it with his own insights. In other words, the coach's conclusions are far more likely to create insight and energy for growth if they are prepared and positioned as hypotheses—insight hypotheses—that the coach and Nigel will test together.

An *insight hypothesis* is a prediction or supposition, based on objective data or input, about a learner's behavior or personality patterns and how those tendencies could affect performance in likely future leadership situations. An example of an insight hypothesis about Nigel:

> *Nigel's interpersonal agility is likely to make him very adept at navigating the political dynamics inherent at more senior levels. However, if given responsibility for an entire business unit or function, he may not always show the leadership initiative that is required to ensure that his unit adapts as business conditions or limitations change. While he may respond to crises and quickly fix problems, he may not be proactive in addressing potential performance inhibitors.*

For this prediction to become a concept that animates and focuses Nigel's developmental energy, it will need to be brought to the center of the feedback discussion, bantered about collaboratively, and ultimately defined and owned by Nigel. It will need to become part of his world, in his job and career context, relating to his personal needs. This won't happen because of the coach's wisdom or eloquence. Nigel will bring his own perspectives to the conversation and will add important insights to those presented to him. The feedback coach would need to be prepared for the many different directions that Nigel's reactions might go.

Appendix 6.2
Structuring a Great Feedback Discussion

Great feedback is *guided self-discovery.* When handled skillfully, the feedback discussion inspires bold action, because the learner makes new discoveries about how to advance and succeed as a professional as well as how to make a bigger difference in the business.

Start with business and role issues, and then work toward behavior and personality patterns. Leaders making the transition to roles that have more business impact benefit most when business context is discussed first, followed by specific competency and personality insights. This ensures that the participant hears feedback first through the lens of the top strategic priorities, cascading to his or her role requirements and then to personal needs. Feedback coaches gain trust more readily when they demonstrate that

> Accelerated growth happens when a learner can pinpoint specific behaviors within a competency that will improve effectiveness.

they are first seeking to understand the business and the participant's role in it. An early exchange about the participant's current role focus, pressing business challenges, future aspirations, and self-perception of strengths and weaknesses allows the person to feel heard and recognized as a unique individual. This tailors the feedback to the learner and also equips the coach to anticipate how the person will react to feedback and to predict objections. It also helps the coach gauge how to best package messages for maximum insight and influence and, in turn, clearly tie results to future implications for success or failure.

Use Key Actions to be specific. It's one thing to understand the concept of competencies such as *Leading Change* or *Strategic Influence;* it's quite another to know precisely what actions to take to become better at living them. Competencies are clusters of related behaviors, but being effective does not mean being good at every behavior. Nor does a development need require improvement across all behaviors. Accelerated growth happens when a learner can pinpoint specific behaviors that will improve effectiveness. Unfortunately, the value of this specificity evades many. Table 6.1 illustrates the point with a powerful example.

6.1 Table

The Importance of Key Actions in Feedback

Strategic Influence—*Creating and executing influence strategies that gain commitment to one's ideas and persuade key stakeholders to take action that will advance shared interests and business goals.*

The Story

A large medical system was in the midst of a major consolidation and business model shift driven by recent acquisitions, soaring cost pressures, and increased transparency around quality outcomes. Synergies demanded by integration of systems and cross-functional interdependencies also led to a more highly integrated structure.

Complexities associated with these changes created new performance challenges for system leaders who were accustomed to achieving objectives through formal authority. Martin Weaver was one of those leaders; although brilliant, logical, and highly articulate, emerging collaboration and execution issues led to his participation in a developmental assessment.

Overall, Martin's results reflected his strong intellect, forceful personality, and strategic orientation. He received many **proficient** and **strength** ratings, with the exception of a development need in the competency Strategic Influence.

Initially, he objected to his competency rating, as he took pride in the ability to present strong business cases for functional initiatives, such as a new order-to-cash system. His resistance began to thaw as his coach pointed to Key Action gaps, most notably around proactively building an influence strategy that better considered shared goals across functions and constituents. He also gained insight around how to adjust this strategy when required and how to confirm commitment to action.

Based on the Key Action insights, Martin focused his development plan on tailoring his influence approach to both the personal and practical needs of diverse partners and stakeholders. One year later he had developed a solid reputation for building coalitions and was described by the organization's CEO as a model leader for the emerging "System-ness" era.

Key Actions

- **Develops influence strategy**—Devises an influence approach that favorably positions one's ideas and own agenda while focusing on the shared goals of key decision makers; prepares an influence strategy that leverages supporting factors and breaks through barriers; adjusts influence strategy based on stakeholder reactions and perspectives.

- **Ensures mutual understanding**—Uses open-ended questions to explore issues and clarify others' perspectives and goals; shares information to clarify the situation; discloses own goals, insights, and the rationale behind decisions, ideas, or changes.

- **Makes a compelling case**—Presents logical rationale and recommendations in a manner that clearly links them to critical organizational, group, and individual priorities.

- **Gains commitment**—Leverages shared goals to convince others to take action; seeks ideas; asks for agreement to next steps.

- **Demonstrates interpersonal diplomacy**—Builds trust during the influence process by demonstrating sensitivity to others' needs, maintaining self-esteem, showing empathy, and offering support.

Martin (the learner in the table's example) was confused at first about the suggestion that he needed to develop in Strategic Influence. However, the specificity of the Key Actions within the competency not only clarified the issue, but also built a stronger case for Martin's development.[i]

In addition to behavioral information (Key Actions), data on personal attributes such as personality and motivation can provide important specifics. In Martin's case the data related his forceful personality to his tendency to take a more blunt approach when influencing partners. Such links often can be the keys to isolating the behaviors that, if learned or modified, will make the biggest and swiftest impact on growth. For instance, a participant who has demonstrated weak business savvy in a business-planning simulation might receive personality data pointing to an aversion to numerical concepts. This should lead to the recognition that she will struggle to build her business savvy until she stops avoiding financials.

Don't be satisfied with agreement. A good feedback coach comes equipped with a well-prepared point of view about the individual, backed by reliable data and observations from an assessment process. But a good feedback coach also is prepared to be wrong—or at least somewhat off target. Because the goal is to translate observations into insights and actions, the learner must fully process feedback messages into his or her own terms and context. This means asking the learner to state an understanding of the messages and personally interpret them. Such a conversation might play out like this:

> **Coach:** *What do you make of the fact that you received a "Development Opportunity" rating in the competency, Driving Execution? It seems to me that this may be part of a tendency to focus on conceptual issues and perhaps shy away from tactical ones.*
>
> **Participant:** *I think you're right. That's probably true.*
>
> **Coach:** *I appreciate that, but actually I'm not satisfied with being right. Tell me how you interpret this. Why does it make sense?*

Participant: *Well, I hadn't really thought about it this way before, but the truth is that I do rely on other people to handle details, and I probably do it too much. I tend to get good marks for being creative, but I know I've alienated people at times because of my aversion to clarifying plans for how we'll get things done.*

Simply accepting the coach's interpretation is not sufficient. An inspirational feedback session pushes the learner to take ownership of the feedback message by encouraging the person to challenge the coach's words and perspectives and make them his or her own. This happens when healthy, respectful debate is a planned aspect of the discussion.

> Simply accepting the coach's interpretation is not sufficient. An inspirational feedback session pushes the learner to take ownership of the feedback message.

Envision a future star who has learned from past failures. Feedback often fails to have impact because it overemphasizes the person in the past. *"You were very informal and unstructured in that board presentation. You lost credibility, causing the chairman to question whether we've made the right investments. I'd like you to work on your presentation style."* This is obviously important feedback, and a broad-shouldered leader would take it in stride and do some things differently. But exactly what he might do differently would be open to question, and it wouldn't do much to inspire the kind of accelerated growth we're explaining here.

When working with learners to uncover inspiring insights, instead of focusing on the negative impact of their past actions, it is far more energizing to concentrate on how new, different behaviors will positively impact *future* situations. This doesn't mean abandoning the description of the past. The points about the board presentation were important to convey. But they would have more positive developmental impact if balanced with a specific description of what good performance looks like and a discussion of the positive impact of change. An alternative approach: *"Influencing our board is crucial, and I'm going to need your help to be stronger in your presentations. Next time, I'd like to see you adjust your informal style to be more confident and fact based. I can see you being highly influential in this setting, but it will mean adopting a more poised and formal approach."*

Provoke personal reflection. The role of feedback coach is, in large measure, that of provocateur. Many learners come to feedback discussions already hesitant, for fear that the talks will become too personal. But a healthy feedback discussion stimulates reflection without becoming overly intrusive. Feedback coaches can make their insights more personal by reframing problems with stories of other executives or with relevant benchmarking data or research.

Questions, and how coaches frame them, also heavily influence the learner's openness to reflection. Recognize that tolerance for question-based discovery is limited and will require a balance between questions and open sharing of perspectives. As coaches dig deeper and challenge the learner to think more rigorously about different approaches, they can use "why" and "what if" questions to increase the person's role in explaining trends and surfacing their implications. Feedback coaches also need to push for what needs to be different: *"If making change was easy, you'd have done it already and without my help. What will make this uniquely challenging for you?"* The feedback discussion affords an important opportunity to challenge learners to think of development solutions, as opposed to supplying them yourself. For example, *"What are two or three ways you might be able to work through this challenge today?"* And when asking questions, coaches should use silence and allow space for reflection. They should cultivate an environment in which the learner does most of the reflecting, while providing support and helping to steer the conversation productively.

Stay focused on the right kind of tension. Feedback can evoke anxiety in both coach and learner, and it takes hard work to make it successful. So, it can feel extremely reinforcing (to both parties) to sort through all the data and discussion to uncover the real truth about an individual. But be

> Once you have arrived at the peaceful moment of clarity about the learner, it is essential to turn immediately to building a case for why growth is both essential and valuable for the person and for the business.

careful. A feedback session that reduces anxiety or arrives at an accurate shared conclusion about the meaning of assessment results has not yet been successful. While dispatching the tensions associated with the feedback session itself, it is important to remain focused on a healthy, optimistic tension between the learner and the future—the Success Profile that represents the leadership level toward which the learner aspires. Once you have arrived at the peaceful moment of clarity about the learner, it's essential to turn immediately to building a case for why growth is both essential and valuable for the person and for the business. Bear in mind that building tension should be coupled with building confidence. Feedback coaches should emphasize how strengths can be maximized and aspirations met by addressing underlying growth areas.

Appendix 6.3

Special Challenges and Opportunities in Feedback

Difficult manager relationship: Occasionally, a learner has a poor relationship with his or her manager. It might be described as a personality conflict, or ongoing disagreements about role focus, or simply a lack of access (e.g., *"We rarely talk."*). In these scenarios trust issues will reduce the learner's confidence in candidly presenting development needs. Understandably, the person might be less than confident about getting support, empathy, or encouragement to try on new behaviors. Coaches will need to help learners strategize how to present their results in a nondefensive manner, ask for what they need, and demonstrate commitment to working on themselves and for the benefit of the business. It also will be helpful to brainstorm mitigation strategies (e.g., seek help from Talent Management).

Weak manager: At times, managers are seen as well-intended but less than competent. While this is still frustrating, participants can more easily maneuver complementary support from informal/formal mentors, peers, and the internal talent management function instead. As in the previous scenario, however, they'll need to work with their manager on development. In a positive light, the coach may help the participant see how collaborating with the manager may develop them both or even their broader team simultaneously. For example, if the learner is working on improving technology acumen, she might present a series of brown-bag lunches to her manager and team that shares the same need.

Perceived gender or cultural issues: This is a delicate topic, especially when the issues are described as overt or extreme. It actually might be more challenging but equally damaging when the issues are less obvious to outside observers. Of course, it also is possible that the participant has overinterpreted or unfairly attributed concerns to gender or culture bias. There is not a one-size-fits-all answer to these concerns, but the coach will have to help the learner explore root issues and potential mitigation strategies. These may range from engaging HR to reaching out to others who have faced similar issues.

Fear of failure or resistance to change: Individuals oriented toward personal risk aversion may have a deeply rooted fear that their weaknesses will be exposed. Worse yet, some are certain that they eventually will be revealed as a "fraud" who has advanced due to circumstances versus earning their way. Individuals who suffer from fear of failure may be especially anxious about the assessment experience and the transparency it creates around their vulnerabilities. They also may be reluctant to pursue stretch development that pulls them out of their comfort zone. Others may be naturally cautious or change resistant. Coaches need to help these individuals recognize personal triggers for risk aversion (e.g., ambiguous challenges with no right answer). They also should encourage participants to push themselves toward stretch development focused on change and/or complexity. Throwing them in the deep end on a high-risk, visible assignment may create a productive opportunity to confront their anxiety.

Appendix 6.4

Individual Development Plan

PART 1: Development Goal

- ☐ Competency (Skill)
- ☐ Knowledge
- ☐ Experience
- ☐ Personal Attribute/Derailer

Goal:

Group or organizational payoff:	Personal payoff:	Due Date:

PART 2: The Plan

Learning Acquisition Plan

How will you acquire the knowledge/skill/experience?

How will you learn alternative approaches to derailing behaviors (if appropriate)?

Application Plan

How will you apply the knowledge/skill/experience in your role once you have achieved mastery?

PART 3: Support and Measurement Plan

What barriers/challenges do you expect?

What support/resources will you need?

How will you know you are making progress?

PART 4: The Results

Learning Acquisition Results

Did you learn what you set out to learn (Competency/Knowledge/Skill)?
Why/Why not?

Application Results

Did you achieve your development goal? □ Yes □ No □ Partially
Completion date:

How did you apply what you learned?

What were the personal and organizational payoffs?

PART 5: Insights from Your Development Efforts

Reflect on some of the following questions and write your comments below:

What worked well? What didn't? Why?

What was most unexpected, gratifying, or challenging in this development
process?

As a result of this development experience, what will you do differently in the
future?

What additional opportunities do you have to apply your new knowledge/skill/
experience?

What unplanned opportunities did you have to build knowledge/skill/experience?
What were the results?

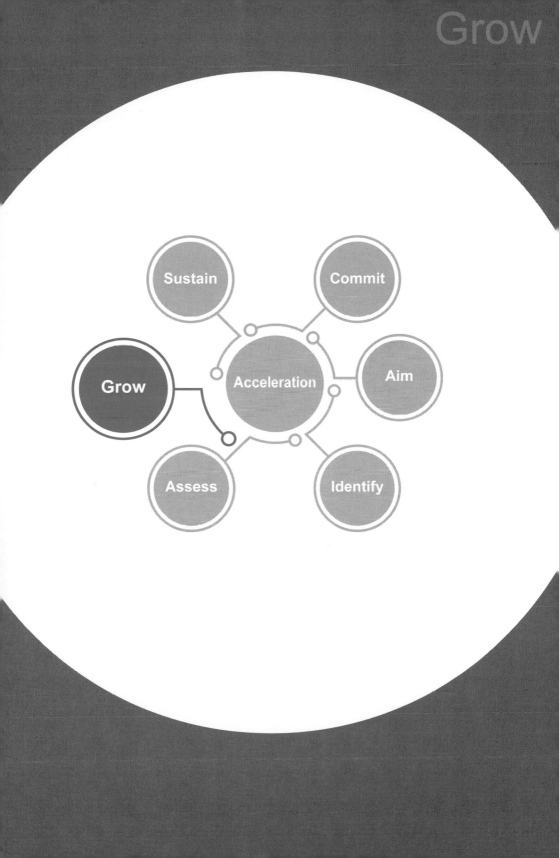

Grow　Make the right development happen.

In this section…

Chapters 7 through 11 outline how organizations become great at the GROW imperative. The practices they employ generate energy in the following ways:

- **Less talk, more action:** Learning and development methods—not just learning activities—spark application of new leadership approaches that the business needs.

- **Personalized learning:** Learners become more engaged by creating learning pathways that are specific to their unique growth needs and motivations.

- **Better leveraging of unique personal attributes:** Individuals learn to embrace their stable individual dispositions and manage the risks of their negative tendencies while capitalizing on their natural strengths.

- **Bigger, bolder development assignments—and more of them:** Management learns practical ways to generate, assign, and track developmental assignments that can dramatically increase the rate and frequency of growth.

- **Shared growth experiences that electrify groups of leaders:** Learning journeys combine group learning and application activities that energize leaders and reinforce the growth process.

 Denotes that tools and information on this topic are available at the *Leaders Ready Now* website (www.leadersreadynow.com). Use this code to access content: LRN2016.

APPLY MORE DISCIPLINE TO DEVELOPING LEADERSHIP SKILLS

7 | Developing Competencies and Key Actions

This chapter introduces the fifth Acceleration Imperative, Grow, which confronts the challenge of how leaders learn—particularly, what helps them learn faster and make larger contributions to the business sooner. Keep in mind that following this imperative is nothing like following a step-by-step recipe in a cookbook. The next five chapters outline the principles and practices that will help you hone your processes to make the right development happen.

As we've said, learning is not the same as growth. Learning becomes growth only when it is sustained and applied. And to convert leaders from *not ready* to *ready now,* growth must happen consistently. But sadly, the general track record of achieving it is not good. As organizations beef up their investments in leadership development, leaders themselves are showing little growth.[1]

---

1 If you need supporting evidence, at the end of this chapter we have provided a list of data points from a series of studies that show the disappointing state of leadership development at large (see Appendix 7.1).

> Across all organizations in the research, 93 percent saw improvements, with a 36 percent increase in leader readiness, on average.

But some organizations apply approaches that generate significant returns. Drawing from the lessons of 161 research studies conducted with our client partners, we know that when the principles of leadership learning (see next section) are applied, positive change (growth) occurs faster and the respective organizations' financial metrics improve. Across all organizations in the research, 93 percent saw improvements, with a 36 percent increase in leader readiness, on average. Clearly, accelerated growth can, and does, happen.[i]

Fundamental Principles of Leadership Learning That Lead to Growth

If you're a veteran of learning design, you know that the highest-impact solutions adjust to accommodate the unique learning needs of leaders at different levels. More senior-level leaders require more specialized approaches like executive coaching and customized learning designs for executive teams. First-time leaders often share common development needs, allowing for more standardized (and scalable) solutions. Mid-level leaders require a mix of solutions.

But regardless of level, the organizations that have succeeded in more quickly growing leaders toward higher-level success profiles have done so by following some basic principles. They have proven these fundamentals to be universal in their positive impact on speed, retention, and application of learning for leaders at all phases of their careers. When implementing learning processes, these organizations:[ii]

- **Don't skimp on assessment.** Growth builds on accurate insight about strengths, weaknesses, and development priorities. While measuring the entire success profile is essential, companies that get better results also include more granular (Key Action-level) measures in their assessments. Learners at all levels need the full picture, but also need specifics about how to grow.

- **Design processes for *practicing* skills, not just learning them.** The goal of skill practicing is to boost the capability and confidence to use and improve the skill. Practice with feedback must be built into the learning process and not left to chance.

- **Create a powerful "why."** The purpose (payoff) of learning is as important as how it takes place. The most successful organizations don't just mention it; they go deep into both business and personal benefits to build wide engagement and support.

- **Create opportunities for learners to observe strong models.** When it comes to learning new skills, there is no substitute for seeing someone using them well. The most effective skill-acquisition processes include opportunities to observe positive models in action, effectively applying the target skills. Even senior executives benefit from strong models.

- **Regard manager support as vital.** Individual learners should meet with their managers early and often to share successes, clear up issues or barriers, and get coaching where needed. This has value at all levels and does not require managers to be superior leaders or to have all the answers.

- **Charge up processes with learning accelerators.** Learning accelerators reinforce content after learning events by facilitating self-measurement, building competition and community, and providing opportunities to share hints, tips, and insights just when they are needed. These accelerators are simple tools (mobile apps, social networking tools, etc.) that keep the learning process vibrant and learners connected.

- **Avoid being misled by the 70/20/10 model.** Formal learning (i.e., the 10 percent that includes classroom, e-learning, etc.) is often deemphasized due to the broad misinterpretation of the 70/20/10 research. But it does not suggest that formal learning should be downplayed or skipped. Our research and experience have actually shown that in organizations where development has the greatest impact, more time is spent on formal learning, often much more than 10 percent.

163

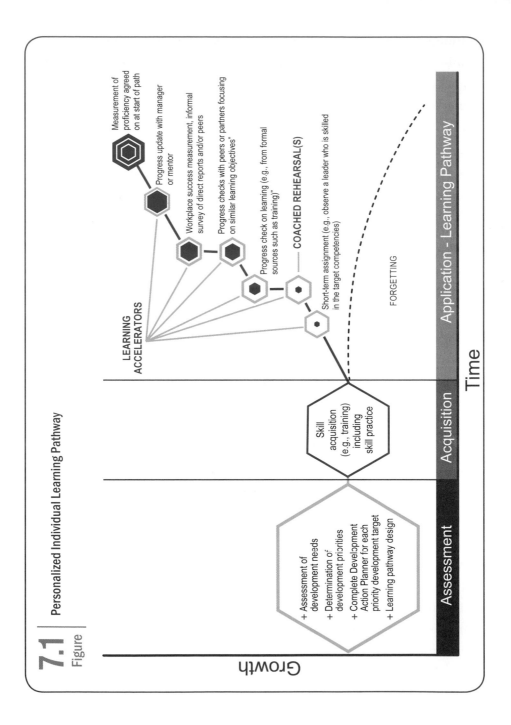

7.1 Figure | Personalized Individual Learning Pathway

- **Commit to a complete learning pathway.** Skill acquisition most likely will lead to growth when it is coupled with a commitment to follow a learning pathway to increase proficiency and confidence. A lack of follow-up allows skills to decline and results in no payoff for the development effort (see Figure 7.1).

The Development Plan

Throughout this chapter and those that follow, we often refer to development plans. Appendix 6.4 shows the format that we have found to be most effective for documenting plans and progress.

When Developing the Skills Your Business Needs, Key Action Focus Is Critical

Here's a key point that many (maybe most) organizations miss: As you take action to cultivate your leaders' skills, make sure they are the specific skills *your business needs,* now and in the near future. In Chapter 3 we outlined how to ensure that your success profiles articulate those behaviors and how to align them to your business. Business Drivers define the broad leadership priorities in your unique context. Competencies, wired to the Business Drivers, provide focus on the right skill sets. And Key Actions supply the behavioral precision that shows exactly how to develop each competency. Without a focus on Key Actions, aligned to competencies and your business context (Business Drivers), development is unlikely to drive your business in the way, or at the speed, you need. Here's why:

Skill is behavior. Leaders build skill by changing their behaviors—learning new ones, adjusting old ones—to conquer new challenges. It sounds simple enough, yet the typical learning experience fails to create much behavior change. As it stands, leaders

> Without a focus on Key Actions, aligned to competencies and your business context (Business Drivers), development is unlikely to drive your business in the way, or at the speed, you need.

need much more than an experience to make that happen. It's not enough to want to change. Nor is it enough to recognize the right behavior. That's why outdoor adventures and mountain retreats seldom have real impact on leadership capability. Building leadership skill requires commitment, planning, and effort by your organization—not just to administer training or assign coaches (that's the easy part), but to provide the resources and incentives necessary to spark people to follow through on their learning goals and grow the skills they need to succeed.

Remember that competencies are the language of leadership skill. They should spell out the behaviors that lead to effectiveness in a given skill, like *Strategic Influence* or *Leading Change.* But as we said in Chapter 3, not all competencies do, and this lack of specificity can cripple your efforts to help leaders build their skills. Developing competencies requires drilling down to the *Key Actions*—the specific behavioral components of a competency—that an individual must practice to become more effective.

An example: Carlo's boss says, *"I want you to improve your influencing skills."* As a person focused on his own growth, Carlo's reaction would be to ask for specifics. It wouldn't be enough for his boss to recite the definition of the *Strategic Influence* competency. That might help a bit, but Carlo knows (or has a general idea) what *Strategic Influence* is. What he really needs to know is exactly what skills to improve and how. Does Carlo need to ask more questions? Be more diplomatic? Does he give in too easily? Does he not make his case effectively? Carlo needs details about which aspects of *Strategic Influence* he needs to work on. Without them, he would be guessing about what to do differently and likely wouldn't sustain his effort to improve.

The first lever to pull in making competency development happen faster is to ensure that the learner understands the Key Actions in the target competency and that he or she focuses on the highest-payoff Key Actions.[2] This makes

---

2 Key Actions that are part of multiple target competencies (i.e., Interaction Essentials, Chapter 3) should get the greatest emphasis because addressing them in one competency has a positive impact on all the competencies of which they are a part.

feedback, training, coaching, practice, and ongoing measurement much more precise and meaningful. As simple as this point might seem, we see company after company underemphasize it or miss it entirely.

If a coach, mentor, facilitator, or instructor knows a learner needs to develop a specific Key Action, it could mean pairing the learner with a leader who is strong in that area or assigning the learner to a team with people who are good models of it. These (and other) seemingly minor adjustments can (and do) result in major differences in the impact of competency-development efforts.

In your organization, learners, managers, mentors, and all the players in the acceleration process need easy access to the specific behaviors that drive effective leadership performance. Think of it like the Olympics. Figure skaters, gymnasts, divers, snowboarders, and all the other athletes know precisely how they're being judged, and that determines how they practice and prepare. As you push leaders into more challenging assignments, it's too risky to assume they will know how to develop competence. (The many stories of leadership failure remind us that they often don't.) To understand and practice the behaviors that will lead to success, they need specifics. Your job is to provide the scorecards in advance so that they can be ready for the games. Every training or development activity you ask leaders to undertake to accelerate their competency growth should provide Key Action precision to guide their efforts.

> Figure skaters, gymnasts, divers, snowboarders, and all the other athletes know precisely how they're being judged, and that determines how they practice and prepare. Your job is to provide the scorecards in advance so that they can be ready for the games.

Acquiring Skills

Understanding the Key Actions required for competency success is one thing; demonstrating them is quite another. Everyone has, at some point, attempted to learn a difficult skill: music, art, athletics, craftwork, technology, architecture. All of these are complex, multifaceted skill sets requiring formal instruction

7.2 Top Barriers to Formal Learning in Order of Rated Importance[3]

Figure

Barriers to Formal Learning

Low Relevance to the Job

Low Relevance to Business Challenges

Weak Connection to Personal Development Plans

Not Enough Opportunities to Apply the Learning

Not Being Held Accountable for Using the Learning

Poor Post-Learning Feedback from Manager

(courses, demonstrations, e-learning, webinars, video, etc.) to learn the basics and to advance proficiency.

There are basics to be learned with every new leadership assignment at every level in the organization. But even with the best instruction, learning a complex skill for the first time can be challenging and frustrating. Giving up is easy. Settling for mediocrity (or less) is common. The point is that learning new skills involves more than just trying out new behaviors. It requires motivation and confidence to do so in situations where it matters and to get feedback about how it worked (or didn't).

Motivation to develop competencies requires relevance—to personal and organizational needs. We have referred to this as the "why" of development, and its absence is the top barrier to learning from formal instruction (see Figure 7.2).

Confidence in developing leadership skill also increases when learning methods match the individual's competency development needs. For that reason, many organizations offer a variety of skill-acquisition methodologies (e.g., training courses, online self-development content, peer networks, coaching/mentoring). Some fit better with particular competencies or Key Actions and accommodate learners' varying needs and motivations. With the right mix of methods, and

---

3 As rated by learners (*Global Leadership Forecast*, 2015).

high business-relevance, you will keep your learners engaged as they get deep into learning new Key Actions and competencies.

Develop Competencies and Key Actions Using Skill Practice and Positive Models

Leaders at all levels, no matter how knowledgeable or experienced, need practice as they step up to more challenging competencies. Training shows leaders

> Training shows leaders how to practice.

how to practice. Whether it is delivered to groups of new supervisors in classroom settings or to senior executives in one-to-one coaching engagements, two key practices differentiate learning that creates real change from efforts that don't.

First, don't bother with training (or any learning approach) that omits skill practice. Leadership competencies might seem easy to understand conceptually, but leadership doesn't happen inside one's mind. It happens through the demonstration of Key Actions that change the attitudes and behaviors of others, which proves difficult for every leader at times. Practice is vital, starting

> Leadership competencies might seem easy to understand conceptually, but leadership doesn't happen inside one's mind.

from the moment of initial formal learning (e.g., a classroom or virtual learning experience) to repeated applications in the workplace. Great training begins with the clear articulation of the competencies and Key Actions required for success, and then provides learners with a safe environment in which to try out new behaviors for the first time and receive feedback for improvement. Repeated attempts can then be taken to the workplace with the support of a manager, coach, and other learning aids (more on this shortly). This approach builds both skill and confidence—and in turn, confidence breeds a willingness to pursue greater application.

Second, there is no substitute for positive models when developing competencies and Key Actions. In the same way a picture paints a thousand words, one positive model of effective behavior teaches many lessons. Albert

Bandura demonstrated this in 1971 when he showed the effectiveness of behavior modeling. Starting in 1975, DDI began using behavior modeling as a key ingredient of most leadership development models. The method has evolved considerably since then, as it is used by many of our most successful client partners. Modeling effective skills for learners has been shown over hundreds of studies to be one of the most effective methods of making growth happen faster. So, touting the virtues of such a tried-and-true method might seem superfluous, and we would agree if not for all the organizations that have abandoned or shortchanged the approach out of concern for efficiency and speed. This often backfires and actually slows growth.

To illustrate these two tenets, let's go back to Carlo's hypothetical need to develop *Strategic Influence* skills and look more closely at how a) clear articulation of Key Actions, b) a positive model, and c) skill practice with feedback actually play out.

Let's start by assuming that Carlo participated in a virtual course focused on *Strategic Influence*. In the course he learned the Key Actions associated with the competency, viewed several positive models (via video), and had several opportunities to practice influence skills with partners in a virtual classroom. Later, back at his job, Carlo's boss sits in on several meetings with him and some internal partners. She observes that Carlo's primary challenge is *making a compelling case* for his point of view (a specific Key Action in *Strategic Influence*). She shares examples and helps Carlo understand what he might have done differently to state his point of view more assertively and clearly.

She then invites Carlo to listen in on a telephone call in which she plans to negotiate an agreement with one of her internal partners about how to allocate resources between the two groups. She is known to be a strong, diplomatic leader who has impact in the organization. Before the meeting she shares her perspective about the issue and desired outcome and invites Carlo to observe and evaluate how she positions her point of view (now Carlo is like the Olympic judge with the scorecard). As he listens to the discussion, he takes notes and gathers insights about his boss' technique. After the phone call, Carlo and his boss discuss her approach, and he shares his observations about her influence behaviors—specifically, how she made a case for her most important discussion points.

It is difficult to overstate the power of an experience like this, because what started as a broad need to improve influence skills has transformed into an ongoing conversation about specific behaviors that work (and don't) in real situations, and has blossomed into continued practice, feedback, and discussion. As Carlo progresses, his manager might invite him to take on more challenging influence assignments that will test his mettle against not just one but all the Key Actions required for *Strategic Influence*. This is *deliberate practice,* which continues until proficiency, at which point Carlo and his boss can move on to work together on the next development challenge.

Here's a key point: The goal is not to achieve complete, perfect mastery of *Strategic Influence*. Rather, it is to build enough capability to practice and hone the skill (see Figure 7.1). Understanding Key Actions, having a positive

> The goal is not to achieve complete mastery. Rather, it is to build enough capability to practice and hone the skill.

model, and practicing with feedback is like attaching a rocket booster to development. It clarifies the importance of the competency and provides a tangible reference point from which to practice all the Key Actions. Along the way, it reinforces the value of giving and receiving feedback and highlights the essential role of reflecting on learning experiences to solidify commitment and understanding of what actions to take in the future.

With our client partners we have applied these practices in the successful development of more than 10 million leaders around the globe, often in ways that Albert Bandura wouldn't recognize. Games, virtual (web-based) classrooms, online simulations, custom one-to-one coaching courses, and many other methods have been applied successfully to make these approaches work. And, indeed, it works—at all levels of leadership. A meta-analysis including 161 research studies attests to its effectiveness in changing workplace behavior.[iii]

Applying Learning

> Training alone does not create more-skilled leaders. It simply focuses their practice so that they can become proficient more quickly.

Training alone does not create more-skilled leaders. It simply focuses their practice so that they can become proficient more quickly. It's what happens *after* the training that leads to its permanent use in the leader's behavioral repertoire. Scores of formal and informal research studies support this point. For example, a 2008 study by the CEB Corporate Leadership Council found that 68 percent of the success of an HR program depends on the quality and quantity of reinforcement of newly learned skills in the workplace.[iv] The *Global Leadership Forecast* by DDI and The Conference Board found that the top two barriers to workplace applications of training were poor post-learning coaching and feedback from the manager and insufficient opportunities to apply the learning at work (see Figure 7.3).

Many learners, and often their managers, view training experiences as something to endure—not the start of a journey to make new skills a permanent part of a leader's repertoire. Meanwhile, many senior leaders prescribe training as the sole vehicle for accelerating growth. In both cases, the focus is too narrow.

Make rehearsal a routine. Learning to apply a newly acquired skill benefits from rehearsal with coaching from a manager, mentor, or peer before trying it

> Actors, golfers, firefighters, and many other professionals who depend on their skills for success thrive on rehearsal. But how often do leaders rehearse before a difficult conversation?

in a high-risk situation. This aspect of learning often is overlooked. Most individuals coming out of training experiences—no matter how good the program is and how much practice they've been afforded—benefit from the extra learning and confidence provided by a rehearsal. Bands often rehearse songs hundreds of times

7.3 Figure | Barriers to Workplace Learning in Order of Rated Importance[4]

Barriers to Workplace Learning

Poor Post-Learning Feedback from Manager

Not Enough Opportunities to Apply the Learning

Not Being Held Accountable for Using the Learning

Weak Connection to Personal Development Plans

Low Relevance to Business Challenges

Low Relevance to the Job

before an audience ever hears them. Actors, golfers, firefighters, and many other professionals who depend on their skills for success thrive on rehearsal. But how often do leaders, particularly new or emerging ones, rehearse before a difficult conversation? As a senior executive, how often do you sit with accelerated learners and rather than simply talking about a skill, you actually practice it together?

Interpersonal skills, like communicating and influencing, are the most obvious examples of where this can have impact. But many other leadership skills, such as *Inspiring Others, Coaching and Developing Others, Gaining Commitment,* and *Leading Change,* can be learned and applied far more rapidly and successfully if coached rehearsal is built into the development process.[v] Often, less-experienced leaders can be successfully groomed for assignments far beyond their levels of experience by leveraging coached practices. Board presentations, major negotiations (with customers or labor unions), alliance meetings, and important internal organizational speeches or communications are just a few examples of where rehearsal can pay off.

Elevate the role of feedback. The CEO of a large, global retail corporation has begun to change the way his organization views and uses feedback. Each time a claim is made that a leader (often an accelerated learner) has made

---

4 As rated by learners (DDI *Global Leadership Forecast,* 2015).

A Bit of Structure Makes Rehearsal Easier and More Repeatable

Rehearsal is notoriously unstructured. Time pressure often makes it seem nearly impossible to wedge a practice session into busy schedules. But just a small amount of structure can change those perceptions as well as the frequency and effectiveness of the rehearsal. Many of our most successful client partners make routine use of Discussion Planners (like the one shown in Appendix 7.2). The planner's simple structure organizes the user's thinking and prompts the leader to anticipate how the discussion will flow and consider what points likely will emerge during the discussion. It takes only minutes to complete the planner, and it has a powerful impact on planning and rehearsals. Many leaders come to find such tools indispensable as they work through challenging leadership situations.

developmental progress, he asks, *"What did the feedback say?"* He follows up with questions about how the feedback was gathered, by whom, and how it was used. His goal is to increase the use of feedback in the organization and heighten the rigor with which development progress is evaluated, ensuring that learners make continual use of feedback. As he has been known to say, *"Our best leaders should have reputations as feedback seekers."*

Feedback is vital to the learning process, and as leaders advance, knowing how to gather and use it not only enables faster skill development, but also helps leaders avoid costly mistakes and potential failure. It is essential that accelerated learners seek feedback on their use of newly learned skills. Colleagues are usually glad to share private feedback about progress on competency-development efforts—particularly if they are told they will be asked for feedback in advance. This increases positive performance tension and promotes a culture where feedback is valued and sought by the best performers.

Feedback becomes an invaluable leadership asset when it is part of a routine. Authors such as Malcolm Gladwell (*Outliers: The Story of Success,* 2008) have written about the need for 10,000 hours of deliberate practice to achieve

Social Media as a Key Source of Feedback

Savvy users of social media understand that what one contributes to a social network determines what one gains from it, and even a small contribution can generate meaningful advantages. For accelerated learners the process of cultivating a network of colleagues and friends who are mutually interested in a topic related to leadership growth can become a rich source of insight, data, benchmarks, and resources when new challenges occur. Most organizations have adopted internal social networking applications (e.g., Yammer), and public venues (Twitter, Facebook) are useful as well. The high volume of sharing across many varied situations creates insight that is difficult to gather in any other way. Many users leverage their networks for just-in-time advice and tips as well as for feedback after the fact. A tweet like the following could yield quite a bit of help in just minutes:

Help! New job. Have my own P&L for the first time. Anyone have tips for how to get smart fast? #petrified

Or an entry like the following could generate interesting insights into how best to apply better coaching skills:

Working on my coaching. Trying to ask more questions, but all I get is griping from my team. What am I doing wrong? #frustrated

Participating in and contributing to communities with shared interest in skill development is a powerful way for learners to strengthen their ability to gather and use feedback to grow more quickly. Strong learning programs build and maintain communities as a core component of the design.

---

excellence. But most executives don't need to be excellent; they simply need to be proficient. So, we don't pretend that 10,000 hours of practice with feedback are required to be an effective coach, change leader, or delegator; but surely, those skills should be practiced and feedback given more often than a few times a year.[vi] As you evaluate the progress of accelerated learners, make the application and use of feedback a standard element among your criteria.

> If people don't have a way to know what happens when they apply their skills, they'll quickly lose interest in trying to improve them.

Keep score in real time. Imagine a basketball player who is blocked from seeing whether his shots go through the net. Or a comedienne who can't see the audience or hear its laughter. Or a marksman who can't see the target. Get the idea? If people don't have a way to know what happens when they apply their skills, they'll quickly lose interest in trying to improve them. Why? Because they have been robbed of one of the main reasons they tried it in the first place: to feel the satisfaction of scoring, succeeding, and improving. If your accelerated learners are expected to sustain their efforts at growing their leadership skills, they need to keep score and feel that same sense of satisfaction.

This requires real-time measures, not just the ones that are easily observed after the game or at the end of the fiscal year. If all the basketball player could see was the team's win-loss record, it wouldn't be much incentive to work on his shooting form.

When most leaders think about measuring the impact of competency growth, they look for evidence in related business metrics such as sales, margin, productivity, turnover, etc. These are important measures to consider, but they don't have the same impact on behavior as real-time measures—those that happen very near in time to the behavior. When a leader with a development need in *Driving Execution* manages a project that meets its deadline and comes in under budget, that's a score. A leader practicing her *Coaching* skills scores when a direct report whom she coached recently returns to say that the coaching helped, and then asks for more. *Planning and Organizing* can be tracked by meeting project milestones. *Delegation* can be measured by the frequency with which follow-up is needed to clarify assignments or address confusion. The key is that every competency-development effort must have specific real-time measures associated with it. Key Actions help to determine exactly what those measures should be and illustrate how a learner can score on his or her development plan.

Use learning accelerators. There are a number of ways the Talent Management function can support accelerated learners in developing competencies and Key Actions after formal training or other development experiences. We call them *learning accelerators* (see Figure 7.1). A few examples:

- **Learning support apps.** Support via mobile apps optimized for tablets and smartphones allows participants to check or refresh their learning on a just-in-time basis. Such support can include content reminders in the form of questions, videos, text messages, and emails. Or, they might appear as quick tips, reminders of application opportunities, or online support discussions that extend the training to the workplace. Reminders also may prompt learners about development commitments that were made at the end of the training.

- **Video learning tests.** These short "pop quizzes" evaluate development progress in a target competency or Key Action, and learners receive a score, creating a game-like experience to sharpen skills, evaluate progress, and enhance positive learning tension.

- **Learning communities.** Many people prefer to learn with and among others and do so more productively by sharing ideas and experiences. Communities can be live or virtual and can focus on any aspect of the learning process or content. Gathering information on others' progress toward their learning goals develops healthy competition, particularly on common goals. Learning communities also use virtual check-ins to reinforce key learning points and provide a forum for learners. In these networks learners can share success stores and discuss challenges with their peers.

- **Multiple-perspective (360°) pulse surveys.** Some organizations create brief surveys (often five items or fewer) tailored to the competencies or Key Actions a learner is trying to develop. Multiple, easy-to-use technology platforms generate standard or custom items while maintaining respondents' anonymity.

- **Practice simulations.** Designed to target specific competencies, automated practice simulations are often very brief and can be completed at the learner's discretion, from any device at any time. Repeat attempts hone skills and prepare learners for live practice in the workplace. For example, an automated coaching simulation might invite the learner to select ideal behaviors (from a list of possible alternatives) while viewing a coaching meeting between a leader and a team member.

Creating Energy (Performance Tension)

All the critical aspects of skill development we have discussed so far—training with behavior modeling and skill practice, rehearsal, feedback, measurement, and learning accelerators—generate energy in the growth process. But there is another enhancement you can make to create the positive tension that causes learners to devote their full energy to skill development.

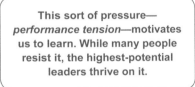

This sort of pressure—performance tension—motivates us to learn. While many people resist it, the highest-potential leaders thrive on it.

At one time or another, we all experience performance tension—whether performing in a musical group, competing on a sports team, or representing a school or company at a big event—where performance is both critical to success and on display. People clearly see how our contribution has an impact on success. Others are depending on us. This sort of pressure—*performance tension*—motivates us to learn. While many people resist it, the highest-potential leaders thrive on it. Examples common to learning processes include:

- Having learners (individually or in teams) make presentations to senior management about important business issues or questions (as a concluding exercise when analyzing or participating in an important business challenge), and then answering difficult questions about their recommendations.

- Detailing one's own development progress in update meetings with one or more senior managers and discussing the business impact of what has been learned and how it has been applied.

- Presenting a business- or process-improvement idea to a group of highly skeptical stakeholders, such as critical customers who have had bad experiences with the organization's products or services.

Following are more actual examples of how we have seen performance tension facilitate ongoing skill growth:

- **Ensuring the retention and use of interviewing skills.** DDI invented behavioral interviewing in 1970 and since then has done a great deal of research on managerial interviewing skills—an important leadership competency. In Targeted Selection® interviewer training, participants learn behavioral interviewing skills and then practice them in simulated interviews, receiving feedback after each one. Interviewers trained in this manner consistently make better hiring decisions, and their organizations receive more positive reactions from interviewees.

But in spite of effective training and early success, our follow-up research shows that the skills of *some* trained interviewers had deteriorated over time. This was not the case, however, for managers who participated in *data integration* meetings after interviews of all candidates were complete. In fact, these interviewing managers showed continued skill improvement and also made better hiring decisions. Data integration is a group discussion in which interviewers share observations on each of the candidate's competencies being evaluated. By verbalizing their findings, they gain valuable insights into the individual, and they learn additional interviewing skills from other interviewers. Performance tension is quite high in these meetings, because interviewers don't want to look bad to their fellow managers and their boss, who is often in attendance. Colleagues who are listening to an interviewer's report can readily determine if that person has done a thorough job.

- **Helping leaders retain and apply media-relations skills.** An energy company involved with hydraulic fracturing was facing intense media attention and scrutiny. Even though the organization had provided in-depth skills training to key leaders who frequently dealt with the media, most had forgotten the skills or hadn't fully acquired them from the start. These skill lapses led to unflattering news stories that tarnished the organization's reputation for safety and environmental responsibility. The solution involved dividing managers into groups to practice interviewing each other, with one manager playing the role of a news reporter. The groups made a contest of it. After each simulated interview, they listened to each discussion and critiqued one another.

Learning Pathways

Considering all we've discussed in this chapter, it is easy to understand why we collectively describe the effort to change behavior as a learning pathway. A map of a *learning pathway* is shown in Figure 7.1. We discuss learning pathways in more detail in Chapter 11, where we also describe group learning journeys, in which a cohort of accelerated learners go through a series of development activities together.

In Appendices 7.3 and 7.4, you'll find discussions of common competency development strategies by organizational level.

Appendix 7.1

The Disappointing Status of Leadership Development

In *Global Leadership Forecast 2014|2015,* comprising 1,528 HR professionals and 13,124 leaders, only 32 percent of HR professionals and 37 percent of leaders viewed their organization's leadership development programs as highly effective. Only 15 percent of HR professionals reported strong bench strength to meet future business needs, and on average, they could fill only 46 percent of critical positions immediately with internal candidates. Even more concerning, virtually no progress had been made on these metrics since a similar survey was conducted three years earlier. Other disappointing findings from DDI research include:

- Only 24 percent of HR professionals viewed their organization's succession-planning systems as effective.

  (Evan F. Sinar, Richard S. Wellins, Rebecca Ray, Amy Lui Abel, & Stephanie Neal, *Global Leadership Forecast 2014|2015: Ready-Now Leaders* [Pittsburgh, PA: DDI, 2014], supplemental information.)

- Only 46 percent of nonmanagement employees said their managers are committed to their development.

  (Patterson S. Weaver & Simon Mitchell, "Lessons for Leaders from the People Who Matter: How Employees Around the World View Their Leaders" [Pittsburgh, PA: DDI, 2012], supplemental information.)

- On average, leaders were able to apply only 54 percent of what they've learned in leadership development activities back to the job.

  (Sinar et al, *Global Leadership Forecast 2014|2015* [Pittsburgh, PA: DDI, 2014], supplemental information.)

- Only 58 percent of frontline leaders felt their manager is effective at developing them as a leader.

  (Ibid.)

- Only 51 percent of leaders felt they receive the right amount of active involvement in their development as a leader from their manager; even fewer (42 percent) believed the level of involvement of senior management and HR is right.

  (Ibid.)

- Only 33 percent of first-level leaders had a written and up-to-date—and, therefore, actionable—development plan in place.

  (Ibid.)

- Only 53 percent of managers said that their own development assignments were worthwhile learning experiences.

  (Scott Erker & Bradford Thomas, "Finding the First Rung: A Study on the Challenges Facing Today's Frontline Leader" [Pittsburgh, PA: DDI, 2010], supplemental information.)

- Only 50 percent of frontline leaders perceived their senior executives as committed to developing their organization's leaders.

  (Sinar et al, *Global Leadership Forecast 2014|2015* [Pittsburgh, PA: DDI, 2014], supplemental information.)

- Only 56 percent of frontline leaders felt their manager has the necessary knowledge to adequately support their development.

  (Erker & Thomas, "Finding the First Rung" [Pittsburgh, PA: DDI, 2010], supplemental information.)

- Only 40 percent of frontline managers were satisfied with their organization's development offerings.

  (Erker & Thomas, "Finding the First Rung" [Pittsburgh, PA: DDI, 2010], 3.)

Appendix 7.2

Discussion Planner

Discussion with: _____ Date: _____

Topic/Issue to discuss: _____

Key Principles *(to meet personal needs)*

☐ **Esteem**
  • Be specific and sincere

☐ **Empathy**
  • Describe facts and feelings

☐ **Involvement**
  • Unleash ideas with questions

☐ **Share**
  • Disclose feelings and insights to build trust

☐ **Support**
  • Specify the level of support you'll provide

My Approach

What are my objectives for this discussion?

How will I know I've accomplished these objectives?

What personal needs of the person/team do I need to consider?

Interaction Guidelines *(to meet practical needs)*

Time

☐ 1. OPEN
  • Describe purpose of discussion
  • Identify importance

☐ Make procedural suggestions
☐ Check for understanding

☐ 2. CLARIFY
  • Seek and share information about the situation
  • Identify issues and concerns

☐ Make procedural suggestions
☐ Check for understanding

[continued at top of next page]

··
[continued from previous page]

☐ 3. DEVELOP

 • Seek and discuss ideas
 • Explore needed resources/support

☐ Make procedural suggestions
☐ Check for understanding

☐ 4. AGREE

 • Specify actions, including contingency plans
 • Confirm how to track progress and measure results

☐ Make procedural suggestions
☐ Check for understanding

☐ 5. CLOSE

 • Highlight important features of plan
 • Confirm confidence and commitment

☐ Make procedural suggestions
☐ Check for understanding

Post-Discussion Notes

 • What did I say or do to use the skills effectively?

 • What could I say or do to use the skills more effectively next time?

Appendix 7.3

Competency Development That Works for High-Potential, Mid-Level Leaders

The most effective leadership training for middle managers is cohort-based (in groups) to maximize networking and create a sharing environment (see Chapter 11). Typical programs may be one or two days per quarter or a week-long residential program that focuses on common leadership competencies needed at that level. Alternatively, the focus may be on competencies that relate to a major organization initiative, such as innovation, making change happen, or building employee engagement. See the sidebar for a common curriculum.

Sample Two-Year Course Curriculum Configured Around Common Competency Needs for a Cohort of Mid-Level Managers

Year 1

1. Translating Strategy into Results (Decision Making, Driving Execution, Establishing Strategic Direction, Planning and Organizing)

2. Making Change Happen (Facilitating Change, Leading Change)

3. Mastering Emotional Intelligence (Authenticity, Building Strategic Work Relationships, Creating a Culture of Trust, Interaction Essentials, Personal Growth Orientation, Stress Tolerance)

4. Influencing for Organizational Impact (Gaining Commitment, Influence)

5. Developing Organizational Talent (Building Organizational Talent, Coaching, Developing Others)

Year 2

1. Instilling a Culture of Innovation (Customer Focus, Entrepreneurship, Facilitating Change, Driving Innovation, Leading Change)

2. Mastering Decision Dynamics (Courage, Decision Making, Navigating Complexity, Operational Decision Making, Strategic Decision Making)

[continued at top of next page]

[continued from previous page]

3. Cultivating Networks and Partnerships (Building Partnerships, Building Networks)

4. Coaching for High Performance (Building Organizational Talent, Creating a Culture of Trust, Coaching, Coaching and Developing Others)

5. Leading with a Global Perspective (Decision Making, Global Acumen, Leveraging Diversity, Optimizing Diversity, Strategic Decision Making)

As with first-level programs, mid-level management programs are built around competency Key Actions, and content can be tailored to meet individuals' specific development needs.

Interaction Essentials (see Chapter 3)

Middle managers are in a central position in the organization. They need to motivate and engage people within and outside their team and across organizational boundaries. They also lead and develop talent and make and communicate difficult decisions. These challenges require skillful use of the Interaction Essentials to enhance emotional intelligence (EQ).

While managers should have already mastered the Interaction Essentials before reaching middle management, there are many who still do not routinely apply them (in fact we know CEOs who don't). Thus, a foundational course in many mid-level curricula includes the topic of emotional intelligence. In 1999 the Emotional Intelligence Consortium sanctioned DDI's leadership development courses using the Interaction Essentials as model programs for increasing emotional intelligence.

Typical cohort-based, mid-level programs feature group discussions, thereby creating opportunities for participants to seek, connect, and share job challenges and solutions. Once a climate of sharing and trust has been established, most middle managers are ready to admit and discuss their shortcomings relative to the competencies being developed and learn from group feedback when they try new skills.

Getting Outside the Classroom

The Institute for Executive Development (IED) and DDI (2011) found that the approaches organizations are taking to develop mid-level leaders are changing just as quickly as their roles. Some approaches that we have tried successfully include:

Virtual Classroom Training

In virtual classroom training designs, participants have exactly the same learning experience they would have in an instructor-led classroom, except that they are sitting at their own PC, laptop, or tablet miles away from fellow learners.

Virtual classroom training is not synonymous with web-based training, which is asynchronous self-study. Instead, it involves a number of participants interacting in real-time discussion, Q&A, game playing, skill practicing, and receiving feedback. The instructor presents content, makes lighthearted small talk, answers questions, and monitors skill practice sessions when the participants divide into subgroups (enabled by virtual classroom technology). The learning tension created by learning as part of a team or receiving feedback after a skill practice is still very much a part of the experience.

Advantages

- **Travel time and transportation costs are cut, but outcomes remain strong.** When the outcomes of virtual classroom training were calculated for Nissan, DDI found that measured leader behavior change was comparable—even superior—to measured behavior change after classroom delivery of DDI courses.

- **Training can be segmented to optimize learning.** Research has shown that five half-day training programs conducted a week apart produce better learning and on-the-job application than two-and-a-half-day programs covering the same material. People can become fatigued with too much training in a short period, even when provided in an extremely dynamic and interactive way. The advantage of spacing training units is that participants can try out the program concepts/skills between sessions, and then discuss their experiences with other participants in their next meeting.

- **Training can be scheduled immediately prior to planned applications, allowing immediate skill use.** Interviewer training, for example, is much more effective when delivered right before a manager has to fill an important position. Training on setting performance goals is learned best the month before yearly goals are to be submitted.

- **Training can speed teams' success.** When an organization is setting up a cross-organizational project team to handle a technical or other type of issue, it's very important that the team works together effectively. If members don't have experience in cross-organizational teams, it is quite likely that team progress will be slowed as they encounter communication and interpersonal challenges. A virtual training session on team building and team interaction skills can prove quite valuable.

- **Timely training is a key to making major organizational changes successful.** After a major reorganization or downsizing, senior leaders face many challenges. How will managers throughout the organization communicate the new direction? How effective will they be in selling the benefits to their direct reports? Senior leaders would like to equip their supervisors and managers with the skills needed to handle these challenges, but rarely have time to do so. Virtual training provides that time.

Disadvantages

- **Cost.** Instructor costs can be higher than the cost of conventional training because often two instructors are needed.

- **Loss of casual interactions before or after a conventional training experience.** Participants appreciate being physically together as a group to network and establish stronger relationships with coworkers. The absence of those connections can erode the perceived quality of the experience. That said, however, there often is quite a bit of casual and planned conversations before and after virtual training sessions.

Web-Based Training with Learning Practice Labs

Web-based training provides the same content as live classroom training, except that the learners' insights are gained in very different ways. Good web-based training programs are highly interactive and engaging, checking participants' learning as they go through the program. They also are fun—using games and other learning challenges. The downside is that web-based courses don't allow the immediate practice/feedback and reinforcement that are important for most people's learning.

Web-based skill development can be substantially enhanced by adding *learning practice labs,* where learners engage in discussion, demonstrate skills, and receive feedback on several competencies in half- or full-day, live or virtual sessions. The web-based courses deliver the cognitive aspect of training along with some skill development in advance of the learning practice labs.

One problem with combining web-based training with learning practice labs can be the timing. Many organizations wait for weeks or months after their web-based sessions to conduct the learning labs. In that time lapse and without application opportunities, users often forget what they had learned. Then, when convening the learning practice labs, organizations must backtrack or move off the intended course flow to provide a refresher that gets participants mentally into the lab activities.

Action Learning

Action learning is a well-tested methodology commonly used in developing mid-level, accelerated learners. CEOs routinely tell us that their investments in these cadre-based learning efforts reap significant ROI for the business. In teams, participants explore compelling, real-life business issues and recommend solutions to senior management, while simultaneously honing their competency skills. Personal learning distinguishes action learning from other assignments, such as serving on a task force. Team members receive feedback from many sources—teammates, management, professional coaches assigned to their action learning team—on their contributions to the decision-making process along with their use of the Interaction Essentials and other focus Key Actions. (See Chapter 11 on the development of learning journeys that involve action learning components.)

Learning by Teaching

Peter F. Drucker once stated, *"No one learns as much about a subject as one who is forced to teach it."* To develop their skills in key competencies and Interaction Essentials, accelerated middle managers benefit by being assigned to conduct some first-level leadership training on competencies in which they are weak. To become qualified to instruct, they must complete rigorous facilitator training and demonstrate teaching proficiency. Some will need additional support before they are ready for solo delivery. Their facilitation training and experience gained while conducting a few courses boost accelerated learners' confidence in using the target competencies as well as their teaching and assessment skills. Insights gleaned from observing skill growth in the trainees help them to really believe in the effectiveness of the training content they deliver.

Well-trained middle managers have a high success rate in changing the behavior of first-level leaders, who interpret their superiors' involvement as a sign of management support. Also, middle managers' work with frontline leaders provides a unique window into what's happening throughout the organization. Finally, teaching builds their reputation as someone who is willing to give up his or her own precious time to help others. And there's no loss of face for the individual. In fact, it's an honor to be made an instructor.

See Chapter 11 for examples of developing mid-level competencies along with other development goals in learning journeys.

Appendix 7.4

Competency Development That Works for Senior Executives

Many senior-level leaders have competency development needs similar to those of lower-level leaders, and the learning approaches already discussed can (and often do) work just as well for them. But because role demands are so unique among senior executives, participation in formal competency development programs often does not meet the need to individualize the content so that it can be readily applied. For that reason, most executives prefer to take on skill development challenges with the help of an executive coach who can adapt relevant content from formal learning programs to the executive's. In this way, skill development for senior leaders often is much like a one-person competency training course. Target competencies and focus Key Actions are equally relevant and instrumental to successful growth, but learning segments are aligned to suit the executive's needs and applied in ways that are often more integrated with real-time work activities.

The Importance of Interaction Essentials for Senior-Level Leaders

With specific regard to competencies, the Interaction Essentials (Chapter 3) play a particularly important role. Senior executives are held to higher standards by their organizations and public constituents, leaving little room for error around the fundamentals. For that reason, the need to apply the Interaction Essentials effectively becomes greater as individuals climb the organizational ladder. In addition, some Essentials become more important because personality derailers tend to become more detrimental to performance at higher levels where there is more decision risk and stress. The impact of derailers often can be mitigated by using appropriate Essentials (see Chapter 8).

A High-Speed Competency Development Process for a Senior Executive Team

A global energy corporation faced a crisis. Their business and culture were struggling following a global economic downturn and a series of business setbacks. Scrutiny on the organization was intense, both from outside and within. Performance languished, and the senior management team struggled to get it back on track. Deadlines were missed, budgets ran high, and performance targets were far below expectations.

So, the CEO and Talent Management SVP isolated the *Driving Execution* competency and started with the senior management team as the primary group to be developed. Acceleration was desperately needed. The primary objective of the process was to (urgently) enhance strategy execution by providing one-to-one coaching (training) to each senior executive. For the sake of brevity, we share only the details of the competency-development aspects of the process:

Pre-Interviews: Following project stage setting, planning, and establishing stakeholder alignment, executive coaches conducted one-to-one interviews with each senior team member. The goal was twofold: 1) diagnose and understand the issues and challenges facing the team, and 2) preview the individual coaching process and the *Driving Execution* competency. During the interviews each executive gained specific insight into the Key Actions associated with *Driving Execution,* and coaches gathered input about each team member's personal needs and role challenges.

Assessment: Each executive participated in an Acceleration Center experience (Chapter 5) that was customized to emphasize the execution components of senior-level leadership. Also included were a multi-perspective (360°) feedback survey, personality inventories, and multi-perspective interviews to allow participants to provide insights on one another.

Feedback and initial coaching: Each participant then engaged in DDI's executive coaching process, which begins with feedback from the Acceleration Center experience, and then launches a high-speed journey examining the business, role, and individual challenges that each leader faced, with specific emphasis on *Driving Execution*. With help from a coach and using the behavioral detail from the Acceleration Center feedback, each executive drafted a development plan aimed directly at how to enhance his or her skills in *Driving Execution*. The plan was then shared with other key stakeholders for review and input. Of course, each executive focused on the Key Actions that he or she needed to develop.

Team learning event: Following initial feedback and coaching, the senior team participated in a two-hour training event on the principles of world-class strategy execution. The lead executive coaches served as instructors for the event, which was highly customized to the organization's context and business, but also very focused on establishing a shared understanding of the Key Actions associated with *Driving Execution* and their relevance to the current business situation. Each senior team member also had Acceleration Center results in hand and was able to share personal observations and learning from the Acceleration Center experience and to further refine his or her development plans based on what was learned.

Group development update: After the formal learning event, the senior team met again to review and refine their individual development objectives. They reviewed group assessment trends and data (again with special emphasis on *Driving Execution*), discussed common development opportunities, shared personal development objectives publicly, and exchanged feedback about the expected impact of their development efforts on the business—specifically on enhancing strategy execution. Development plans were scrutinized for their focus on the application of the Key Actions to be developed. Each leader was put to task among the rest of the team to demonstrate exactly how he or she would apply the new skills.

Individual development updates: Approximately six weeks into the coaching process, participants conducted individual updates with the CEO to review development progress and discuss how their actions were having an impact on the execution of critical initiatives. Each person's coach participated in the meetings, and development action plans were revised and enhanced to continue to push leaders to enhance their skills and continually apply them in ever-more-challenging ways. Updates also were shared regularly with the Talent Management SVP.

Three-month checkpoint: At the three-month point, all participants had taken at least initial actions on their development plans, and most had demonstrated some preliminary growth. At this juncture all participants were invited (with the input of the CEO and Talent Management SVP) to continue development with or without their coach's support. Decisions to continue coaching or not were based on the nature of the development plan, support needed, and anticipation of future challenges or opportunities that might warrant coaching support. Most elected to continue working with their coaches, and some elected to work independently. With or without coaches, updates with the CEO and Talent Management SVP continued regularly.

Outcomes: All participants accomplished and documented behavioral evidence of their personal growth in *Driving Execution*. Strategy execution was significantly enhanced, resulting in dramatically improved progress against critical efficiency metrics, cost reductions, and margin enhancement. Board meetings became easier for the CEO to manage as performance began to have a positive impact on the stock price and on public perceptions of a positive response to the disaster. In addition, the team discussed and penetrated critical barriers to their effectiveness and achieved new levels of candor and trust in discussing sensitive issues. They engaged in further team development to address issues uncovered in the coaching process such as decision-making efficiency and talent development. And finally, strategy execution has been significantly enhanced and has become, in the words of the CEO, "a process that I can manage more effectively because we all practice it together."

UNLEASH THE INNER STRENGTH OF YOUR LEADERS

8 | Helping Leaders Overcome Personality Derailers, Motivation, or EQ Challenges

Big leaps in leadership take courage. In riskier assignments failure comes with great business and personal costs. To avoid it, most leaders must bring their full and complete effort. We won't rehash all the reasons that higher-level roles are more difficult; that has been well documented in previous chapters. But it is important to start this chapter by reiterating that as leaders face more challenging assignments, they must exert themselves more heavily to keep up with the complexity and speed at which challenges come at them. Amid the chaos they're less able to control their reactions. As leaders step up, their unique nature, hard-wired dispositions, or in our terms, *personal attributes* have a stronger pull. And because they are so often unaccounted for, personal attributes—more so than competencies, experience, or knowledge—tend to hold the key to why executives fail.

None of us can change our most fundamental hard-wiring, and it is fruitless to try. That said, leaders can learn to adapt their behaviors to mitigate the negative effects of their dysfunctional tendencies (of which we all have some) and learn how to capitalize on their natural gifts without over-relying on them. This is no simple task. And for that reason, your acceleration efforts must carefully consider your learners' personal attributes as you plan for their accelerated growth.

When Do Personal Attributes Matter Most?

Personal attributes underlie and steer behavior. They are stable, enduring characteristics that don't change—not much anyway and not quickly. Personality, motivation, and emotional intelligence are the focus of our attention, as they have the greatest relevance to accelerated growth.[1] The stronger these attributes are (either positive or negative), the more consistent their effect is on behavior across situations and the more difficult it is for individuals to engage in alternative behaviors. Consider the impulsive leader who can be relied on to quickly mobilize his organization around new initiatives, but can't be patient enough to involve key stakeholders, even after he commits to doing so. He might generate action, but he alienates his internal partners. Or, think about the argumentative executive who is a shrewd negotiator but can't help but focus on one minor problem in her team's business proposal, even though their overall plan is exceptional. Sure, she's a reliable business advisor, but she's draining her team's self-confidence.

Some attributes are universal enablers, such as ambition, resilience, creativity, learning orientation, and self-efficacy; others are more universally problematic, such as volatility, lack of interpersonal awareness, argumentativeness, and passive aggressiveness. Very often, derailers are rooted in enablers that have been overused or that are so extreme that they have a dysfunctional effect.[i]

---

1 Cognitive ability is the other major component of personal attributes, and because it is uniquely difficult to develop, we don't discuss it here. We do address the topic in Chapter 5, focusing more on when and how to apply cognitive testing to ensure positive impact in your acceleration efforts.

Examples include confidence that morphs into arrogance and unwillingness to accept feedback, or passion that spills over into emotional instability and unstable relationships, or emotional steadiness that is so extreme that it transforms into a lack of empathy and a difficulty in building trust.

There's a long list of fascinating and relevant personal attributes, but our purpose is not to define them all here. Instead, our goal is to focus on your role as a leader of acceleration and to highlight the following actions you must take to ensure that your acceleration efforts address personal attributes effectively:

Ensure the accurate measurement of personal attributes. As the saying goes, "opinions are cheap," and that is particularly relevant to personal attributes. Few senior executives hesitate to share their beliefs about the personalities and motivations of high-potential leaders, and very often, they are wrong. Having accurate, objective data about personal attributes is essential to accelerated development. Chapter 5 examines assessment approaches to provide that data.

> "Opinions are cheap," and that is particularly relevant to personal attributes.

Ensure that management receives an accurate interpretation of personal attributes. Having accurate data helps in development planning only if management receives results in an appropriate way. We've seen extensive personality-assessment reports on individuals sent directly to management without interpretation. We've also seen these same reports reduced to a single bullet point in a slide show. Both tactics result in misinterpretation. The process of providing data on personal attributes to management is as important as the information itself. Trained experts, either internal to your organization or contracted from outside, are essential to help management understand the meaning and implications of this data.

Don't permit leaders to wear derailers as badges of honor. If you've ever introduced personality assessment to management, you probably know that senior executives sometimes recognize their own characteristics as they review the accelerated learners' profiles. Some executives actually take pride in their most dysfunctional attributes. We've seen many of them smile broadly when told that others perceive them as overly aggressive and overconfident, or other executives who claim proudly that they don't hesitate to speak their minds and that if others can't handle it—their insensitivity, that is—well, tough luck. These executives frequently reason that if they have managed to be successful in their careers, then why should the same trait be a concern for the learner? These are dangerous viewpoints that should be countered with emphasis on your success profile and the business consequences of derailing patterns in your context.

Don't allow leaders to be branded by their personal attributes. While it's important to recognize that personal attributes are stable, this does not mean that leaders are unable to replace unproductive tendencies with more productive ones. As your organization gathers and uses data on personal attributes, that data should neither be dismissed nor used to permanently brand leaders as certain types.

Identify derailers before they do damage, and be sure to put development plans in place to ensure success. The purpose of having good data on personal attributes is twofold. First, it helps management assess the fit between leaders and prospective roles or assignments for which they are being considered (see Chapter 5 for more on this topic). Second, and a key focus in this chapter, it helps leaders learn to apply behaviors that mitigate the risks of their dysfunctional tendencies.

The following sections focus on strategies that can change or enhance behaviors associated with three types of personal attributes most relevant for leaders developing toward senior positions: personality, leadership motivation, and emotional intelligence.

Personality—Managing Derailers and Optimizing Enablers

As we've said, there's no such thing as a good or bad personality; it's the behavior that matters. Personality interacts with the situation or context to influence the effectiveness of behavior. Attributes can be positive (enablers), as in the case of a naturally sociable leader who must build a network of partners in a new role. He feels energized by reaching out and interacting with many people, quickly cultivating a diverse group of alliances. Or, they can be negative (derailers), such as when the same leader's sociability spills over into attention seeking, and he struggles to operate in a very analytical environment where relationships are built over time (and with less frequent interaction). His approach becomes too flamboyant for the culture, and he loses credibility by appearing unwilling or unable to engage in deep analysis. He also loses motivation because the environment doesn't fit his natural approach.

Some leaders have somewhat neutral personality patterns that are more receptive to different behavioral approaches, and these individuals can be developed to alter their behaviors across a variety of situations. But other leaders have such strong derailers that they represent barriers to effectiveness in almost any leadership context. When your high-potential leaders show dysfunctional tendencies, they must be addressed proactively to avoid failure in larger assignments.

> When your high-potential leaders show **dysfunctional** tendencies, they must be addressed proactively to avoid failure in larger assignments.

Anticipating and Managing Derailers

Although leaders may have gained the skill, experience, and knowledge needed for success, even the best performers can fail because of a strong derailer. The danger comes from the fact that derailers typically are rooted in attributes that had contributed to early career success, but have backfired as leaders make the transition to the uncertainty and exposure associated with executive roles. This can be surprising and disorienting, given that many leaders fail to recognize it until after the negative effects have begun to manifest themselves. Consider the highly successful salesperson who struggles when stepping up to a leadership role. She may be at risk for the very same reasons she was successful as a sales professional—confidence can veer into arrogance, passion may translate into volatility, and interpersonal skillfulness can be interpreted as being manipulative.

But not all derailers are tied to strengths; some are traits that were ignored at one level, but then balloon into problems as the leader advances. Consider the perfectionistic leader whose high standards lead him to be controlling of others and overly critical when things go wrong. With a greater scope of responsibility and more pressure on his decisions, he might find it difficult to delegate, leading to overload and a failure to develop others behind him.

Derailers are most likely to show up during times of stress, when managing a heavy workload, and especially when making a transition to a new challenge or role. Conversely, derailers also can emerge when individuals become complacent and stop paying attention to their behavior in known areas of risk. And the reality is that derailers are not always directly observable—that is, until they wreak havoc on the leader's career or, worse yet, on the careers of those around the leader. Long is the list of leaders whose tenures as CEO were characterized by failure that emanated from their derailers—Lay (Enron), Ebbers (Worldcom), Ivester (Coca-Cola), Nardelli (Home Depot), Dunlap (Sunbeam), For these and others, it was not lack of knowledge or skill that hurt them most. Rather, characteristics like arrogance, recklessness, insensitivity, and impulsiveness derailed their success.

Both context and timing play a role in whether derailers actually lead to failure or not. In the right settings, leaders with severe derailers can accomplish great things; in the wrong environments, the same leaders fail. The many biographical accounts of Steve Jobs describe derailers that threatened his career and impact, including arrogance, argumentativeness, and volatility. While by most standards Jobs was ultimately a success, he derailed several times in his career—most famously, when he was fired from Apple, the company he founded.

There are four tactics that accelerated learners must develop to avoid being derailed. They are most effective when personalized to the individual's goals and learning needs:

- **Understand and accept** personal derailers and the need to avoid them.

- **Anticipate** when derailing behaviors are likely to be triggered.

- **Practice** alternative approaches in situations where derailing behaviors occur.

- **Stay focused** on maintaining new behaviors.

Understand and accept personal derailers and the need to avoid them. Avoiding derailers won't happen unless the individuals also acknowledge the real risks and negative implications associated with them. Why do they matter? How will they hurt individuals' own effectiveness or, worse yet, that of others? An example: Attention-seeking individuals are commonly outgoing and gregarious and enjoy being the center of attention. This can cause them to appear charming and socially magnetic. However, as leaders, they also may be perceived as self-promoting, seeking recognition and credit over those they are assigned to advocate.

> Derailers are not always directly observable— that is, until they wreak havoc on the leader's career or, worse yet, on the careers of those around the leader.

They are sometimes described as "taking the air out of the room," usurping the energy and spotlight from less-confident partners and subordinates they are assigned to develop and champion. Although unintentional, their attention seeking hurts those they care about most. Most attention-seeking individuals truly enjoy relationships and interactions. Many recognize and even joke about their overabundance of extraversion as spilling into an attention-seeking derailer. But because these individuals are fundamentally concerned about others' feelings, they typically value deeper understanding of how to manage the risks associated with their derailer.

Personality and behavioral assessments (e.g., Acceleration Centers) help to spot potential derailers among emerging high-potential leaders (Chapter 5). Feedback around derailers can trigger sensitivity and even resistance. This is particularly true when derailers have not yet been obviously detrimental to someone's career. In this case, real evidence and skillful persuasion often are needed to convince people that they have a possible derailer. This is understandable because many executive derailers represent too much of a good thing. It's very difficult for people to see the potential negative consequences of doing what they have been doing successfully for years. Some common responses include:

- **Dodging.** Saying they plan to change the behavior, but then failing to take meaningful or consistent action.

- **Rationalizing.** Recognizing that it is a problem without searching for an alternative to the derailer. In their mind, the derailing behavior is an appropriate way to handle a given situation.

- **Denying.** Refusing to believe there is a problem, citing early career success.

- **Delaying.** Seeing how a particular derailer might cause problems at higher levels, but thinking they will deal with it when they get there.

- **Accepting.** Admitting the need to improve and initiate action to avoid the derailer and stay on track.

Individuals should be encouraged to seek evidence of derailers by gathering feedback and insight from colleagues (the right kind of 360° feedback works well). Friends and relatives also can be trustworthy sources. We have heard many leaders describe reactions of coworkers, spouses, and others who verify derailers with their own observations and, at times, frustrations (e.g., *"Because I respect you so much, I live with it, but I don't like it."*). Coaches often are assigned to "hold up a mirror" to help talented executives recognize

A Coach Helps a Derailing Leader

Scott ran a tight ship as plant manager. His personal warmth softened the command-and-control style he had learned in the Navy. This mix resulted in a style that was highly effective with plant associates. However, Scott's directive, albeit friendly, approach became a liability after he was promoted to director of quality assurance. Success in his new job became dependent on his power of persuasion and influence rather than formal authority, and Scott didn't recognize the changes he needed to make in his style.

An executive coach interviewed Scott's internal stakeholders. These people felt Scott was far too controlling, rather than consultative, when discussing methods to improve quality.

After several discussions with his coach and some serious reflection, Scott acknowledged the issue and began to address it by more actively seeking others' input before promoting his own solutions. This created a stronger sense of shared ownership around quality solutions from those he worked with and led to significant, ongoing improvements in both quality metrics and partnership scorecards.

the implications of derailers and to work on behavioral approaches so they can avoid negative impact.

Anticipate when derailing behaviors are likely to be triggered. An important first step is being aware that role transitions represent times of increased risk of derailment. But there are other factors that can trigger derailing behaviors. Triggers differ for each individual, but not everyone is aware of their own. They include a wide range of variables such as environment, physical condition or fatigue, criticism, moods and attitudes, offenses to values and sensibilities, and even business events or interactions that involve exposure or competition for resources. Triggers cause emotional responses (frustration, anger, impatience, etc.), and the more sudden and unexpected they are, the more likely they will be to elicit derailing behaviors.

Helping Leaders Identify Personal Triggers

- I get mad when…
- I don't like it when…
- I get tired of…
- I think it's rude to…
- I wish people would…
- I think work would be a better place if people would stop…
- If people would only…
- I get irritated when I get to work and…

Exploring and confronting one's own derailers enables leaders to anticipate situations that might trigger them. That leads to the ability to develop alternative or coping behaviors.

> When people first see that a different behavior can achieve better results, it often catalyzes a shift toward using it.

Practice alternative approaches in situations where derailing behaviors occur. Once a leader understands his or her derailers and when they are likely to occur, the next step is to apply productive behaviors to replace the dysfunctional ones. This takes some practice and, as we discussed with the development of competencies in the previous chapter, requires commitment. But when people first see that a different behavior can achieve better results, it often catalyzes a shift toward using it.

Consider the real case of a technology executive—an argumentative leader who was seen as skeptical, tense, defensive, and at times even paranoid or suspicious. He often was accused of protecting his own interests and resisting feedback. He exhausted people who had to work closely with him and ultimately lost credibility even when he made a good case. As difficult as it was to give him feedback, people eventually convinced him that practicing alternative behaviors would make a significant difference in his performance.

For instance, a useful exercise with this leader has been to reconsider a direct report's "bad idea" (according to him) and practice alternative questioning techniques to explore the impact of how different approaches might be perceived. These approaches are then rehearsed in private with a coach and later tested live. In live situations the coach sits out while the technology leader enlists help from one of several trusted colleagues to provide feedback. He uses the feedback to reflect on what might have worked better and to plan different (better) approaches in the future. Not only has this leader made great progress in how he manages his argumentative derailer, but colleagues also have come to notice his effort. They have gone out of their way to compliment him on the positive effect he is having on the culture. Bear in mind that this leader is far from perfect—his argumentative derailer always will be with him, and at times it still causes disruptive behavior. But he has significantly improved his behavior, which has been recognized and appreciated, and his continual practicing in this area has created a healthy dynamic in the organization.

Stay focused on maintaining new behaviors. Managing one's derailing behavior is a lifelong commitment, like adhering to a fitness regimen or changing eating habits. It's very easy to slip back to old behaviors unless one is constantly on guard. It requires focus, motivation, self-awareness, and usually some help from others. So, a system that monitors success is essential. Focusing on positive behavior can make a big difference. It's much easier to get feedback on how frequently a positive behavior is used than on how often a derailer resurfaces.Relying on colleagues for feedback also fosters their support and makes them more accepting when the derailer seeps out.

> It's much easier to get feedback on how frequently a positive behavior is used than on how often a derailer resurfaces.

Many leaders also track their behaviors independently. A finance executive we know makes a tick mark in his notebook each time he asks an open-ended question to get others' input. He is consciously trying to be less directive and controlling. Another leader has made a habit of asking members of her team to quickly recap what has been agreed to in meetings. She had received feedback that her enthusiasm sometimes has overshadowed the team's need for clear direction. Tracking progress in managing derailers doesn't have to be complex or arduous, but it does need to be continual.

Optimizing Enablers

Just as there are derailers that can cause executives to fail, there also are enabling personality characteristics that act as catalysts for positive behavior. With respect to acceleration, the opportunity is in creating assignments that allow leaders to bring out their best and create positive impact for the business. For example, accelerated learners who are naturally open to change will be quicker to offer innovative ideas during an organizational restructuring than would equally capable peers who are more cautious and pragmatic by nature. Those who are emotionally resilient are more likely to channel energy in the right places in the midst of stressful, ambiguous leadership challenges than those who are anxious and prone to second-guessing themselves. Awareness of enablers helps accelerated learners to consciously leverage their strengths and better understand behavior-based competency feedback.

Leadership Motivation

Tapping into the motivations of learners is one of the most important things you can do to inject energy into your accelerated-development processes

> Leaders choose
> to lead for very
> different reasons.

and ensure good fits between leaders and higher-level assignments. The point is so fundamental that it might seem obvious, but understanding motivation can be complex. Leaders choose to lead for very different reasons. Many people, particularly ambitious, high-potential leaders, present themselves in ways that do not fully reflect (and may at times even misrepresent) their core motivations. In your acceleration system the first task is to fully understand (and potentially

Why Worry About Derailers? Why Not Simply Leverage Strengths?

If derailers are hardwired aspects of personality, then why try to manage them? Why shouldn't leaders simply surrender to their natural tendencies by maximizing already existing advantages?

It's easy to understand the appeal of this premise. Every leader should, in fact, find ways to sharpen innate strengths. For example, an individual with natural charisma might do well to get additional training that polishes his delivery style, elevating this area to a towering strength.

It's also tempting for leaders or their managers to excuse or even encourage derailers as the inevitable "dark side" of strengths. Take Mitch, a marketing director recognized for his extraordinary creativity and contribution. Mitch might be described as both inspiring and infuriating, the latter attribute emerging when he expresses unfiltered ideas and monopolizes discussions, disrupting input from others. Based on past feedback, Mitch tries to manage his behavior. But his passion generally overrules his self-control, resulting in predictable lapses into dysfunction. While both Mitch and his manager acknowledge the consequence, they also shrug off this pattern to his eccentricity, characterizing it as part of Mitch's "charm" and implying that it's simply part of the package that comes with his talent.

Mitch's behavior illustrates why driving a singular focus on developing one's strengths is unwise. Ignoring development needs just because they are rooted in personal attributes is shortsighted, as it assumes that strengths sufficiently compensate for weakness, which clearly is not true.

influence) individuals' motivation to lead, after which it is useful to look at more specific leadership motivations to help fuel accelerated growth.

Fostering the motivation to lead. Research has continually shown that differences in leadership motivation start at a very young age—in elementary school or even earlier. People who were schoolyard or classroom leaders are more likely to be leaders later in life. Part of this is skill, but a great deal of it is motivation as well as self-efficacy. Some never attempt leadership and therefore never receive the positive reinforcement that comes from doing it well. Leadership motivation also is informed by exposure to role models, including parents, teachers, early mentors, and coaches. Those who have not observed strong leaders might not understand the opportunity for impact they would have if they stepped up to a leadership role.

> Motivation evolves, and the desire to lead can be purposefully increased.

It's a mistake to assume that everyone wants to be a leader, but it's also erroneous to conclude that people who convey disinterest in leadership will always feel that way. Motivation evolves, and the desire to lead can be purposefully increased, particularly through experiences that reinforce the positive aspects of being a leader. Sometimes the best leaders are people who never thought of themselves as leaders until they were asked to try on the role.

Encouraging those without inherent leadership motivation does not happen instantaneously, but there are many situations where individuals have the competencies, knowledge, experience, and personal attributes that otherwise would make them good leaders. Some scenarios are characterized by deep leadership voids because very few people step up to lead (e.g., technical disciplines like health care, engineering, finance, and IT). In these cases, it's worthwhile to engender leadership motivation in capable individuals whenever possible.

There are two very straightforward ways to boost motivation for leadership. First, managers can slowly and incrementally increase the informal leadership role an individual plays. Heading up a small project or subgroup or being the coleader of a larger group can help introduce individuals to leadership. Naturally, it is important for them to be complemented by a more experienced coleader or mentor. But once in a leadership position, they often discover aspects that are inherently interesting to them and that feed their motivation in unexpected ways.

Second, managers can experiment by placing reluctant individuals into leadership roles and surrounding them with coaching, training, and support. In fact, this is the situation in which many organizations find themselves. Often, after a company has identified the person believed to be a perfect fit, the individual will profess not to want a leadership job. Sometimes this reluctance is a legitimate absence of leadership motivation, which should be respected. But again, sometimes the lack of leadership motivation is rooted in a lack of confidence. In either case, providing support, guidance, and skill building in leadership fundamentals may diminish this barrier and lead to success. We have seen many people placed into both small and large leadership situations who, with the appropriate support, have changed their minds about their leadership motivation. As they tally leadership successes, they discover the role to be more appealing than they had thought previously.

Understanding and capitalizing on specific motivations. Establishing an individual's motivation to lead is a key building block to accelerating growth. But tapping into a person's real passion requires a deeper look at work-related motives like having a desire to help others, forming strong bonds with coworkers, being rewarded or recognized for one's work, having influence, having fun, and many others. Each leader has personal motivations, and as he or she takes on more responsibility, motivation is a prime source of the energy needed to conquer each new assignment.

A leader who values relationships at work may thrive in a consultative role that requires long-term connections with customers and partners, but may struggle in an engineering environment where people are more task oriented and prefer less interaction with others. An altruistic individual put in charge of a major organizational transformation likely will focus on how to help people cope with the change and may emphasize messaging that clarifies how it will make their lives better in the long run. In contrast, a different leader who values quality and excellence may handle the same challenge by reminding people that their efforts will create better products, provide greater value to customers, and have a positive effect in the marketplace.

> Simply asking someone, *"What motivates you?"* won't produce the insights you'll need.

Motivation influences fit—with situations (leadership assignments) and people. This has important implications for how accelerated development plans are made. It is essential to understand how each accelerated learner's motivations intersect with the people and scenarios into which the individual will be placed. Simply asking someone, *"What motivates you?"* won't produce the insights you'll need. Like personality, motivation can and should be measured accurately, using the right methods and tools (Chapter 5). Well-designed interviews using trained interviewers[2] can help to not only ask the right basic questions about motivation, but also determine how to probe into individuals' responses to gather more accurate insights. Validated motivational inventories also can add objective insight that enables a more specific understanding of motivation. Leveraging these methods can help to ensure that you fully understand your learners' motivations so that you can best capitalize on them.

Emotional Intelligence (EQ)

> Many leaders fail to execute on their leadership intentions, because they are unable to manage their behavior in response to their own and others' emotions.

The notion that one's emotional intelligence is as important in leadership as cognitive intelligence not only is logically appealing,[ii] but there also is considerable evidence of its legitimacy as a predictor of leadership growth and success.[iii] Adele Lynn's definition of EQ is particularly relevant to acceleration because it speaks to the importance of developing self-management behaviors to enhance EQ.[iv] Lynn describes EQ as the *"ability to manage yourself and relationships with others so that you truly live your*

---

2 Targeted Selection® pioneered the world's first and, now, most widely applied method of interviewing for motivation. It uses a behavioral approach to probing individuals' past work experiences and how specific behavioral approaches relate to satisfaction, energy, and success.

intentions." This might seem like a lofty aspiration, but it points to the crux of the EQ dilemma: Many leaders with exceptional skills and knowledge fail to execute on their leadership intentions, because they are unable to manage their behavior in response to their own and others' emotions.

People with high emotional intelligence demonstrate strong self-awareness, social expertness, and empathy toward others. They are attuned to others' feelings as well as to their personal and practical needs. They are self-reflective and recognize the impact of their actions on others. This helps them build trust, sustain relationships, and effectively influence others.

Those with average emotional intelligence might not be naturally sensitive to others' emotions and personal needs, so their insight into themselves and others may be inconsistent. They may genuinely care, but sometimes overlook the implications of their own and others' behavior. As Lynn points out, their opportunity is to develop techniques to better connect to others' needs so they can behave accordingly.

Individuals with very low EQ are commonly described as being interpersonally obtuse, being insensitive, or having severe blind spots when it comes to interacting and building relationships with others. They routinely damage relationships by failing to attend to others' important emotional cues or needs. People with low EQ make others feel unappreciated, unrecognized, and undermined, and most of them do so unintentionally. But in the absence of a concerted effort to increase one's EQ, others will question the individual's intentions over time, presuming that the leader actually doesn't care about the emotional well-being of others. For this reason, when leaders with very low EQ reach positions of influence, the effect is toxic to the culture and the business.

As we've said in other parts of this chapter, while the problem may be rooted in hardwired personal attributes, the solution to an EQ deficit is behavioral. This highlights why we at DDI have come to believe so deeply in the fundamental value of the Interaction Essentials (Chapter 3). Increasing

> While the problem may be rooted in hardwired personal attributes, the solution to an EQ deficit is behavioral.

emotional intelligence requires training and practice using new, more emotionally appropriate behaviors, and the Essentials are the behavioral foundations of EQ. Responding to others' concerns with empathetic statements, sharing one's thoughts and feelings, asking for help—these and the other Interaction Essentials behaviors can be learned (with practice) by all leaders, regardless of their EQ level.

To be clear, we are not pretending that training can change one's personal attributes. Some leaders always will be inclined to miss emotional cues. However, for leaders who are committed to the effort, training and practice can help them recognize situations where their behavior (or lack of) could create damage and then demonstrate more emotionally sensitive behavior instead.

8.1 Figure

The Interaction Essentials Represent the "Flip Side" of Emotional Intelligence

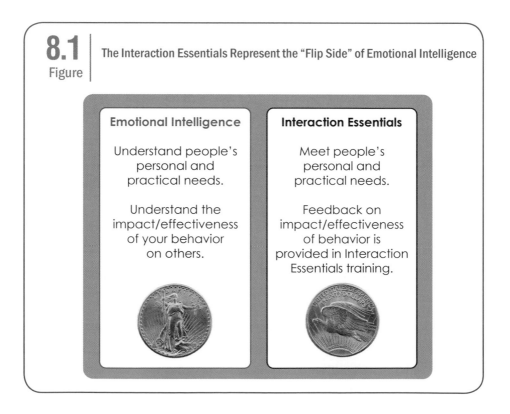

Emotional Intelligence

Understand people's personal and practical needs.

Understand the impact/effectiveness of your behavior on others.

Interaction Essentials

Meet people's personal and practical needs.

Feedback on impact/effectiveness of behavior is provided in Interaction Essentials training.

When they see that the alternative behavior produces better results than the original behavior, they become more sensitive over time to the impact of their behaviors, and their emotional intelligence will advance. (See Figure 8.1.)

Training in the Interaction Essentials helps people develop the appropriate responses and, at the same time, makes them more aware of others' emotions. This relationship is true at all levels of management. One of the primary reasons for coaching senior managers in the Essentials is to increase their expression of emotional intelligence.

How Leaders Can Increase Their Emotional Intelligence

Confront worries. Help leaders accurately recognize their own and others' underlying concerns, insecurities, and fears (e.g., feeling intimidated by the skills or intellect of others, risk-averse, or chronically under-recognized).

Confirm understanding of others' emotions. Encourage leaders to check their understanding of emotions by identifying the emotion they believe others to be feeling (e.g., *"You seem very proud of your work on this project."*). If the empathetic statement is correct, it will seem supportive. If it is incorrect, it becomes an opportunity to clarify and discuss how the other feels. Either way, the emotions become clear to the leader.

Practice predicting others' responses. Encourage leaders to predict others' responses to upcoming situations or to remarks they are soon to make. *"How do you expect Stephan to respond when you ask him to take over the project?"* It is often true that individuals are not blind to their effect on others; they simply don't take time to consider it. The more thought they give to others' reactions, the more accurate their insights become.

Pause before responding. Challenge leaders to take time before responding to others' comments, emails, or actions. This can be a pause for a few seconds in the moment or a decision to sleep on it before responding. *"The right word may be effective, but no word was ever as effective as a rightly timed pause."* (Mark Twain)

[continued at top of next page]

213

[continued from previous page]

Confirm others' reactions. Encourage leaders to actively check on reactions to what they've said or done. Simple questions can have positive impact on others and sharpen a leader's accuracy in understanding them. For example, *"How do you feel about that?"* or *"Did my comment in the meeting upset you?"*

Get good data about themselves. Help leaders gain insights into their emotional intelligence by considering acceleration center results that include personality inventories and multiple-perspective (360°) survey data—ideally focused on evaluating facets of emotional intelligence. Most useful are the written comments, which should be encouraged.

Get good data about how others are feeling. Suggest that leaders leverage engagement surveys to identify where emotional or values-based outcomes are being achieved. Engagement surveys have advantages over 360° surveys in that they deal with emotional outcomes such as feelings of trust, empowerment, and cooperation. In general, positive changes in a leader's emotional intelligence should, over time, show up in these measures.

Share their emotional selves. Encourage leaders to appropriately share their thoughts, feelings, and rationale with the people they interact with. Doing so develops trust and openness. Disclosure of feelings is the greatest trust builder, as it encourages others to reciprocate and reveal their true feelings.

Enlist trusted advisors. Encourage leaders to recruit one or more people who are knowledgeable of the Interaction Essentials to discuss the projected emotional flow of an upcoming conversation or to review a recent interaction. If such meetings are open, honest, and repeated over time, real insights and learning will occur.

Identify triggers. Help leaders identify personal *triggers* that emotionally *hijack* them, getting in the way of behaving the way they intend or want to (see the previous section on "Anticipating and Managing Derailers").

Adele Lynn, 2004

GET LEADERS IN THE GAME SOONER

9 | Generating Assignments That Rapidly Build Skill, Knowledge, and Experience

We have discussed the need to get your leaders in the game. Well, it's game time, and the growth you need won't happen with your future stars on the sidelines. You will need to take some risks, and you might have to rethink the concept of *experience*. If your organization is like most, there are high-performing players with leadership potential who don't yet have enough experience to be placed into key roles. It's simply too risky, which raises a dilemma: You need to get less-experienced leaders more involved in the business, but they don't have enough experience to step in where the business really needs them.

This is where many organizations make a costly mistake: They wait. They default to the assumption that experience comes with time. In talent reviews they make time-based readiness estimates like *"ready in two years"* or *"ready in five years."* But it's not sufficient to let time dictate how quickly your leaders

> It's not sufficient
> to let time dictate how
> quickly your leaders gain
> the skill and experience
> needed to be ready for
> larger roles.

gain the skill and experience needed to be ready for larger roles. Readiness does not come with having the same job title for a period of time; it evolves as leaders face challenges. We call them *growth challenges,* and you can develop skill, knowledge, and experience much faster by providing accelerated learners with the right ones at the right time.

Think of growth challenges as *missions* for your accelerated learners. Business missions. Leadership missions. Crucial errands to be carried out—not reckless, haphazard pursuits that put careers and the business at risk. Growth challenges are intentional assignments that make a targeted impact on individual leaders and the organization. They are not simply identified; they are *designed* by you and your management team to meet business objectives while growing the specific leadership skills, knowledge, and experience that your accelerated learners need.

When this aspect of your acceleration system is functioning, your senior leaders will be continually scanning the business for leadership needs that can become growth challenges. Then, senior managers will match these challenges to accelerated learners whose development needs would be well served by conquering them. It's not complex work, but with a bit of discipline and application of some foundational principles, your senior management team will quickly build proficiency in this crucial component of your acceleration process.

Stop Thinking About Jobs and Start Thinking About Growth Challenges

Senior leaders typically equate growth challenges with jobs—a view that severely inhibits acceleration. Here's why: In a traditional scenario, leaders on their way up the organizational ladder are moved from one position to the next, ideally through a progression that, over time, educates them about important aspects of the business and presents them with incrementally more difficult assignments that build leadership experience. Under this job-by-job development approach, acceleration can be accomplished only by a) shortening a leader's tenure in a given job and offering a promotion sooner, b) taking a risk to place a leader into a job in unfamiliar functional territory, or c) promoting a leader two or more levels beyond his or her current role. These tactics can be useful, but when applied as the sole means of accelerating leadership readiness, they often lead to damaging consequences such as:

- **Leaders change jobs, but don't grow leadership skills.** Development goals tend to be nonspecific, with no ties to learning outcomes, because senior leaders wrongly presume the requisite learning will occur automatically as part of the new job. It doesn't—not without the right planning.

- **Senior management becomes overly cautious in developing leaders.** Organizations with severe leadership shortages are forced to consider high-risk job moves, because they tend to represent major leaps of responsibility. Without the right preparation, however, the success rate of leaders making these jumps will be mixed at best, offering little reinforcement for continuing to take such risks. With no developmental alternative to job moves, management learns to take no risks at all.

- **The rate of leadership growth grinds to a standstill.** The organization quickly runs short of job openings, leaving no developmental opportunities for many accelerated learners.

If you aim to accelerate the growth of more leaders earlier in their careers, you'll need to plan for more than just job moves (rotations, promotions, lateral transfers). With your senior management team, generate growth challenges that meet accelerated learners' unique needs so that they can prepare quickly for larger business leadership roles without having to change jobs.[i]

> If you aim to accelerate the growth of more leaders earlier in their careers, you'll need to plan for more than just job moves.

Growth challenges are assignments that prepare accelerated learners to perform effectively against the success profile of higher levels of leadership.

Specifically, growth challenges:

- Help leaders quickly gain experience important for success in future jobs.
- Enable leaders to develop competencies and overcome derailers.
- Provide leaders with broader insights, understanding, knowledge, and confidence, which prepares them for higher-level roles.
- Can be short-term (one to six months) or long-term (one year or longer).
- Can be part of a job change, but very often are not.

Examples of High-Impact Growth Challenges

- Building and presenting a business case for (or against) a merger, acquisition, joint venture, or strategic alliance.
- Implementing an organizationwide process or system change.
- Developing and implementing a plan to cut business costs or control inventories.
- Negotiating agreements with external alliance partners or regulatory organizations.
- Leading in a high-pressure or high-visibility situation, such as a media relations challenge.
- Leading a reduction in force (RIF).

Shifting the focus from job moves to growth challenges promotes more acceleration, but there is an important caution: Some senior executives lack acumen for this sort of growth planning and might even resist taking it on, viewing it as Talent Management's (HR's) responsibility to generate accelerated-development assignments. But to create the *missions* that challenge your emerging leaders in ways that truly elevate their readiness for larger roles, senior business leaders need to *join* Talent Management in identifying assignments that best match learners' development needs. Remember, the goal is to get your players in the game—the business game—so your senior leaders must generate growth challenges that do so.

Growth Challenges Offer a Faster Way to Prepare Leaders for Big Roles

Consider the risk your organization might be willing to take in elevating an unproven leader two levels above her mid-level leadership position, or by placing a staff executive into a product leadership position for which he has no experience. Failure in key assignments is not only costly to the business, but it also can ruin promising careers. On the other hand, success can be an exhilarating career turning point and can create great value to the organization.

Testing an individual's ability to conquer new challenges is worth the risk if the person has the right success profile. That includes skills (competencies), knowledge, experience, and personal attributes. But many organizations place too much weight on experience, assuming that it only comes with time in a certain job. To the contrary, with the right success profile, experience can be gained very rapidly. The far greater risk is when an individual has personal attributes (particularly personality derailers) that would likely prevent success in the target assignment. In these cases, the accelerated learner has a much greater chance of failure, even with the motivation to learn and succeed.

> The goal is to get your players in the game— the business game—so your senior leaders must generate growth challenges that do so.

Consider this situation, which occurred recently in a global chemicals corporation: Two leaders were being considered for the role of country manager for a business unit in France. The incumbent was scheduled to retire in a year, and no successor had been named yet. The first candidate, Desh, had limited management experience and would have been required to jump two leadership levels, from a different business unit and to a culture that was literally foreign to him. Known for having a "smart business mind," Desh was an exceptional performer. He was a quick learner who sought and accepted feedback readily, easily adapted to different environments, networked effectively, and used the Interaction Essentials consistently.

The second candidate, Irina, had more management experience and would have needed to jump only one level. She had been a leader in this business unit, but in a different country. Although she was a solid performer, some potential derailing patterns had emerged recently. As Irina's responsibilities expanded, she became far more controlling. To make matters worse, she began to have difficulty keeping her emotions in check. She displayed angry outbursts coupled with demands for her team to rework large-scale efforts at the last minute. Irina was receptive to feedback on these issues, however, and seemed motivated to overcome them.

The outcome? The European VP took the riskier path and selected Desh over Irina, who would have had to overcome behavior patterns rooted in underlying personal attributes. But the company didn't simply place Desh into the new role and let him sink or swim. The European VP identified a key need in his business unit—revamping the customer relationship management system—and assigned Desh to tackle it. So, the organization relocated Desh to France, and he went to work on a highly critical growth assignment that provided business-relevant experience and knowledge of the France unit. Desh's assignment included:

- Interviewing and spending time with key leaders and associates in the France business unit, learning about issues, challenges, initiatives, people, processes, etc.

- Assisting with an in-progress analysis to alter the branding of a struggling product line in France.

- Participating in reviews with key French customers to understand their needs and concerns.

- Collaborating with a sales process-improvement team that had been deployed to reduce the cost of sales in France.

- Debriefing his experiences with the very successful country manager of Germany to get coaching and insight.

Desh also participated in leadership training aimed directly at the challenges he was expected to encounter in his new role. Through a combination of formal learning and working with an internal executive coach, he learned more sophisticated strategy execution methods, tactics for building talent in a larger and more complex unit, and advanced *influence* techniques. With his coach he learned and practiced focus Key Actions in advance of his new role and developed plans to apply them immediately upon starting it.

In less than a year, Desh gained extensive knowledge, skill, and insight into the unit he soon would lead, helping him get off to a fast start and establish strong performance early in his tenure. The growth challenge he completed was instrumental to his success and soon became a model of how the organization could rapidly elevate the readiness of its high-potential leaders without having to risk placing them into key jobs prematurely.

In this instance a need to fill a vacant position precipitated the high-speed learning process for the leader, but the right growth challenges can have a rapid effect on skills and knowledge whether there is a job waiting or not. Powerful

> The right growth challenges can have a rapid effect on skills and knowledge whether there is a job waiting or not.

learning assignments like the ones identified by the chemicals company are plentiful in every organization. They can be identified quickly, with little or no disruption to business as usual. Some are short-term assignments (one to six months); others are longer term (a year or more). Some represent small risks; others carry significant risk and require more support from managers, mentors, coaches, and HR. With a bit of structure and discipline (which we focus on next), you can hone your management team's ability to generate the right growth assignments and dramatically increase the rate at which your leaders gain the experience they need to take on bigger roles.

With Planning, Growth Challenges Offer Sizeable Returns

Positive learning outcomes won't just *happen*. The mid-level leader won't develop her skill in *Leading Change* if she doesn't intentionally practice the behaviors most essential to her growth. Success requires that long-term growth challenges be assigned with discipline. We call it *Assignment Science,* because it is informed by the lessons of hundreds of organizations and hundreds of research studies pointing to the practices that cause individuals to learn from their experiences.[ii] Applying these principles will ensure that decisions about assignments are purposeful and reliable in generating the learning that leaders need.

Before Assignments...

Identify the essential preparatory challenges for key job levels. Identifying the right growth challenges for individual leaders is much more efficient when you first establish the key challenges that all leaders should meet before assuming a target job level (e.g., executive level or C-suite). Some organizations articulate a generic list of must-have assignments, such as leading multiple functions, managing a unit with responsibility for profit and loss, taking on an international assignment, working on a business integration team, and so on. Other organizations apply a variation of a *3x3x3 plan*, which requires experience in three countries or regions, three company functions or businesses, and three types of jobs (e.g., corporate, field, and staff). An organization's list of challenges often is more aspirational than truly required. An individual does not need to meet every challenge (indeed, some cannot be met in the time allotted) to be ready for the next level, but gaining experience with a critical mass of these challenges typically is essential to prepare individuals for a particular level.

Determine if any target challenges have been met already. With the tight time constraints facing most organizations, it's a waste of time and money to assign accelerated learners to job challenges they have already met and overcome. Because HR records might not specify job challenges faced, the outcome, and what was learned, it's worthwhile to do some research. Beware of job titles; they don't necessarily convey meaningful experience. It's possible to have the title "manager" but never manage, or to have a role in the finance department but know very little about finance.

Check assumptions about the individual's commitment to growth. Successful executives often wrongly project their own motivation for advancement onto others. Don't assume a person desires to move faster and entertain development risks, such as taking on a high-profile growth challenge. Also, check on current restrictions to development, such as health concerns among family members, the need to care for an aging parent, or other personal issues that could prevent someone from fully committing to a long-term assignment.

When Creating Assignments...

Target and prioritize learning objectives in the growth challenge. Will the individual focus on developing key competencies, overcoming derailers, gaining knowledge, or facing important challenges?

> Beware of job titles; they don't necessarily convey meaningful experience.

For longer-range development (i.e., when there is no near-term job for the individual), it is relatively easy to find assignments that will meet several of these categories at once, and we recommend leveraging assignments to do so. But needs change dramatically when, for example, a leader is one step away from a senior management position and has a significant experience gap, such as never having had profit-and-loss responsibility, never having developed and implemented a business growth strategy, or never having had responsibility for leading a major organizational change. In these situations the learning targets become highly specific, aiming to provide the missing experience, knowledge, or skill in the shortest possible time.

Get creative. Rapid development requires some creativity as you decide on the growth challenges to assign. Consider the following:

- **Target multiple learning goals in one growth challenge.** In the interest of speed, multiple development goals can be accomplished with each assignment. For example, a leader might take on a two-year assignment as a product manager, seeking to:

  - Leverage her strength in coaching.

  - Develop the competency *Entrepreneurship.*

  - Correct her Impulsivity derailer.

  - Develop her knowledge of *Global Operations.*

  - Gain experience introducing a technology-oriented product.

- **Provide networking opportunities.** Our research has shown repeatedly that when looking back on critical career transitions, leaders regard networking as one of the most essential ingredients to success.[iii] A leader's network is an indispensable asset that includes peers and coaches both within and outside the organization, long-term mentors, organizational leaders, direct reports, and other professionals or groups that have unique skills, knowledge, or additional connections. In general, increasing network size, diversity, and representation of key content domains is essential, and as leaders take on growth assignments, it's important to emphasize the cultivation of one's network along the way.

- **Offer high-quality support.** Some managers and mentors are better at growing leaders and make more time for it. This is a key success factor in most growth challenges. Excellent developers of people spend time coaching and working with accelerated learners to review and discuss their applications of new knowledge, experiences, and competencies. They prepare individuals for situations they will face and how to handle them. A poor manager can disrupt an otherwise solid development strategy.

Consider lateral moves. As we have said, if you wait until job promotions are available for accelerated learners, growth almost certainly will happen too slowly. Lateral moves offer excellent learning in situations where promotions aren't available or appropriate. More growth-oriented organizations often downplay or eliminate the concept of the *career ladder,* replacing it with *development ladders* that feature lateral moves to provide the appropriate experiences. We find that high potentials are likely to accept lateral moves if the development value is clear and the assignment isn't too long (e.g., two years or less). For them, the attraction is a new job challenge in which they can demonstrate a major impact.

Collaboratively assess the value of the growth challenge. Individuals need to know that a growth challenge is not just for the organization's benefit. If planned well, it provides career-altering experiences vital for advancement as well as the chance to develop target competencies, knowledge, and experience. Learners at every phase of their careers, whether taking their first leadership jobs or preparing for the C-suite, expect—and deserve—to play an active role in choosing their assignments without negative consequences. It is important that a person considering a risky growth challenge fully understands the pros and cons of the assignment before making a decision.

Surprises that reveal themselves when, for example, the individual and family are already moved to a new city, can be very costly. Personal constraints, such as an upcoming marriage, children, or educational plans, need to be discussed. Sometimes they can be accommodated; sometimes they can't. Very often, what seems to be a constraint fails to materialize as such. For example, we know of a young, high-potential individual who was being considered for a major assignment in a Middle Eastern country. The week before he was offered the assignment, he received his acceptance letter from a prestigious executive M.B.A. program in the United States, his home country. Upon investigation, he found that the university had a weekend executive M.B.A. program in a nearby country in the Middle East (a two-hour drive from his new assignment) that was a better fit for his career plans than the program in the United States.

Balance long-term growth needs with immediate position requirements. When leaders are candidates for key positions, it's essential to consider the trade-offs between an individual's long-term competency, experience, or knowledge needs and his or her needs relative to the position being filled. At middle and senior management levels, there is always a tension between accelerated learners' long-term development needs and the job assignment's short-term needs. Long-term needs include the competencies, derailers, or knowledge identified as high priorities to prepare an individual for a senior position. Short-term needs are the competencies that need to be developed to make individuals successful in their new assignment. When assignments are identified to achieve short-term needs, it's important to keep the long-term needs in sight. Adjustments typically can be made to plan for both.

To Ensure That Assignments Have the Desired Effect...

Check progress and measure success at the end of the challenge. When checking on the learning gained as part of a growth challenge, be careful not to accept general answers such as *"I'm learning a lot."* Ask for specifics. Measurements likely will be imprecise, but reviewing progress will clarify what an accelerated learner is expected to accomplish in the assignment and helps to target efforts. It also is important to measure development success at the end of the assignment. Consider how learning progress might have been stepped up; doing so will inform actions on the next assignment.

Don't keep leaders in growth assignments too long. Move accelerated learners to new assignments as soon as the needed development is accomplished— not necessarily when projects are completed. Many organizations mistakenly keep people in development assignments too long—beyond when they have achieved the required learning. Managers naturally prefer to keep these high achievers as long as possible, because they become indispensable to their operation. In fact, these managers generate many reasons why a learner's continued experience in the assignment

> Many organizations mistakenly keep people in development assignments too long.

would be advantageous. And of course, their rationale is typically rooted in business priorities that might suffer if the high potential on assignment is prematurely moved. This balance must be managed carefully. Managers should not have the power to retain accelerated learners longer than they are needed in a given role, and senior management should not endanger the business by moving people before they are able to make a positive business contribution.

Short-Term Growth Challenges Enable Rapid Preparation

Short-term growth challenges become increasingly important as organizations seek to develop leaders who are unable to be moved geographically or who have other constraints preventing them from taking on long-term assignments (a common reality these days). Challenges lasting a day to several months offer high-speed opportunities to confront new business situations. These challenges might include leading important projects, making major presentations, participating in strategic planning efforts, conducting organizationwide research or analysis, or serving on action learning teams. Short-term challenges provide insights and knowledge with a shorter turnaround, often with less risk but, of course, with less significant business impact than longer-term assignments.

Short-term development challenges have a number of advantages beyond the fact that they don't take too much time. They:

- Meet unique job challenges (e.g., run a major project; speak to a large group of people).

- Provide growth opportunities not present in the current job.

- Develop the person's confidence in dealing with people and groups at higher levels.

- Afford opportunities to practice behavior that addresses derailers (e.g., dominating conversations during meetings).

When possible, short-term challenges should be planned using the principles of Assignment Science associated with long-term challenges. However, because the best assignments often come up unexpectedly, it will be incumbent on management to seize these opportunities as they occur.

Many organizations have realized spectacular payoffs from short-term job challenges. In one organization an up-and-coming executive sometimes made poor presentations, while on other occasions she did an excellent job. The problem was not a lack of skill, but rather a lack of preparation. Although the executive had been advised to devote more time preparing for her presentations, she remained adamant that the immediate task of running her unit was more important than diverting time to prepare. At her mentor's suggestion she was asked on two occasions to watch the CEO rehearse a presentation and then give him feedback. By seeing how much time and effort the CEO put into his presentations, she came to appreciate the importance of preparation and how to best accomplish her presentation objectives.

Action Learning Assignments

The technique of action learning has been widely applied for developing decision-making and interpersonal skills, and has been proven effective at all levels of leadership. It is also quite popular for increasing general organizational knowledge by providing high-level job challenges to high-potential individuals. Taking on an action learning assignment is like being a copilot in a small aircraft—it allows participants to try important real-life skills in an environment where coaching and other support are available. Teams of four to eight leaders research and provide recommendations on strategic issues facing the organization or real-life business challenges outside their usual area of expertise.

An action learning assignment might involve finding answers to questions such as:

- *"How can we change the fundamental rules of competition in our industry?"*
- *"Is the market for Product X ready for a new player?"*
- *"Could we actually change the basic market assumptions about our products, and, if so, how?"*
- *"How could we start operations in India? Should we?"*
- *"How could HR add more value to our business?"*
- *"How can we develop a new strategy for acquiring new clients?"*
- *"What back-office operations should we outsource?"*

There is wide variation across organizations regarding how to configure action learning programs. At its best, action learning provides an opportunity to experience making a high-level, strategic decision that involves a broad array of constituencies and to apply a number of competencies in doing so. Depending on the program's design, participants can learn:

- Decision-making styles represented by other members of their own action learning team.
- Leadership skills. (We have been involved in several programs where action learning and leadership competency development goals were combined. This works very well because the team offers an excellent opportunity for skill practice and feedback.)
- How to solve problems collaboratively in small groups.
- Global acumen (if team members are from different countries or if their assignment has global issues).
- The importance of networking and strategies for being effective at it.
- Different perspectives on the business.

Success is measured by accomplishing the assignment and receiving feedback from other team members as well as executives who are assigned to work with the team. Skill levels can be markedly accelerated if team members seize the opportunity to:

- Get involved in analysis and decisions, and not merely observe the action.

- Share leadership responsibilities and, if possible, align the learning to individual growth targets.

- Try out new management or technical skills and not just rely on skills they already have. Too often, people volunteer to use their specialty (e.g., analysis of finance systems), which results in slight improvement of areas where they already are proficient, instead of developing new skills.

- Develop meeting leadership and presentation skills. Before starting an assignment, some organizations assess all participants to determine their EQ needs. Participants share their personal needs and establish ways to provide feedback.

- Develop interaction skills (e.g., the Interaction Essentials) if they seek feedback from other participants and managers or coaches who work with the team.

Final Advice: Urgent Business Situations Contain Valuable Growth Challenges

Getting your players in the game and sending them on business *missions* requires some planning. Your high-potential leaders should be involved in as many long- and short-term growth challenges as possible. But remain watchful: Many of the most powerful development experiences cannot be planned. CEOs and executives routinely look back on their careers and recall a time when they were suddenly thrust into an event, opportunity, or dilemma, such as responding to a natural disaster, making a major acquisition decision under time pressure, or determining how to navigate an economic crisis. These events often call for lower-level managers to step up and become directly involved

What Action Learning Is and Is Not

Action learning IS:

- A combination of learning and doing.
- About solutions and recommendations regarding implementation of the solutions.
- Often part of a many-faceted development plan (see Chapter 11 regarding learning journeys).
- Often aimed at addressing important business problems or opportunities.

Action learning IS NOT:

- Another task force or committee.
- Group therapy.
- A stand-alone solution.
- An end in itself.
- Usually implemented for frontline leaders.

in higher-level decisions. The needs of a larger group of constituents must be considered in making decisions. Time is of the essence. Top management is watching. These are often ideal learning opportunities.

There also are more prosaic surprises. A delegation from another country decides to visit the corporate office with little or no notice. Or, unexpected news arrives that the company has been chosen as the corporate flagship for a high-profile community charity campaign. You and your management team must be constantly alert for new challenges and be prepared to move swiftly to assign high-potential individuals when opportunities arise that would enable them to experience key challenges and meet development goals.

MAKE EXECUTIVE COACHING WORK BETTER

10 | Leveraging Executive Coaches as Growth Catalysts

Imagine your senior executive team seated around a conference table while they discuss key leaders in your organization and how to help them grow faster. You probably can recite many of these conversations from memory, including the predictable moment when someone suggests, *"Let's get him a coach."* This often coincides with a particularly difficult or urgent development challenge for which the traditional learning alternatives, such as a special assignment or a formal learning course, would be insufficient.

Relationship challenges. Political savvy. Public communication skills. Self-awareness. Or simply an anticipated jump that is extremely high-risk. All these and more might cause your senior management team to decide that executive coaching is the best alternative, and they might be right. But to be sure, and to maximize the chances of success in this and all coaching engagements, you need to be prepared with a clear understanding of the situations in which coaching works best, where it tends to fail, and what you can do to ensure that assigning a coach to an accelerated learner achieves the desired outcome— faster growth.

Because acceleration is our focus, we won't be covering the totality of what has become a vast field of practice in executive coaching. Books, articles, conferences, communities (online and live), and more are dedicated to the selection, training, certification, and practice of effective executive coaching. There are many models and approaches, and we won't review them here. Instead, we have isolated the topics that are most critical when deploying executive coaching as part of an effort to accelerate growth. We'll also focus primarily on executive leadership levels, where professional coaching is most common and most valuable.

Three Types of Coaching That Catalyze Acceleration

As you select and deploy coaches to fuel your leaders' acceleration, it's important to distinguish between three primary types of coaching: feedback coaching (covered in Chapter 6), acceleration coaching, and classic executive coaching. Each has distinct objectives and activities, as shown in Table 10.1.

Feedback Coaching

In Chapter 6 we outlined a unique, powerful approach to feedback that can inspire leaders to take on more substantial developmental challenges in their quest to learn and grow more quickly. Mastering feedback that reframes a leader's mind-set is the vital foundational skill for a coach. Far more than a single session, feedback permeates all coaching engagements from start to finish, regardless of duration, and any coach supporting an acceleration process needs to be expert in delivering feedback that adds value. Post-assessment feedback coaching typically occupies one or two sessions and is completed when development priorities and a preliminary action plan have been drafted.

After that, individuals typically track their own progress and are expected to collaborate with their manager or a mentor who can help secure the support and resources required to carry out the plan.

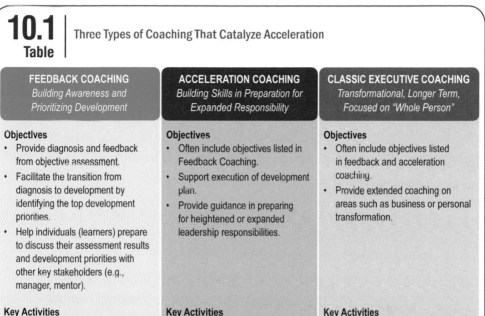

10.1 Table | Three Types of Coaching That Catalyze Acceleration

FEEDBACK COACHING *Building Awareness and Prioritizing Development*	ACCELERATION COACHING *Building Skills in Preparation for Expanded Responsibility*	CLASSIC EXECUTIVE COACHING *Transformational, Longer Term, Focused on "Whole Person"*
Objectives • Provide diagnosis and feedback from objective assessment. • Facilitate the transition from diagnosis to development by identifying the top development priorities. • Help individuals (learners) prepare to discuss their assessment results and development priorities with other key stakeholders (e.g., manager, mentor).	**Objectives** • Often include objectives listed in Feedback Coaching. • Support execution of development plan. • Provide guidance in preparing for heightened or expanded leadership responsibilities.	**Objectives** • Often include objectives listed in feedback and acceleration coaching. • Provide extended coaching on areas such as business or personal transformation.
Key Activities • Help learners understand strengths and development areas. • Help learners determine development priorities. • Prepare learners to discuss assessment results and development priorities with other key stakeholders. • Draft preliminary Development Action Plan.	**Key Activities** • In partnership with manager or mentor, review development priorities and facilitate commitment to actionable, measurable objectives. • Finalize and document Development Action Plan. • Provide feedback, guidance, and support through learning and application opportunities. • Track progress and provide support in gathering feedback and progress measurement.	**Key Activities** • Focus on execution of business priorities. • Penetrate more deeply into role responsibilities, performance habits and trends, and means for optimizing efforts to achieve personal growth and job accountabilities at once. • Focus on individualized process, "whole person" (e.g., career) goals. • Serve as routine sounding board, feedback provider, and provocateur. • Assess progress toward business, role-related, and personal goals. • Challenge growth and facilitate sustained focus on areas needing continued development and growth. • Refine, adjust, and evolve tactics and growth strategies.

Acceleration Coaching

> An acceleration coach helps a learner better understand his or her leadership profile against potential future roles.

As coaching moves beyond feedback into executing a plan for accelerated growth, careful and constant attention to the business context becomes pivotal to success. An acceleration coach helps a learner better understand his or her leadership profile against potential future roles related to the business challenges the organization must meet, such as building alliances, driving integration, launching new products, optimizing processes, cultivating innovation, and so on. A strong coach plays out possible future scenarios and helps learners anticipate situations in which they might struggle to be successful or fall prey to derailing behaviors.

> **Coach:** *"For the last 18 months, you've been a member of the team that's been generating a new product strategy, and we know that increasing speed to market is crucial. Your colleagues often marvel at your creativity and unique point of view. Now, let's imagine that you lead the team. Given the history of creative ideas that haven't been implemented in this organization, what would you need to do to make sure that history doesn't repeat itself? Given that you can at times be undisciplined, what would you need to do to ensure that the new product strategy is one that moves with speed?"*

In many instances, acceleration coaching is part of a broader learning journey (see Chapter 11) in which the learner encounters a variety of learning activities over a period (perhaps 3 to 12 months) and has multiple opportunities to learn and apply new concepts and approaches. As learners practice new behaviors in the learning journey, acceleration coaches facilitate objective, candid reflection and evaluation of the effectiveness of those efforts against likely future situations. As the learning and application attempts accumulate, the coach adjusts the action plan to emphasize practicing behaviors that require more attention and to accentuate those behaviors that will serve as strengths in future roles.

Some organizations outsource acceleration coaching to third-party providers, often because they value the objectivity of the external perspective or simply due to capacity constraints. For less-mature talent management processes, professional executive coaches fill gaps by making sure development plans meet quality standards and that there is sufficient, structured guidance and support after feedback. In addition to helping learners construct concrete development plans, coaches help them build in means to measure and monitor progress.

Classic Executive Coaching

Beyond the mainstream agenda for accelerated development and preparing leaders for future roles, coaches often are engaged to increase leaders' likelihood of success as they step into new roles or take on new assignments. Also, coaches may be deployed to help rescue valued individuals whose contributions are overshadowed by deeply entrenched dysfunctional behaviors or other ongoing performance challenges. These relationships typically are more enduring, extending for periods as long as one year and beyond. Many executives retain the same executive coach for years. (Note that these do not always achieve the result of accelerated growth.)

Classic executive coaching is more likely to take aim at supporting a whole-person development plan, uniquely tailored to each individual's role challenges as well as career and personal interests. In these scenarios the coach becomes deeply embedded in the business, the specifics of the learner's role, and the nuances of his or her assessment profile, including detailed behavioral and personality tendencies. Classic executive coaching may target a wide spectrum of professional opportunities and challenges, including support in driving business ventures or initiatives, formulating decision-making and execution strategies, building influence networks, avoiding political landmines, and adhering to a personal wellness regimen (e.g., work-life balance). Any of these applications could be the primary means of achieving accelerated growth. Coaches engaged in these types of relationships may contract for a retainer (i.e., as needed, on-call services) or build a service agreement with defined deliverables and scheduled sessions (e.g., monthly, quarterly).

Real Life: How Coaching Accelerates Growth and Transforms Leadership Capability

Melanie was a rising star in the global oil corporation where she had worked for the last decade. A whip-smart Harvard M.B.A. known for her extraordinary intellect and activism in industry boards, she had been identified as a successor to the incumbent CFO. Melanie had recently returned from a three-year expat assignment where she led a successful initiative to reengineer global project estimation and contracting processes, to the tune of $100 million savings in the first year.

However, Melanie's repatriation had not gone smoothly. Her aggressive interpersonal style had ruffled the feathers of the male-dominated senior leadership team and was exacerbated by her transparent ambition to join the C-suite. Her relationship network had eroded during her absence. And Melanie's intolerance for weak performers had gained her a reputation for being unapproachable.

Melanie was aware of the scrutiny pointed at her, and she was frustrated with the *laissez-faire* attitude of her manager, the CFO, who was focused on his own career. So, Melanie had become a retention risk. In the prime of her career, she wondered if she had a future at her current firm.

Could Melanie be saved? The organization engaged an executive coach for her. Early on, the coach conducted stakeholder interviews to paint Melanie a candid picture of how she was being perceived. At first, Melanie was angry and in denial; she considered leaving the company. But her coach helped her recognize underlying trends that, in truth,

[continued at top of next page]

. . . .
[continued from previous page]

reflected issues that had limited her for years—through her education, previous roles, and even her marriage. Melanie ultimately recognized that her values included developing talent and treating others with respect, so she chose to face her challenges.

Over the next 12 months, Melanie and her coach worked on explicitly defining what they called her *leadership brand*. They zeroed in on developing her Interaction Essentials and a purposeful network to enhance her strategic partnerships. She also focused on how to become more effective at influencing others. For example, she and her coach built a cross-business strategy for selling the importance of a major financial initiative. With her coach's help, she gained other stakeholders' commitment, and in short order the initiative had sweeping impact.

During a subsequent C-level talent review discussion, the CEO noted that there had been a "truly remarkable turnaround" with Melanie. The CEO reaffirmed her as a C-level successor and placed her in a coveted developmental assignment to accelerate her readiness. Melanie reported that she had never been more engaged, that her relationships across the enterprise were far richer, and that her team was performing at peak levels. She appreciated the investment her organization had made in an executive coach. And, she was having fun again!

What Should You Expect Executive Coaching to Achieve?

As you accelerate leaders into executive-level assignments and roles, they quickly learn that the support systems that once helped them succeed are gone. There are simply fewer resources and people who have the perspective, skill, and time to advise them. They face complexities they never saw coming and often can't anticipate how shifts in risk, visibility, constituencies, and span of control will affect their ability to focus, make good decisions, and demonstrate effective behavior. Past approaches that fueled success no longer have that same effect. Pressure and isolation mount in tandem, increasing both the risk of derailment and the appeal (or necessity) of a coach who can help.

> In the context of acceleration, a coach's role is quite specific: *catalyst and facilitator of rapid, high-impact growth.*

The title *executive coach* has been bestowed on a wide-ranging category of professionals. But in the context of acceleration, a coach's role is quite specific: *catalyst and facilitator of rapid, high-impact growth.* As such, your approaches to the selection, deployment, and evaluation of executive coaches should be anchored on their ability to fulfill that role. You may assign coaches to help emerging leaders accelerate readiness, to develop skills crucial for larger assignments, or to support seasoned executives who face difficult challenges in the midst of business crises. Coaching adds value for accelerated learners, whether they are new or experienced executives, who are in the midst of:

- Making large career leaps.
- Acquiring new skills quickly.
- Transitioning to a new executive team.
- Assembling a new team.
- Fixing a performance crisis.
- Moving into a high-risk role.
- Implementing a new business process or initiative.
- Experiencing relationship challenges (e.g., with peers, across boundaries).
- Overcoming personal derailers.

The coach's goal is to help develop and sometimes execute a development action plan that integrates business needs, the individual's responsibilities, and his or her individual strengths and development needs to ensure that the person gains and applies the right skills at the right times. This action plan always should be built on some type of objective assessment and include progress measurements and stakeholder progress reports at logical intervals. A leader working on elevating her ability to delegate to more experienced leaders, for example, might plan to gather feedback quarterly from key members of her team to ask about the quality and clarity of her delegations. Depending upon the depth, duration, and type of coaching chartered, coaches also may act as a complementary guide or mentor charged with helping their clients navigate these objectives across time.

Great coaches establish credibility and trust in a way that makes it safe for executives to shed their egos long enough to benefit from diagnostic insights, candid feedback, performance suggestions, and career advice. They are assertive about adhering

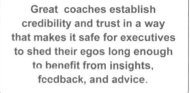

Great coaches establish credibility and trust in a way that makes it safe for executives to shed their egos long enough to benefit from insights, feedback, and advice.

to the right amount of structure and accountability in the relationship. This generates momentum and tangible progress from session to session. Coaches must be fluid enough to adapt their approach to an individual's business and personal needs, which is essential to sustain busy executives' interest and participation over time.

As Figure 10.1 illustrates, executive coaching can be a powerful catalyst and source of support throughout the acceleration process, from feedback and establishment of development priorities to more in-depth guidance on applying new behaviors and supporting progress measurement. Bear in mind also that the acceleration process does not simply apply to emerging leaders. These steps often play out with senior-level executives who face accelerated growth needs, in which case the coach may provide support via a longer-term, deeper engagement (e.g., transformational or remedial coaching).

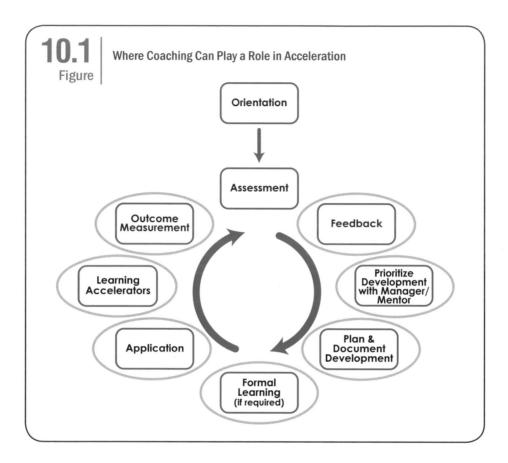

10.1 Figure | Where Coaching Can Play a Role in Acceleration

When Does Coaching Have the Greatest Impact on Acceleration?

Executive coaching is sometimes treated as a panacea for development. While coaching can be a powerful intervention, it should be seen as just one of many development alternatives used for the right reasons. That means it is also important to clarify when coaching is not appropriate. Coaching would not be a good alternative in the following scenarios:

- In advance of imminent terminations. (Coaching seldom works to "save" struggling leaders.)

- As a replacement for performance management or as a vehicle to deliver performance feedback that should be delivered by the manager.

- In the absence of a robust behavioral assessment.

- Without the full involvement and support of management and Human Resources.

- Without clear objectives and a shared understanding of the indicators that the engagement has achieved its goals.

With respect to acceleration, coaches should be employed when they can make growth happen faster and better. Without discretion and thoughtful criteria as to who gets a coach and why, executive coaches can become viewed as an entitlement or a unique symbol of organizational value. Some organizations make a blanket decision to offer a coach to Acceleration Pool members or executives at a specific level (which usually fails to provide a positive return on investment). Others have learned to be more selective, deploying coaches in three key categories:

- For accelerated leadership transitions.

- To address acute business or individual needs.

- To avoid derailment.

Coaching for Accelerated Leadership Transitions

- **Experiencing big leadership jumps.** In a 2007 study on leadership transitions, mid-level and strategic leaders reported that moving into a major new role at work was more stressful than most other life challenges, including divorce, starting a new job, raising teenagers, or health issues.[i] Helping executives prepare for and move more quickly and successfully through significant leadership jumps is one of the most fertile areas for executive coaching. Coaches assume the role of scout by helping executives anticipate common landmines associated with the transition (e.g., a jump between levels, a broadening role, or leading functions without having

243

> The major benefit a coach offers during these transitional phases lies in helping executives pause, take stock of the bridge they are attempting to cross, and determine how to proceed.

experience in them). These include helping the leader navigate increased complexity, visibility, spans of control, diverse stakeholders, and the ambiguity and costs of failure that arise with senior leadership responsibility. Coaches also can help executives who are working to manage their succession and leave a legacy to devise a plan to do both simultaneously. The major benefit a coach offers during these transitional phases lies in helping executives pause, take stock of the bridge they are attempting to cross, and determine how to proceed, given their skills, motivations, and available time.

- **Accelerated on-boarding into a new assignment.** Assimilating executives as they arrive in new assignments is another powerful application of coaching, because it can significantly reduce time to proficiency. Coaches can play a powerful reconnaissance role by collecting data about the new environment (including key business and relationship dynamics) through interviews, team observations, and a targeted diagnosis of the individual relative to the new team's needs and expectations. Even seasoned leaders can benefit from the advance scouting a coach can offer—it often prevents them from relying too much on past strengths, assumptions, or points of view that might cloud a fresh approach to new challenges. Coaches also can help to proactively shape the reputations of newly appointed executives in unfamiliar environments (new function, geography, market) that require quick assimilation or perceived sure-footedness. Novice executives or experienced leaders in surprise assignments will be watched closely both by internal and external stakeholders (including investors and competitors), and past dynamics will matter. For example, a new unit executive may be following in the footsteps of a treasured leader, creating a special need to establish his or her own leadership brand.

- **Assuming a first-time global leadership role.** Those who step into global leadership roles outside their home country inevitably face a learning implosion that affects their perspective on business, leadership, and personal points of view on world issues and politics. However, there are several common arenas in which an executive coach can help the individual assimilate more quickly into a new global role:

— *Providing cross-cultural insights:* Coaches versed in global interpersonal effectiveness and decision styles can help their charges anticipate how their style/approach will interact with others in the new environment.

— *Offering accelerated global business acumen:* Most new global leaders learn the hard way that the manner in which their organization makes decisions and generates revenue is vastly different across geographies. Unique market expectations, regulatory requirements, business models, competitor sets, social norms, and economies all inform these differences.

— *Anticipating impact on family and friends:* Coaches help heighten the new leader's sensitivity to ensuring that his or her expatriate family is prepared and cared for during assimilation into the new environment. This is crucial as the success of expatriate global leaders relates directly to how well their family adjusts.

Coaching for Acute Business or Personal Needs

- **Fast-tracking development in a targeted area.** Many coaching interventions have one objective: Facilitate the development of a targeted skill or competency. This is a very common application of coaching for Acceleration Pool members, particularly when there is a dearth of internal models. Consider, for example, a pool member who has a development need in strategic thinking and financial acumen. A coach might provide side-by-side support for the learner through his or her first business-planning and budgeting cycle.

- **Supporting major strategy shifts or execution challenges.** Another arena in which coaches can have strong impact is as advisors for relatively inexperienced leaders engaged in high-profile, high-risk roles. Like all other coaching, these types of support interventions still must start with a holistic evaluation of the leader's readiness and vulnerabilities across the success profile. Coaching then can zero in on balancing the strategy-execution goals with ensuring that development is adequately framed, reflected upon, and debriefed both during and after the engagement. Example opportunities include:

– Executing a large-scale project.

– Leading a global change initiative.

– Restructuring or consolidating an organization.

– Launching a new product or process.

– Driving innovation.

• **Facing team or peer issues.** Targeted interventions might partner a coach with an executive to address team dynamics and/or business-related changes that are diminishing a team's effectiveness. A coach can help the executive to recognize the root cause of rifts or conflicts, respond appropriately to a crisis in leadership confidence, or better empower the team to address its own challenges.

• **Overcoming interpersonal and relationship challenges.** This is a classic coaching scenario focused on refining the behaviors of an otherwise-promising leader who may be perceived as abrasive, socially unpolished, or politically clumsy. Left unaddressed, interpersonal skill gaps can become significant career limiters. This risk rises with executives who are poor listeners, argumentative, or socially obtuse (i.e., they fail to recognize how their actions affect others). The good news is that the interpersonal arena is highly developable for motivated individuals (see Chapter 7). Coaches can help interpersonally challenged leaders envision an alternative future with a dramatically enhanced likelihood of success if they address their challenges and build new skills.

• **Dealing with diversity issues.** For organizations/industries that still have meaningful obstacles to the progress of target populations (i.e., women, minorities, age or cultural groups), coaches can serve as advisors or even role models for members of these groups who might feel isolated in a homogeneous (i.e., predominantly white male) executive culture. Coaches provide a safe haven for open expression and offer a balanced perspective on real versus perceived obstacles.

Coaching to Avoid Derailment

Using a coach to chaperone executives around blind spots can help them remedy derailers that might otherwise trip up a successful career. Navigational assistance often is needed because most executive derailers represent too much of a good thing: Confidence turns to arrogance, conscientiousness and dependability evolve into rigidity/risk aversion, and assertiveness

> Coaches offer a mirror to talented executives to help them recognize when their overreliance on familiar behavior patterns is affecting performance.

manifests itself as defensiveness or being argumentative. Ironically, executives often are derailed by the same behaviors that drove their success in previous roles. Coaching to avoid problem areas also includes helping executives to get unstuck or break bad habits. Coaches offer a mirror to talented executives to help them recognize when their overreliance on familiar behavior patterns is affecting performance and perceived organizational credibility. Sometimes coaches need to go further and wield a "velvet hammer" to get through to executives who would otherwise derail. Following are some examples:

- **Emotional intelligence and volatility challenges.** Rory was a highly strategic and innovative VP of Information Technology who was well on track to become his organization's first global chief technology officer. He was a personal favorite of the CEO, who valued Rory's strong customer focus and market acumen above all others' in the technology organization. In addition to being recognized for his future focus, Rory also had earned a reputation for having a "Jekyll and Hyde" personality. Partners and direct reports alike often referred to encountering "Good Rory" or "Bad Rory." At his best, he was a creative, resourceful problem solver. Unfortunately, his moodiness and quick temper emerged on an increasingly more frequent basis, creating trust issues with partners across the organization.

Rory received several rounds of direct feedback about his volatility, and he made several attempts to manage the behavior. Nevertheless, after periods of brief improvement, Rory's impulsive, negative reactions persisted. The company hired an executive coach who helped Rory get to the heart of his emotional "triggers" (the situations and circumstances that activated his emotions). Ultimately, Rory determined that he was most likely to react negatively when others pointed to problems, issues, or questions of IT competence without offering alternative solutions or courses of action. He resented being in incessant problem-solving mode unless he felt others had equal "skin in the game" around solving problems and challenges. With his improved self-awareness, Rory had the confidence to commit to better self-management. He routinely solicited feedback from others and continued working on this issue with his executive coach. While Rory believes he will always struggle to overcome his volatility, he credits his coach with helping him better live his intentions.

- **Resistance to change.** Sarah was a long-tenured marketing team leader known for her phenomenal execution skills. This was a desirable skill in the highly complex, process-oriented matrix organization she served. Her reputation for driving role clarity and accountability in high-profile product launches was unparalleled. As a result, the Marketing SVP held Sarah in great regard and considered her his likely successor when he retired in two years.

  However, in the estimation of her stakeholders, Sarah's process management orientation was too much of a good thing. Specifically, they hoped she would adapt the manner in which she collected, processed, and integrated market intelligence into her positioning. Sarah's determination to adhere to tried-and-true processes was frustrating to those who felt like every other approach suffered under her reconsideration.

Sarah's executive coach helped her understand that what had made her successful in the past was now a liability in a more iterative product management context. The coach helped Sarah identify her triggers for resistance and pointed to an observed tendency that he labeled "listening to refute." He helped Sarah see that success in the new context depended on her powers of persuasion and influence rather than formal authority. The coach also laid out specific examples of alternative approaches that she could use to reshape new-paradigm launch processes that preserved both flexibility and execution discipline.

- **Feedback receptivity issues.** Coaches offer neutrality and the opportunity for candid, direct feedback to executives who otherwise might not want to hear it. For example, a coach respected at senior levels might offer

> Coaches offer neutrality and the opportunity for candid, direct feedback to executives who otherwise might not want to hear it.

"outsider" insights that would carry more perceived credibility than the same message delivered by an insider. This is particularly true when there is a lack of trust within the management ranks, when there are no dependable observers who can provide specific behavior examples, or when an individual's history of personal resistance has limited meaningful feedback.

Finally, leaders in some industry segments have been lauded for technical acumen and other traits or skills that run counter to strong leadership in a collective environment (e.g., extreme confidence, independence, decisiveness). A common example of the phenomenon can be found in the physician leadership ranks for health care organizations (e.g., university and hospital systems). Physician leadership development has become a ripe topic in these environments as the transformation of health care into big business has driven many physicians into system leadership roles. And, of course, traditional medical education programs have done little to prepare these individuals for leadership roles. A credible, confident executive coach can convince even the most accomplished physician that what has made him or her successful to date will not necessarily spark the same success as a business leader. Ironically, yet again, common coaching emphasis for this population tends to reside in the basics of the Interaction Essentials, coaching, and influence. The great news is that once emotionally and intellectually captured, physicians are excellent students who believe in skill practice.

Factors That Increase the Likelihood That Coaching Will Work

Senior-Level Sponsorship

The desire to develop an Acceleration Pool member might become irrelevant if there is no one to sponsor the changes to be made. We have seen many coaching engagements fail because they were conducted in a vacuum or in scattered fashion without overarching goals aligned to organizational strategy. Executive coaches are sometimes deployed as surrogate managers who are expected to turn around performance problems that managers themselves have been unable to correct. These approaches rarely succeed, because most development strategies require the involvement of and input from the individual's manager. A triumvirate, consisting of the individual, coach, and manager working together to support a development strategy, is required if performance turnarounds are expected.

Accurate Diagnosis of Development Needs

Coaching relationships often begin with both parties agreeing on development priorities. Once those are established and agreed upon, execution of the development strategy can begin. As we outlined in Chapter 5, knowing what to develop is essential before trying to develop it. A solid coaching relationship begins with reliable data about the individual's development needs. It also bears mentioning that the individual's acceptance of that diagnosis is a must. Because participants typically accept the feedback related to their Acceleration Center findings (more than test results), it is highly advisable to couple Acceleration Centers with professional coaching.

Clear Plan and Objectives

Chapter 7 outlines a developmental strategy based on the importance of crafting a specific development plan with clear measures of progress and success. No coaching engagement should be launched without a clear notion of the expected outcomes.

Business (Strategic) Linkages

Helping individuals appreciate the business impact of their personal development often requires an experienced coach and the input of key internal stakeholders (e.g., the individual's manager). Linking personal development to business strategies creates an inarguable sense of relevance for development. For example, a development objective of improving competitor insights and competitive positioning strategies would be very salient for a leader who is assuming a new role in a new market. There is nothing like performance anxiety to help leaders recommit to the value of personal development. Again, collaboration between the executive coach and the individual's manager is essential to achieve maximum impact.

Desire to Change

We've seen executive coaches assigned to individuals who have no interest or intention of developing themselves. Leaders who do not feel

> Often, initial reactions to the coaching process can be misleading.

the need or see the value of personal development obviously will be far less likely to show improvement. This can change over time, however. Often, initial reactions to the coaching process can be misleading—it can take a while for an individual to embrace the coaching and longer still for it to take hold. As personal chemistry and trust with the coach increase, more windows open for real self-insight, self-determination, and process ownership. Individuals begin to believe that change and growth are instrumental to their ability to achieve their business goals, the responsibilities associated with their role, and their personal objectives. With the coach's help, they eventually demonstrate commitment to, a sense of urgency around, and hard work in accomplishing true behavior change and personal growth.

Matching the Coach to the Leader

One of the most common questions we hear is, *"Should coaches be assigned to or chosen by the individual executive or Acceleration Pool member?"* The answer depends upon the purpose of the coaching engagement. Pool members who need to build specific skills (e.g., oral presentation) might be more willing to accept an assigned coach who has a proven track record in the organization. However, broader objectives, such as managing a major job transition or restoring a reputation after a perceived failure when the executive is feeling very vulnerable, often require a closer look at the personality match between coach and individual. In these cases, the individual's involvement in choosing a coach increases the likelihood of long-term success.

Appendix 10.1

What Is the Profile of an Effective Executive Coach?

In our experience there is no single, ideal profile for an effective coach. Of course, it depends. Chemistry with target executives will be driven by the coach's total package—specifically, the skills, business experience, and personality mix he or she has to offer. More seasoned executives have a greater need for comfort and perceived compatibility with coaches whose experience and style are seen as credible and relevant to their needs. More junior Acceleration Pool members tend to be open-minded about who the coach is, as long as he or she helps to jump-start development through value-added support in feedback and development planning.

From a practical standpoint you need to ensure that someone in the organization plays the role of matchmaker as well as financial sponsor for executive coaching relationships. The Talent Management (HR) function typically researches and recommends coaching options. However, depending on the reason for using the executive coach, the individual's manager or mentor might be involved in defining the specifications for the coach, if not actually selecting the person. Because interpersonal chemistry often is difficult to predict, corporate matchmakers need to make the best possible recommendation, given what they know about the learner's development needs, experience, and personal style.

What to Look For

Most of our client partners have discovered that diversity in background across coaches enables better matches in coaching engagements and brings richer insights and shared learning among teams of coaches. Our organization employs coaches who have arrived at their calling from an amazing array of backgrounds: former CEOs and business executives (banking industry, high-tech, manufacturing, health care), psychologists (industrial/organizational, clinical, and social), social workers, university professors, elementary school teachers, grant development officers, plant managers, physicians, military officers, and law enforcement leaders. These individuals, formally trained and certified in assessment, feedback, and coaching tools and practices, have become exceptional coaches with their own unique abilities in helping accelerate leaders' growth.

Internal vs External

Should coaches come from within or outside the organization? It's a question that has fueled debate, yet one that ought to be a secondary consideration. The quality of the relationship and the coach's skills need to be the primary concerns. Organizations often choose external coaches because of perceived confidentiality or trust issues, time constraints, limitations on internal coaches' skills, or questions regarding the executives' need to receive an external perspective. In some organizations, external advisors might enjoy more credibility than their internal counterparts, simply by virtue of being outsiders. This is a source of frustration to many capable internal HR professionals, but it is a reality. Fairly or not, external coaches might be viewed as untainted by bias and armed with a broader, real-world perspective than insiders. As with any assumption, this view needs to be tested. Notions of superior perspective depend on the external coach's skills, depth of insight, and experience.

The use of internal coaches has its upside as well. While internal coaches are not cost-free, neither are they an out-of-pocket expense. Internal coaches also know more about the organization, industry, and people with whom the executive will be interacting. Ultimately, determining whether to use internal or external executive coaches requires trade-off decisions. Most organizations that routinely use coaches do not exclusively choose one path, finding a mixed model to be the best solution.

Adding Value

On one point there is consensus: An effective executive coach is seen as a "strategic value creator." In other words, leaders improve because of their relationship with the coach. Following are additional observations on the characteristics of executive coaches who have impact:

- **Credibility.** This is earned through demonstrating extensive business or life experience. The coach projects credibility; offers a strategic, high-level perspective; and directly and personally (i.e., not theoretically) relates to the client's world. Being able to "walk in the shoes" of the client is key. Confidence builds as the coach shows the ability to share personal experience and anecdotes relevant to the learner's world.

- **Business experience and acumen.** Coaches who clearly understand the business challenges, priorities, and market drivers that affect their clients offer an expansive sounding board to executives.

> Coaches assigned to more senior executives are undoubtedly more agile when they have their own depth of business experience to rely on.

  Coaches should avoid positioning themselves as a strategy expert when their focus is on leadership effectiveness. Even so, coaches assigned to more senior executives are undoubtedly more agile when they have their own depth of business experience to rely on (e.g., they've been a part of organizational strategy shifts, launched new initiatives, or played an integral role in implementing organizational change processes).

- **Political savvy.** Shrewd coaches impart a degree of protective "radar" to busy executives, offering observations, insight, and guidance on navigating political terrain. Their impact in this domain relates directly to their own natural acumen for recognizing political land mines and their ability to offer survival advice.

- **Future-focused, contemporary point of view.** Seasoned executives fear becoming obsolete—a stereotype of yesterday's style leader. They seek fresh ideas and approaches to keeping their own and their team's perspectives fresh and relevant. To avoid their own obsolescence, coaches who stay ahead of current leadership paradigms—offering a new and different viewpoint on leadership implications associated with tomorrow's challenges—are highly valued. Overreliance on a tired set of tools, assumptions, and approaches renders coaches themselves obsolete.

- **Emotional intelligence.** Strong coaches tend to be personally introspective, which enables them to accurately read individual motivation and organizational dynamics, even from a distance. They also model their interpersonal perception through thinking out loud. Their approach helps clients develop better "lenses" for interpreting behavior around them.

- **Toughness.** Coaches often must deliver difficult messages in a manner that captures attention and buy-in. This requires a delicate balance of extreme candor with an understanding of how to work with diverse individuals who have their own careers and personal motivators. Couple this with the fact that most executives are accustomed to hearing primarily positive feedback about their achievements. Effective coaches understand the best way to get their developmental feedback across without the client shutting down.

- **Chemistry and challenge.** Executives will return to coaches with whom they feel a personal connection on an emotional, intellectual, or social level. Obviously, few formulas adequately predict chemistry; coaches build bonds in many different ways. Executives tend to sustain attention on coaches they find personally stimulating, challenging, or otherwise attractive. These are likely to be individuals with a broad range of interests (or at least similar interests to their own) and a clear abundance of rich life experience. Other traits that might lead to long-term matches include respected intellect, complementary skills (i.e., the coach fills the executive's "gaps"), and technical prowess.

- **Global perspective.** In today's environment most leaders need a far broader market, customer, and societal purview than in the past. Whether they are currently in a global organization or serving in an international role, globalization touches many elements of decision making—market positioning, supply chain, offshoring of manufacturing, alliances and partnerships, financial models, and regulation. As a result, global perspective has risen mightily in importance to an agile coach's repertoire.

- **Creativity.** Executives rarely apply the same creativity to fulfilling personal development needs as they do with their business. Creative coaches can spark thinking outside typical executive self-development paradigms. Such coaches might offer a different "angle" on professional or personal growth, particularly relative to integrating self-development directly into meeting business objectives, work-life balance strategies, and future career directions.

CAPITALIZE ON OPPORTUNITIES TO ACCELERATE LEADERS IN GROUPS

11 | Combining Methods into Learning Journeys That Grow Large-Scale Readiness

Large-scale leadership gaps will not be closed rapidly enough if you accelerate growth one leader at a time. Learning with others sparks faster, more collective progress and should be part of each person's learning pathway (see Figure 7.1).

Your acceleration system can "make the jump to light speed" if you integrate development methods into a sequence that enables groups of leaders to simultaneously make dramatic leaps in readiness. We call these integrated designs *learning journeys*. Cohorts of leaders embark on them together (with the involvement and support of management and HR) and share experiences, insights, feedback, and mutual support to grow their capability faster.

Learning journeys require a bit of rigor in planning and design, but the payoff far eclipses the effort. For example:

- *In just six months a regional bank struggling through crisis achieved major increases (more than 50 percent) in its leaders demonstrating crucial behaviors associated with coaching, influencing, leading change, emotional intelligence, and other skills vital to its culture's health.*

- *A large energy corporation in Southeast Asia took only four months to realize a 70 percent increase (on average) in leadership behaviors needed to execute a major business pivot, including generating more innovative solutions, thinking more strategically, and operating with a more global mind-set.*

- *In less than two years, a large defense contractor more than doubled the availability of ready successors for critical roles across the entire corporation. Ready replacements went from 30 percent of all key positions to more than 70 percent, and performance of newly promoted leaders increased.*

A Learning Journey Success Story—Creating the Conditions for Sustainable Innovation

A European manufacturer of home appliances was losing ground to the competition. The organization had become stifled by both functional and regional silos, making it nearly impossible for leaders to innovate and respond quickly to shifting local market demands. Senior stakeholders and Talent Management (HR) identified three critical business drivers:

- Build strategic partnerships across organizational boundaries.
- Drive innovation.
- Execute competitive strategy.

[continued at top of next page]

[continued from previous page]

Mid-level leaders were identified as the most critical players in translating the organization's growth strategy into action. A six-month learning journey for all directors was constructed with a *red thread of Creating the Conditions for Sustainable Innovation*. Prior to the first session, each director participated in an Acceleration Center, received feedback from an external feedback coach, and drafted a development plan aimed at competencies related to the business drivers.

In the opening session, executives summarized key strategic initiatives and took questions and comments from participants. During the formal learning segments, participants worked together to examine current challenges to strategy execution and worked with tools for overcoming them. Additional formal learning helped the leaders examine their personal organizational networks and presented ways in which they could create better conditions for innovation within their teams. The directors not only learned what they should do, but also how to do it.

Participants came together for on-site learning sessions each quarter. Between sessions, subteams worked together on action-learning assignments that focused on real-world projects within the organization. Because breaking down silos and encouraging innovation across boundaries was so critical, these working teams were purposefully formed with regional and functional diversity. Four indicators of the program's success:

- Teams generated faster response times to new local market challenges.

- A 360° survey revealed that 78 percent of directors improved in ratings of communication and networking skills.

- Cost savings from action-learning teams' efforts exceeded the cost of the learning journey itself.

- Cross-functional multiregion teams remained intact long after the process ended.

> **Sweeping gains in leadership growth are not accomplished with a single developmental experience.**

Leadership behavior can change quickly across large organizations and among entire cadres of leaders. But one fact is certain: These sweeping gains in leadership growth are not accomplished with a single developmental experience. Coordinated events (steps), taken in the right sequence and with the right focus, are required.[i]

How Learning Journeys and Learning Pathways Work Together

- Individual **learning pathways** are personalized to the unique business-specific roles and personal needs of a single leader or professional. Pathways and resulting action plans are built to organize formal and at-work learning experiences completed over a specified time period (see Figure 7.1). Learning pathways focus on achieving proficiency in one or several related competencies or other development goals. A learning journey is one key component along an individual's learning pathway that fuels the achievement of that pathway's objective.

- A **learning journey** is a coordinated series of group development experiences designed to move individuals along their learning pathways. It occurs over time and comprises multiple formal and informal learning components. Usually, several personal development targets (competencies, knowledge, and experience) along with organizational goals, such as changes in strategy or values, are targeted together. A learning journey provides the feedback, psychological support, and encouragement to the cohort as it works to achieve similar goals. It also saves time and money by combining the development of a group of individuals into one coordinated, interactive experience. Learning journeys are most appropriate for accelerating frontline and mid-level leaders or Acceleration Pool members at any level.

Learning Journeys Are Investment Opportunities

Many of us can name the stocks we wish we would have purchased 10 or 20 years ago, and we daydream of someday encountering that *sure thing* investment that pays off handsomely down the road, making us forever glad we took the chance. Learning journeys are like that, except they're not missed opportunities of the past; they're widely available right now. Designed well, learning journeys are the highest-yield investments you will make in leadership acceleration.[ii] But, unfortunately, many organizations squander their opportunities to capitalize on them.

When a group of learners shares a common need for accelerated development, you face a precious opportunity to achieve an unusually large, rapid return on your investment in leadership growth. Learning journeys capitalize on moments of common need—often generated by a crucial business need—and involve groups ranging anywhere from 10 to 1,000 leaders or more to focus on common challenges, learn, and grow in ways and at speeds that would be impossible on their own. The common focus creates situations in which broad and deep learning takes place for all participants, in short bursts of time. Learning journeys combine learning modalities (e.g., classroom or online training, coaching, mentoring) and follow-up activities to build skills covered in the training, including social media (e.g., blogs, peer-learning groups, supplemental online training) and tools that offer on-demand, dynamic, and varied learning experiences.

If you haven't already identified them, chances are you have multiple learning journey opportunities in your organization right now. Learning cohorts can be formed in several different ways to meet varied learning and business objectives (see Table 11.1). These learning cohorts often are assembled to achieve multiple overlapping outcomes and may share elements of the learning process.

11.1
Table | Outcomes and Benefits of Learning Journey Opportunities

LEARNING JOURNEY OPPORTUNITIES	OUTCOMES AND BENEFITS
Leadership Transition Cohorts: *Leaders moving through a common transition in their career (e.g., from a frontline leader to a mid-level role).*	These leaders experience similar challenges and have related questions and learning opportunities, regardless of their specific role or function. Common challenges might be: *How is coaching a leader different from coaching an individual contributor? How do I drive strategy execution as a mid-level leader?* DDI's research[iii] shows that leaders moving through transitions are very unlikely to ask for development even though they might feel highly unprepared. By developing in cohorts, learners have opportunities to learn from one another and gain skills they didn't know they needed.
Acceleration Pools: *Leaders who are part of an accelerated development program to prepare for future roles of greater scope and responsibility.*	It is important that these leaders be exposed to the challenges and opportunities they will encounter at more senior levels well before stepping into them. Special learning accelerators are reserved for these types of cohorts because often they cannot be scaled across the entire leadership population. Some of these specialized accelerators include: • Robust assessment of competencies and potential derailers from an Acceleration Center. • Exposure to successful executives. • Group-based action learning projects.
Cross-Functional Cohorts: *Leaders purposefully drawn from a cross-section of functions and geographies.*	Particularly as leaders move into mid-level leadership and higher, it is important for them to acquire an understanding of the entire enterprise. They need to learn how their role in sales, product development, distribution, or customer service meshes with other functions and business processes. Leaders at these levels also need to develop cross-functional networks so they can help the organization execute and respond to change with confidence and agility. Our studies have revealed that leaders in transition consistently rank *"having a better internal strategic network"* as the single most important factor leading to their success as they move up into new roles.[iv]
Business-Centric Cohorts: *Leaders being developed to help the organization respond to an urgent business challenge.*	Ultimately, all leadership development is conducted in service of business results. At times, leadership cohorts are formed specifically to address current and pressing business challenges. For example: How can we create a more customer-focused culture? How can we drive innovation or process efficiency? These business challenges must be met by leaders who can view them through the right business lens and mobilize their teams to execute against key business priorities. Learning cohorts in these circumstances capitalize on learners' collective mindshare as they build the relevant skills and apply them to meet the targeted business challenges.

Don't Embark on a Learning Journey Without a Map

Learning journeys aren't called tours or excursions. They're called journeys because they chart a longer, more challenging course to a more meaningful destination, with much to be gained along the way. As with any journey, getting to the destination (the growth target) requires a map—a detailed plan for how orientation, assessment, formal learning, skill practice, application, support, follow-up, and any other activities deemed essential will be staged for all who embark. Because learning journeys aim at broad growth objectives, like readying first-time leaders, equipping new mid-level managers, or rapidly arming executives to conquer pressing business dilemmas, they are not created by simply stringing together development curricula aimed at competencies or leadership principles. Proven leadership-development content (e.g., courses,

> Learning journeys work only when they are assembled specifically for your organization's context.

books, models) are useful, but learning journeys work only when they are assembled specifically for your organization's context. Design requires business and cultural savvy, creativity, and experience with a wide variety of learning and learning support methods.

Figure 11.1 shows a basic learning journey aimed at enhancing the readiness of leaders making the transition into mid-level leadership. The map displays the entire series of activities (before, during, and after formal events) that will equip them to tackle the most difficult challenges as they move into new roles. Through formal learning, networking, relationship building, application, and alignment around key organizational issues, groups of leaders come together to gain new perspectives, aligned understanding, enhanced skills, and opportunities for immediate application. Of course, many other options exist around the topic, length and type of training, and whether the curriculum is spaced over time or grouped into a single event. Also, personalized learning accelerators, group learning exercises, and other types of activities and tools are included before, during, and after events to strengthen connections from each learning moment to the next, so that the process builds toward its growth objective.

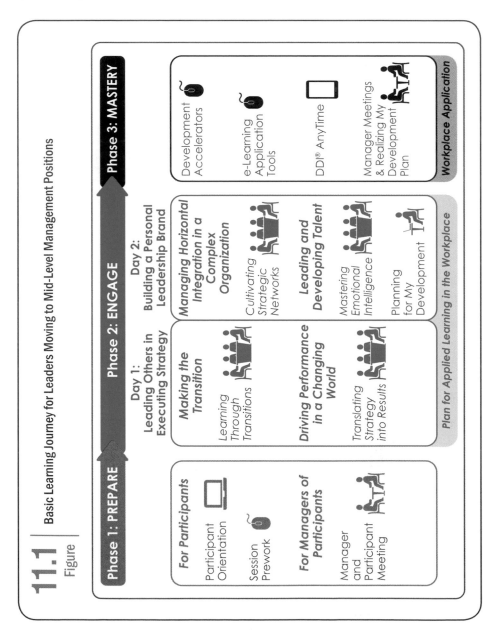

11.1 Figure | Basic Learning Journey for Leaders Moving to Mid-Level Management Positions

Figure 11.2 shows a more multifaceted learning journey aimed at mid-level leaders that brings the benefits of a map into focus. This example shows how a global professional services firm confronted the challenge of more consistently and effectively serving its multinational customers around the world.

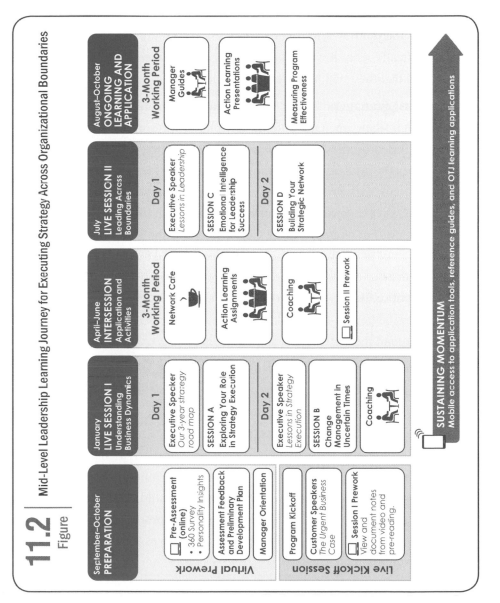

11.2 | Figure | Mid-Level Leadership Learning Journey for Executing Strategy Across Organizational Boundaries

Creating a visual map might seem like a simple task. But mapping out a learning journey is essential for more reasons than simply illustrating the process:

Participants prepare for the entire journey, not just a component of it. Because learning journeys are longer and more challenging developmental experiences, participants benefit by seeing the entire map before they begin. Most know the journey will require some effort, but the map helps them see more specifically what it will entail, how each component fits into the overall picture, and that they will have help along the way.

Participants' managers better understand their roles. Participants need support from their managers (e.g., coaching, prioritizing, finding skill application opportunities). A manager's understanding of the participant's current role and workload helps in finding practical ways to sustain focus on the learning journey without becoming overburdened. Managers and participants also can find ways to make important connections from learning events to real-world concerns. For example, if the CEO kicked off the learning journey with a presentation of the company's strategic priorities and his worries about what will be needed from leaders to achieve them, managers and participants can identify opportunities to focus on those issues in their day-to-day work. This also has the side benefit of stimulating managers' curiosity for more personal reflection around their own skills and readiness.

A map provides a reference point for tailoring learning journeys to different global regions. Rolling out learning journeys in multinational organizations can be particularly valuable for driving consistent methods, experiences, processes, and expectations. Learning journey maps help to ensure purposeful local adaptations and stronger alignment across boundaries. For example, less experienced mid-level leaders in China might benefit from longer time frames for courses or different skill-building activities. Maps facilitate regional customization in which proven approaches are tailored for local needs, while preserving core learning objectives and adhering to the journey's overall intent.

Maps promote creativity in design, and the learning journey becomes more compelling. Producing a visual map has a positive effect on the creative process, resulting in more compelling experiences for learners and the use of a wider variety of methodologies to bring about meaningful change. DDI's *Global Leadership Forecast 2014|2015* found that organizations with the most effective leadership development programs use 32 percent more *development methods* than organizations with ineffective programs. Also, organizations using learning journeys versus single-event-based training are 3.4 times more likely to have learning programs highly rated by learners and 2.9 times more likely to have leaders rated as effective. They also are 2.5 times more likely to demonstrate financial performance in the top 20 percent compared to industry peers.[v]

> Organizations using learning journeys versus single-event-based training are 3.4 times more likely to have learning programs highly rated by learners and 2.9 times more likely to have leaders rated as effective.

Senior management buys in more readily. Although it might seem like the plan will require significant organizational effort, learning journey maps help senior leaders see the benefits of these investments and better understand the alignment with key organizational issues and strategies. Top management should be directly involved in reviewing maps and offering feedback. This has profound impact on the shared understanding of what exactly is happening in one of their highest interest areas—the development of accelerated learners—and makes it far easier for senior executives to learn and own their roles as sponsors of acceleration.

Important Links Between Development Action Plans, Learning Pathways, and Learning Journeys

Development Action Plan (see Appendix 6.4)

Broad development goals targeted at each competency, derailer, assignment, or knowledge after development needs have been identified and prioritized. Articulates what will be developed and when, but not how.

Learning Pathway

Step-by-step approach for how the Development Action Plan will be executed to achieve the learning goal.

Learning Journey

One step along the Learning Pathway that may meet several important development needs. While learning journeys are built to meet the "needs of the many," their ultimate impact depends upon how well the personal and practical needs of individual participants are met and how they are integrated into the group experience.

Design Learning Journeys for Speed and Business Impact

The sample learning journey maps in Figures 11.1 and 11.2 combine formal and informal learning components, which is essential to generate and sustain the appropriate learning. But to ensure that your organization's learning journeys rapidly transform readiness, it's important to address several additional design tenets.

Identify the "Red Thread"

A red thread isn't just a label. Like a compass, it serves as a continual indicator that your journey is on track.

Every learning journey needs a compelling theme—an overarching brand or headline that directs all activities to the journey's ultimate destination. We call it a *red thread* because it knits every aspect of the journey to an objective that matters to all stakeholders (e.g., participants, HR, senior management). But a red thread isn't just a label. Like a compass, it serves as a continual indicator that your journey is on track (or not). A CEO recently remarked, *"The red thread is important because if I ask participants about their experiences in a learning journey, they give me clear answers that show they understand how it all connects to our business."*

Let's go back to the global professional services firm that launched the learning journey to help drive its strategic priority to focus on more effectively serving global customers (Figure 11.2). The learning journey was designed around the red thread of *Driving Excellence for Multinational Customers.* A sound overall objective, but how would the organization ensure that each learning activity was tightly linked to it?

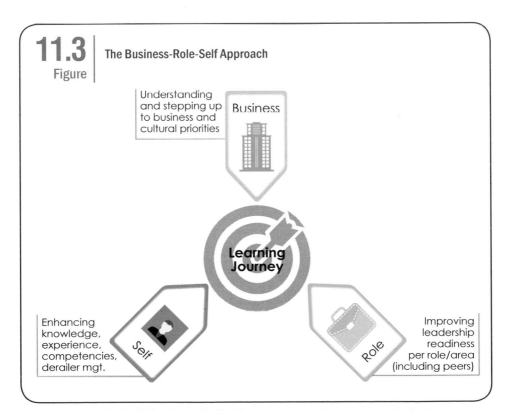

11.3 Figure | The Business-Role-Self Approach

Understanding and stepping up to business and cultural priorities — Business

Learning Journey

Enhancing knowledge, experience, competencies, derailer mgt. — Self

Improving leadership readiness per role/area (including peers) — Role

The firm applied a *business-role-self* approach (see Figure 11.3) to tie the red thread to each activity. Here's how: The learning journey was initiated by customer speakers who built the business case and sense of urgency for improvement (a powerful activity for establishing the business connection). Action-learning teams were constructed to address specific organizational barriers around key issues such as global pricing and technology system alignment. Over several months skill-building courses targeted competencies that leaders would need to achieve their job objectives (connecting the learning to each leader's role), including *Global Acumen, Strategic Partnerships, Cultivating Networks, Driving Change,* and *Execution.* Finally, each leader participated in an individual assessment process to gain insight into competencies and personal attributes, and then received individual feedback and coaching to establish personalized development action plans to elevate the ability to *Drive Excellence for Multinational Customers,* making all aspects of the learning process relevant to each person: *self.*

The red thread rises above specific competencies, courses, and experiences, and ties the learning journey together by creating a strong sense of business purpose, personal relevance, and urgency.

Use Assessment to Unfreeze Mind-Sets

> **Learning journeys provoke change, but people are people, and they will naturally resist if there is no apparent value in it.**

Learning journeys provoke change, but people are people, and they will naturally resist if there is no apparent value in it. Assessment provides insights about participants' orientation to change as they encounter it on their journey. Do they protect legacy ideas? Do they need time to plan how they will make change? Or are they natural change agents who love variety but must learn how to communicate and work with others who are more hesitant? These types of insights alter how participants listen and absorb messages in learning experiences. Assessment enables them to extract the most relevant messages and translate what they learn into development action plans with personal meaning and value.

Assessment insights awaken participants to new ways of thinking about their organization, their role, their motivations, and their behavioral skills (competencies). Well-selected diagnostics heighten the relevance of the learning and provide a sense of urgency to step up development (see Chapter 5).

Personalize the Learning Journey

A learning journey develops a group of leaders together, but for individuals it can be personalized by familiarizing key support partners with a learner's unique development needs. For example, a trainer can partner a learner with others in the session who have high mastery in areas he or she is working to develop, or the trainer could invite the person to play a more active role in discussions of personally relevant topics. A coach can build on activities that take place along the journey and target activities appropriately (e.g., rehearsals, coached practice). Team members familiar with a learner's development goals can collaborate to support growth efforts and provide reinforcement.

Balance Formal Learning Time with Time Spent in Support and Application Activities

It's important to be deliberate about how formal learning is staged relative to other activities. Many organizations design their learning processes with a sole focus on creating time for formal learning (e.g., instructor-led courses, virtual classroom experiences, webinars). It's true that formal learning often is the cornerstone of understanding how to lead more effectively, but in terms of time spent, the formal segments should comprise the smaller parts of the overall equation. Support and application methods reinforce what is learned and enable real change; these should be staged with equal priority. Formal learning components should be the first actions identified on your learning journey map, but they should not replace or drain time from the activities, experiences, and tools that allow participants to put what they have learned into practice.

Design to the Level of Mastery Required and Not Beyond

It's not always necessary to craft learning journeys to achieve full mastery of leadership skills. Proficiency typically is enough. You will face choices regarding what types (and how much) of formal training, special reinforcement, and job application to include. For example, a group of leaders being prepared for international assignments may need some development around global acumen. But their networking and execution skills may be far more essential to the types of leadership challenges they will face. In this case, proportionally more of the group learning journey would focus on the networking and execution skills.

Measure Success on Every Leg of the Journey

A commitment to measurement separates successful learning journeys from those that get sidetracked. In a process with such varied activities, it is essential to remain aware of:

- How each aspect of the journey is performing. Are competencies being developed? Are application assignments clear?

- Whether participants, instructors, coaches, and mentors are attentive, energetic, and engaged.

- Evidence of ROI in advance of program completion. Are there early indicators of success that can be shared when (not if) senior executives ask about progress?

> Any sound measure of a meaningful outcome is better than none.

We have outlined many methods of measuring training and development success in prior chapters, so we won't repeat ourselves here. But one point worth mentioning is that the method must fit the goals of your learning journey. Any sound measure of a meaningful outcome is better than none. We find that a very simple measure is to simply ask participants and their managers, colleagues, and coworkers if they have seen improvement in areas (e.g., competencies) targeted in the learning journey. With very little effort, it's possible to glean a measure of progress that provides important insight into how well the process is working. Figure 11.4 shows an example of such a measure administered six months after the launch of a learning journey. Percentages indicate the proportion of the group that reported progress in the targeted areas. Our clients rely on data like this to continuously improve their leadership development efforts.

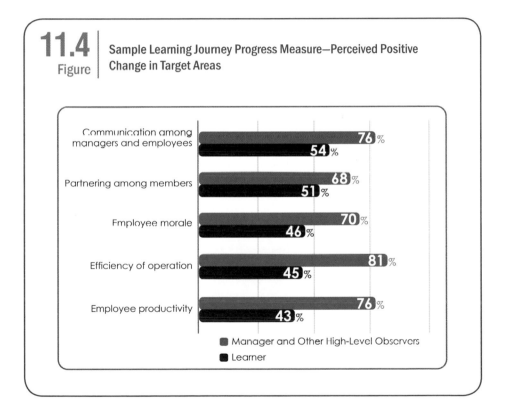

11.4 Figure | Sample Learning Journey Progress Measure—Perceived Positive Change in Target Areas

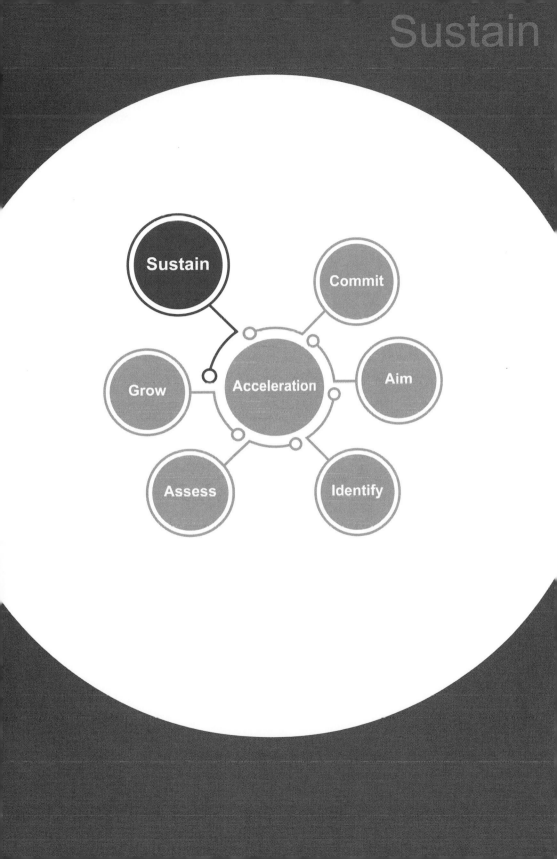

Sustain Aggressively manufacture the energy for growth.

In this section…

Chapter 12 outlines how organizations become great at the SUSTAIN imperative. The practices they employ generate energy in the following ways:

- **Dedication to measuring progress:** The few most-critical metrics are tracked to monitor the most essential measures of growth.

- **A more realistic mind-set:** Management doesn't expect an end point; they acknowledge that acceleration never stops and plan to continually renew their focus on it.

- **More complete ownership of growth:** The CEO and senior team don't just sanction learning activities; they own the accountability to convert leaders from *not ready* to *ready now*.

- **A more productive relationship with failure:** Management gets behind people and helps leaders work through failures to extract valuable lessons that can help the business perform better.

- **A shared experience:** Management grows too, making acceleration something that the entire organization shares. Growth is part of running the business.

 Denotes that tools and information on this topic are available at the *Leaders Ready Now* website (www.leadersreadynow.com). Use this code to access content: LRN2016.

ENERGIZE

12 | Generating the Passion and Commitment That Sustain Growth

"What scares me is the possibility that my CEO, and other CEOs around the world are silently concluding that we in Human Resources and Talent Management are not capable of delivering on our promise to grow more ready leaders."

—Anonymous corporate HR executive

This remark came after a review of the organization's extensive work to accelerate leadership growth. Despite years of effort and numerous well-designed programs, the leadership gap was widening.

This organization is one of many suffering the same fate. As we discussed at the start of this book, the general impact of leadership acceleration programs is not trending upward. DDI's global data suggests that when organizations look to their benches to find ready leaders for key assignments or promotions, half the time no one is there.

Generating more ready-now leaders is about making growth happen faster and better than what is possible under the status quo. And as we have discussed throughout this book, some organizations are showing how it can be done. They generate impressive gains in the form of behavior change, skill enhancement, deeper benches, and stronger leadership performance.

These organizations are not accelerating growth by simply forcing more learning activities into compressed time. At the core, they do one thing differently: They make acceleration a discipline—a continual process that evolves and grows with each business cycle.

> Make acceleration a discipline—a continual process that evolves and grows with each business cycle.

For accelerated growth to become a sustainable discipline, it needs energy. Energy comes from risk, experimentation, and bold attempts to propel and support the development of leaders through challenges that stretch and grow their skills. It sparks when leaders encounter the tension of an intense training course, the plain truth of an in-depth assessment, the thrill of a big assignment, and the fear that failure is possible. It can be exhilarating and at times a bit frightening, but if that energy can be harnessed, it fuels perseverance. Obstacles fall away. Business lessons resonate. Wisdom expands. And leadership growth flourishes.

One thing is sure: You won't generate more energy simply by adding more processes and tools. Instead, in these pages we have outlined how you can convert your current acceleration system from one that burns energy to one that generates it. The Acceleration Imperatives each detail practices that make your acceleration system components not just good enough to garner participation in learning, but great at building passion for growth. And while it's true that the five Imperatives discussed so far—Commit, Aim, Identify, Assess, and Grow—represent proven means for boosting the energy in your system, none of them alone will be sufficient to maintain its flow through your organization's inevitable cycles of opportunity, crisis, and change. There is one more lens through which your acceleration efforts must be examined: How to Sustain acceleration efforts by manufacturing positive energy for growth.

Make It Last

It's much easier to launch programs than it is to sustain their effectiveness through change. Sustainability is a marriage of tactics and mindset. Through the Acceleration Imperatives we have outlined many tactics that will help

> You can create an acceleration system that outlives everyone involved and becomes part of the organization's DNA.

to keep your programs running. But if you focus only on those tactics, you still may repeat the shortfalls that so many others have experienced. As you evaluate your organization against the Acceleration Imperatives and chart a course forward, you can create an acceleration system that outlives everyone involved and becomes part of the organization's DNA. There are several core considerations that must be factored into your plans.

Keep Score (of Growth) or Don't Play

Keeping score creates tension. Virtually every game and competition is more charged with energy when there is a scoreboard. But with regard to leadership acceleration, it's not enough to simply keep score. It's what you measure that matters.

One principal reason that investments in leadership development fail to generate gains in readiness is that often the wrong outcomes are measured. For example, a financial services firm embarking on a major business pivot deemed it too risky to staff the new venture with outside talent. So, management committed to an urgent leadership acceleration initiative. But when selecting the metrics to track success, only two were chosen: retention of high-potential leaders and the existence of development plans. No one should have been surprised when the initiative generated no meaningful growth and the business venture was scrapped.

The CEO of a major shipping corporation faced a coming wave of C-suite retirements—and an empty bench of replacements. His one criterion for evaluating the success of the acceleration program launched to fill the bench was for all participants to "enjoy the process and have fun."

In an acceleration system built to increase leadership readiness, the only score that matters is growth. And as we've said, learning is not growth. In fact, growth happens only when learning is applied to performance, which is how the measurement targets of an acceleration system must be aimed. Learners score when they successfully apply what they have learned. Managers and mentors score when learners score. Senior executive team members score when they can demonstrate that growth has scaled across groups and business units. Did development have business impact? How do we know? Is there evidence that leadership readiness is increasing? Can we present data that shows that our efforts are working, and can we demonstrate improvements in that data over time?

Measurement can be tedious and time consuming, which is why it is important to choose only the most crucial metrics of growth and relentlessly pursue them. It is far better to measure very few things well than to measure many things inaccurately. If the metrics you select truly keep score of your leaders' and your organization's growth, measuring acceleration will generate far more energy than it uses.

Assault Your Organization's Mind-Set

Ready now. When can we safely say that an individual is completely ready for a major assignment or that a business unit's leaders are entirely prepared to pivot to a new approach? Never.

> **Ready now** is not a permanent place at which individuals arrive or a state that organizations achieve.

The truth is no one can ever be fully ready. The world is far too chaotic. But that doesn't mean readiness is unachievable. It simply requires a different mind-set—a vital one. *Ready now* is not a permanent place at which individuals arrive or a state that organizations achieve. Because the only predictable reality is that the world will inevitably present difficult new challenges for leaders, the one viable response is to constantly and continually prepare for what lies ahead. Counterintuitive, perhaps, but if your senior management team doesn't embrace it, your efforts will lose energy quickly.

Without an understanding that readiness comes from perpetual preparation, a program-oriented mind-set will prevail. There will be a persistent expectation of an end point. Talent reviews might be painstakingly organized and executed, followed by a lack of action

> The ready now mind-set means continually looking forward, scanning the environment to anticipate the next challenge, and working with discipline to prepare for it.

on development. Cadres of leaders may participate in learning courses but with no subsequent focus on workplace application. Leaders might be assessed while their development prescriptions go unfulfilled. Energy will surge and then dissipate abruptly. Momentum will stall, and each new initiative will require another painstaking restart.

The ready now mind-set means continually looking forward, scanning the environment to anticipate the next challenge, and working with discipline to prepare for it. The way to make acceleration produce more ready leaders more continuously and with less effort is to ignite a chain reaction. Using the Acceleration Imperatives as guides, your efforts will be more clearly connected to a central business purpose, and the cumulative impact will generate energy that transfers through each program element to the next.

Own It

Think of someone in your organization with leadership potential—a strong performer in whom you see possibility, but who is not yet ready to take on a bigger leadership role. Next, ask yourself a simple question: Who is responsible for converting that person from *not ready* to *ready now*?

Now, scale that question to your entire business. It takes no time to appreciate that the task of acceleration is substantial and that accountability must be shared among senior management, accelerated learners, managers, mentors, and others. But with all those players involved, the upshot teeters dangerously on diffusion of responsibility, which in practice cripples many acceleration efforts. If you have a leadership gap that must be closed urgently, there is no room for ambiguity about who is responsible for what. Ownership and accountability must be specific. And if you are a CEO, business leader, or member of the senior management team, it starts with you.

> When you and your boardroom colleagues agree to take ownership of acceleration, each of you is stepping up to the accountability to transform leaders from not ready to ready now.

When you and your boardroom colleagues agree to take ownership of acceleration, each of you is stepping up to the accountability to transform leaders from not ready to ready now, and to make it happen faster. This is a commitment to *growth*—not just learning— and as we have said, your metrics and rewards must reflect it. To close a large leadership gap, growth goals must be bold, expressed quantitatively as well as qualitatively. For example, if the European Region faces a gap of 18 general managers over the next two years, who owns the responsibility to produce those 18 ready now leaders? If a senior executive has 25 high-potential, accelerated learners in her organization, how will she show that they are increasing their readiness? It's not enough to claim growth; she must demonstrate it.

When senior management takes ownership of growth, they not only shift the dynamics of the talent management system, but also expand the business dialog, adding leadership as a tangible component of how business growth is defined and measured. When you keep score of talent growth as well as financial growth, your executives will begin to compete around it, just as they compete for business success.

This brand of ownership creates powerful energy by driving more aggressive, risk-oriented development. Senior leaders with large leadership growth targets inevitably will need to stretch their leaders into bigger assignments earlier in their careers. Many will instinctively begin to scan the environment for opportunities to expose leaders to key situations or business challenges before they have to step

> This brand of ownership creates powerful energy by driving more aggressive, risk-oriented development.

into bigger roles. With help from HR professionals, they can do all of this reliably and effectively. Successful experiences then help them generate more thoughtful rationale about whom to involve in accelerated learning programs and to think more proactively about how to ensure that learning is applied in the workplace.

When you fully address the ownership of converting leaders from not ready to ready now as well as how you will measure and reward it, the resulting actions will cause senior leaders to look beyond the activities associated with specific programs or initiatives and toward the outcomes of those efforts, fueling a continual focus on growth.

Prove That You Believe in Your People

Acceleration requires experimentation. Failure is not only inevitable, it is indispensable. The most innovative, agile organizations in the world crush the impulse to punish failure and cultivate the practice of capitalizing on it. They

> The most innovative, agile organizations in the world crush the impulse to punish failure and cultivate the practice of capitalizing on it.

ensure that failures are small, frequent, fast, and useful. In the chapters leading up to this one, we have outlined ways to do so, but there is one more detail.

Learning to capitalize on failure has a crucial prerequisite: belief in your people and, more specifically, their ability to grow through struggle and defeat. This proves difficult for many organizations and many individuals. Pressure to produce results in the face of competition, scrutiny, and urgency breeds impatience. We have seen too many stories of the meteoric ascent of a leader who fails in a key assignment and is then relegated to obscurity, having lost the confidence of a senior management team that turns its attention to the next rising star.

> These responses kill energy. Each time you give up on a leader, you drain energy from your acceleration system.

These responses kill energy. Each time you give up on a leader, you drain energy from your acceleration system. But each time you choose to capture the learning from a disappointment and channel it to support a leader in taking on a new and different challenge, energy sparks. And when you replicate that response, you build momentum that fuels acceleration. Fortitude is bolstered. Confidence increases. Performance soars.

And learners are not the only ones who will face failure. Managers, mentors, and senior executives who sponsor and guide learners will find it as well (that is, if your acceleration system is working). As you seek to close urgent leadership gaps, you inevitably will take bigger risks, placing strong performers into situations that put their competence and stamina to the test. Senior executives and managers of learners will similarly struggle to demonstrate that they are affecting change.

As you make choices about how to respond when your organization struggles to gain mastery of acceleration, ask yourself: Am I prepared to be surprised by what my people might do if empowered to take big chances? How prepared am I to demonstrate confidence in a leader immediately after he or she botches an important assignment? How will I respond when one of my senior executives begins to show mediocre results in growing his or her people? Do I fundamentally believe my people can grow into stronger, better leaders? Since you have arrived at this point in this book, we suspect you do. If acceleration is to work and keep working in your organization, you will need to prove it.

Be the Growth You Want to See

Our clients and the many great leaders we have encountered are our teachers. They have taught us that people grow best when they grow together. All the methods, models, approaches, and practices recommended in this book are aimed at helping you and your colleagues do just that.

> People grow best when they grow together.

If you take only one message forward from here, let it be this: Acceleration begins when you sit down with a person, make eye contact, and begin a conversation about how to grow. You might be across from a member of your senior management team or a rising star in your high-potential pool. But if you do it right, all the forms, meetings, tools, processes, and best practices will fade into the background. Doing it right means making an authentic connection and sharing in the experience of learning and the application of new approaches as you confront your organization's most pressing challenges.

The six Acceleration Imperatives offer practices from which you can draw to build on the work you have already begun, and to become great in the areas that will most significantly benefit your organization. If you can do this, you can be a great leader of acceleration. You will not only make growth happen, but also make it happen faster, more consistently, and more completely than you had thought possible.

There is just one thing you must be prepared to do: *Grow.*

Citations

Introduction: Sapped

i   Ben Carroll, Raju Singaraju, and Eunyun Park, *Corporate Learning Factbook 2015: Benchmarks, Trends, and Analysis of the U.S. Training Market* (Oakland, CA: Bersin by Deloitte, 2015).

ii   Robert B. Kaiser, Robert Hogan, and Gordon Curphy, "The Problem With Leadership Development," *Chief Learning Officer* 13, no. 6 (June 2014): 58.

iii Evan Sinar, Richard S. Wellins, Rebecca Ray, Amy Lui Abel, and Stephanie Neal, *Global Leadership Forecast 2014|2015, Ready-Now Leaders: 25 Findings to Meet Tomorrow's Business Challenges* (Pittsburgh, PA: Development Dimensions International, 2014), 13; Laci Loew, "Successful Executive Transition is All about People," Brandon Hall Group (blog), October 19, 2015, http://www.brandonhall.com/blogs/successful-executive-transition-is-all-about-people/; Laci Loew, *State of Succession Management 2015: Increasing Investment and Accelerating Automation* (Delray Beach, FL: Brandon Hall Group, 2015), 4, 7–8; Stuart Crainer, "The New Leadership Special Report," *Business Strategy Review* 22, no. 2 (Summer 2011): 17–22; Kevin Martin and Jay Jamrog, *The Top 10 Critical Human Capital Issues: Enabling Sustained Growth through Talent Transparency* (Seattle, WA: Institute for Corporate Productivity, 2014), 1–2; David F. Larcker and Scott Saslow, *2014 Report on Senior Executive Succession Planning and Talent Development* (Palo Alto, CA: The Institute of Executive Development), 4–5; Suzanne Snowden and Poh-Khim Cheah, eds., *18th Annual Global CEO Survey: A Marketplace Without Boundaries?* (New York: PricewaterhouseCoopers, 2015), 9; Towers Watson, *2014 Global Talent Management and Rewards Study: Making the Most of the Employment Deal* (New York: Towers Watson, 2014), 1–2; Manpower Group, *2015 Talent Shortage Survey* (Milwaukee, WI: Manpower Group, 2015), 5.

iv Pierre Gurdjian, Thomas Halbeisen, and Kevin Lane, "Why Leadership-Development Programs Fail," *McKinsey Quarterly* no. 1 (January 2014).

v   William C. Byham, Audrey B. Smith, and Matthew J. Paese, *Grow Your Own Leaders: How to Identify, Develop, and Retain Leadership Talent* (Pittsburgh, PA: Development Dimensions International, 2002), 15.

vi   Mollie Lombardi, *DDI Clients Finding Succession Success* (Boston: Aberdeen Group, 2011); Jayson Saba and Kimberly Madden, *DDI's Clients Demonstrate Prowess in Succession Management* (Boston: Aberdeen Group, 2009).

vii   Evan Sinar, "Global Leadership Forecast 2014-2015: Match-Up Game" (presentation, DDI Summit, Chicago, IL., 2014), 33; Evan Sinar et al., *Global Leadership Forecast 2014|2015, Ready-Now Leaders: 25 Findings to Meet Tomorrow's Business Challenges* (Pittsburgh, PA: Development Dimensions International, 2014, 13.

viii Evan Sinar, Richard S. Wellins, Matthew J. Paese, Audrey Smith, and Bruce Watt, *High Resolution Leadership: A Synthesis of 15,000 Assessments into Big Data About Today's Leaders* (Pittsburgh, PA: Development Dimensions International, 2015).

Chapter 1: Nail the Basics

i   Evan Sinar et al., *Global Leadership Forecast 2014|2015, Ready-Now Leaders: 25 Findings to Meet Tomorrow's Business Challenges* (Pittsburgh, PA: Development Dimensions International, 2014), 38–39.

ii   Michael Kemp, William C. Byham, and Morgan Blumenfeld, *Interaction Management Impact Analysis: 45 Years of Behavior Change and Business Value* (Pittsburgh, PA: Development Dimensions International 2016).

iii   Evan Sinar et al., *Global Leadership Forecast 2014|2015, Ready-Now Leaders: 25 Findings to Meet Tomorrow's Business Challenges* (Pittsburgh, PA: Development Dimensions International, 2014), 38–39.

Chapter 2: Make Growth Matter

i   Evan Sinar et al., *High Resolution Leadership* (Pittsburgh, PA: Development Dimensions International, 2015).

ii   Evan Sinar et al., *Global Leadership Forecast 2014|2015, Ready-Now Leaders: 25 Findings to Meet Tomorrow's Business Challenges* (Pittsburgh, PA: Development Dimensions International, 2014), 25.

Chapter 3: Become Fluent in the Language of Growth

i   Evan Sinar et al., *High Resolution Leadership* (Pittsburgh, PA: Development Dimensions International, 2015).

ii   Evan Sinar et al., *Global Leadership Forecast 2014|2015, Ready-Now Leaders: 25 Findings to Meet Tomorrow's Business Challenges* (Pittsburgh, PA: Development Dimensions International, 2014), 42–43.

iii   Jennifer Donahue, Kris Routch, and Nancy Thomas, *Strengthening the Middle: Global Challenges and Best Practices in Mid-Level Leader Assessment and Development* (Pittsburgh, PA: Development Dimensions International, 2011).

iv   Evan Sinar and Matt Paese, *Leaders in Transition: Progressing Along a Precarious Path* (Pittsburgh, PA: Development Dimensions International, 2014), 6.

v   Frank L. Schmidt and John E. Hunter, "The Validity and Utility of Selection Methods in Personnel Psychology: Practical and Theoretical Implications of 85 Years of Research Findings," *Psychological Bulletin* 124, no. 2 (September 1998): 262–274.

vi   Evan Sinar, "Part 5: Cognitive Skills in Senior Leaders: Focused Influence, Critical Consequences," *Leadership Insights: A 10-Year Culmination of Executive Analytics* (Pittsburgh, PA: Development Dimensions International, 2013), 1–2.

vii   Allan H. Church and Christopher T. Rotolo, "How Are Top Companies Assessing Their High-Potentials and Senior Executives? A Talent Management Benchmark Study," *Consulting Psychology Journal: Practice & Research* 65, no. 3 (September 2013): 199–223.

viii Allan H. Church et al., "How Are Top Companies Designing and Managing Their High-Potential Programs? A Follow-Up Talent Management Benchmark Study," *Consulting Psychology Journal: Practice & Research* 67, no. 1 (March 2015): 17–47.

ix Robert W. Rogers and Audrey B. Smith, *Finding Future Perfect Senior Leaders: Spotting Executive Potential* (Pittsburgh, PA: Development Dimensions International, 2003–2007), 3–4.

Chapter 4: Have the Right Conversations About the Right People

i Evan Sinar et al., *Global Leadership Forecast 2014|2015, Ready-Now Leaders: 25 Findings to Meet Tomorrow's Business Challenges* (Pittsburgh, PA: Development Dimensions International, 2014), 38–39.

ii William C. Byham, et al., *Grow Your Own Leaders: How to Identify, Develop, and Retain Leadership Talent* (Pittsburgh, PA: Development Dimensions International, 2002), 15.

iii Robert W. Rogers et al., *Finding Future Perfect Senior Leaders: Spotting Executive Potential* (Pittsburgh, PA: Development Dimensions International, 2003), 3–4.

iv Eric Hanson, *Talent Reviews and High-Potential Identification: Overcoming Five Common Challenges* (Pittsburgh, PA: Development Dimensions International, 2011), 3–4.

v Paul Bernthal, Evan F. Sinar, and Douglas H. Reynolds, *Technical Summary for the Leadership Potential Inventory (LPI)* (Pittsburgh, PA: Development Dimensions International, 2009), 1.

vi Matt Paese and Evan Sinar, *The Value of Assessment: Prediction, Validity and Business Impact* (Pittsburgh, PA: Development Dimensions International, 2015). 6.

vii Evan Sinar, "Developmental Assignments Are Vital: Don't Squander Their Potential," *Talent Management Intelligence* (blog), July 23, 2015, www.ddiworld.com/blog/tmi/july-2015/developmental-assignments-are-vital.

Chapter 5: Gather Great Data About Your People

i   Matt Paese et al., *The Value of Assessment: Prediction, Validity and Business Impact* (Pittsburgh, PA: Development Dimensions International, 2015).

ii   Frank L. Schmidt, Jonathan A. Shaffer, and In-Sue Oh, "Increased Accuracy for Range Restriction Corrections: Implications for the Role of Personality and General Mental Ability in Job and Training Performance," *Personnel Psychology* 61, no. 4 (Winter 2008): 827–868; Frank L. Schmidt et al., "The Validity and Utility of Selection Methods in Personnel Psychology: Practical and Theoretical Implications of 85 Years of Research Findings." *Psychological Bulletin* 124, no. 2 (September 1998): 262–274.

iii   Evan Sinar, "Part 5: Cognitive Skills in Senior Leaders: Focused Influence, Critical Consequences," *Leadership Insights: A 10-Year Culmination of Executive Analytics* (Pittsburgh, PA: Development Dimensions International, 2013), 6.

Chapter 6: Rethink Feedback

i   Evan Sinar et al., *Global Leadership Forecast 2014|2015, Ready-Now Leaders: 25 Findings to Meet Tomorrow's Business Challenges* (Pittsburgh, PA: Development Dimensions International, 2014), 42–43.

ii   Marcus Buckingham and Donald O. Clifton, *Now, Discover Your Strengths* (New York: Free Press, 2001).

iii   David L. Dotlich and Peter C. Cairo, *Why CEOs Fail: The 11 Behaviors That Can Derail Your Climb to the Top and How to Manage Them* (San Francisco: Jossey-Bass. 2003); Sydney Finkelstein, *Why Smart Executives Fail: And What You Can Learn from Their Mistakes* (New York: Portfolio, 2003); Robert Hogan, *Personality and the Fate of Organizations* (New York: Psychology Press, 2006); Robert B. Kaiser, ed., *The Perils of Accentuating the Positive* (Tulsa, OK: Hogan Press, 2009).

Chapter 7: Apply More Discipline to Developing Leadership Skills

i   Michael Kemp, William C. Byham, and Morgan Blumenfeld, *Interaction Management Impact Analysis: 45 Years of Behavior Change and Business Value* (Pittsburgh, PA: Development Dimensions International, forthcoming).

ii   Evan Sinar et al., *Global Leadership Forecast 2014|2015, Ready-Now Leaders: 25 Findings to Meet Tomorrow's Business Challenges* (Pittsburgh, PA: Development Dimensions International, 2014).

iii   Kemp et al., *Interaction Management Impact Analysis: 45 Years of Behavior Change and Business Value* (Pittsburgh, PA: Development Dimensions International, forthcoming).

iv   CEB Corporate Leadership Council, *Create Talent Champions: Improve Revenue up to 14% by Transforming Business Leaders into Talent Champions* (Washington, DC: Corporate Executive Board, 2008).

v   Evan Sinar et al., *High Resolution Leadership* (Pittsburgh, PA: Development Dimensions International, 2015), 30–31.

vi   Ibid., 30–31.

Chapter 8: Unleash the Inner Strength of Your Leaders

i   Blaine H. Gaddis and Jeff L. Foster, "Meta-Analysis of Dark Side Personality Characteristics and Critical Work Behaviors Among Leaders Across the Globe: Findings and Implications for Leadership Development and Executive Coaching," *Applied Psychology* 64, no. 1 (January 2015): 25–54; Robert Hogan, Robert Raskin, and Dan Fazzini, "The Dark Side of Charisma," in *Measures of Leadership,* Kenneth E. Clark and Miriam B. Clark, eds. (West Orange, NJ: Leadership Library of America, 1990), 343–354; Joyce Hogan, Robert Hogan, and Robert B. Kaiser, "Management Derailment: Personality Assessment and Mitigation," in *APA Handbook of Industrial and Organizational Psychology,* Sheldon Zedeck, ed. (Washington, DC: American Psychological Association, 2010), 555–575; Timothy A. Judge and Jeffery A. LePine, "The Bright and Dark

Sides of Personality: Implications for Personnel Selection in Individual and Team Contexts," in *Research Companion to the Dysfunctional Workplace: Management Challenges and Symptoms,* Janice Langan-Fox, Cary L. Cooper, and Richard J. Klimoski, eds. (Northampton, MA: Edward Elgar, 2007), 332–355.

ii   Evan Sinar et al., *High Resolution Leadership* (Pittsburgh, PA: Development Dimensions International, 2015), 22–23.

iii Daniel Goleman, *Emotional Intelligence: Why It Can Matter More Than IQ* (New York: Bantam Books, 2005).

iv   Adele B. Lynn, *The EQ Difference: A Powerful Plan for Putting Emotional Intelligence to Work* (New York: Amacom, 2004), 7.

Chapter 9: Get Leaders in the Game Sooner

i   Evan Sinar, "Developmental Assignments Are Vital: Don't Squander Their Potential," *Talent Management Intelligence* (blog), July 23, 2015, www.ddiworld.com/blog/tmi/july-2015/developmental-assignments-are-vital.

ii   Kemp et al., *Interaction Management Impact Analysis: 45 Years of Behavior Change and Business Value,* (Pittsburgh, PA: Development Dimensions International, forthcoming).

iii Matt Paese and Richard S. Wellins, *Leaders in Transition: Stepping Up, Not Off* (Pittsburgh, PA: Development Dimensions International, 2007), 15.

Chapter 10: Make Executive Coaching Work Better

i   Ibid., 6.

Chapter 11: Capitalize on Opportunities to Accelerate Leaders in Groups

i   Evan Sinar et al., *Global Leadership Forecast 2014|2015, Ready-Now Leaders: 25 Findings to Meet Tomorrow's Business Challenges* (Pittsburgh, PA: Development Dimensions International, 2014), 60.

ii   Ibid., 60.

iii   Evan Sinar et al., *Leaders in Transition: Progressing Along a Precarious Path* (Pittsburgh, PA: Development Dimensions International, 2014), 7.

iv   Matt Paese et al., *Leaders in Transition: Stepping Up, Not Off* (Pittsburgh, PA: Development Dimensions International, 2007), 15.

v   Evan Sinar et al., *Global Leadership Forecast 2014|2015, Ready-Now Leaders: 25 Findings to Meet Tomorrow's Business Challenges* (Pittsburgh, PA: Development Dimensions International, 2014), 60.

Acknowledgments

If any parts of this book have been useful, it is probably because of the efforts of one or more of the people listed here.

We (Matt, Audrey, and Bill) could not have completed *Leaders Ready Now* without the instrumental guidance and support of many others at DDI. To each of you, we are deeply grateful and are proud to count you among our advisors, friends, and family.

Tacy Byham, CEO—Having very recently published *Your First Leadership Job* (with Rich Wellins), your insights and thought leadership had significant impact on many elements of *Leaders Ready Now*. Through your experience, your personal commitment to growth, and your own journey to the position of CEO, we have learned so many important lessons. And with you, we've seen firsthand what it looks like when a leader successfully transitions into a major role.

Evan Sinar, Chief Scientist—This book relied heavily on research and thought leadership that you have either conducted, written, or summarized for DDI. Your thoughtful reviews and contemporary insights about both research and practice helped us to be better informed, more relevant, and more clear and consistent throughout the book.

Eric Hanson, Director, Executive Succession and Development—Your expertise in succession, development, and assessment set us straight on numerous topics, particularly around identifying potential and talent reviews. These might be the thorniest subjects in the entire book. But as you have done for so many people for more than two decades at DDI, you made the complex seem simple and helped us clearly articulate the approaches that truly work.

Barry Stern, Senior Vice President—Your experience and wisdom had crucial impact on numerous sections of this book, particularly the Grow section. Piecing together the many lessons DDI has learned about how growth happens and how to make learning stick was challenging. But your guidance focused us on what matters most and isolated the unique practices our clients have employed to get real results.

Jim Kauffman, Product Manager—As a veteran leader and consultant around virtually every topic associated with succession management and accelerated development, your insights helped us frame our thinking in numerous areas. Most significantly, your vast experience with learning approaches for mid-level leaders and executives was essential as we crafted those sections of the book.

Bill Proudfoot, Managing Editor—It's one thing to be a gifted editor, but it's another thing entirely when you are also calm, patient, thoughtful, and almost always right. What a gift it has been having your partnership and skill in writing this book. Your talents have made it so much better, and your disposition has made it a pleasure to do the work.

Sally Seltmann, Consulting Associate—Producing a book is complicated, and to make it work there must be a talented, resilient, focused, organized, collaborative professional to "herd the cats" and keep all the efforts aligned and on track. Sally, you have done all of that and so much more. We are beyond grateful for your leadership and coordination.

Sue Huber, Consultant—You have contributed to *Leaders Ready Now* in more ways than you will ever know. You've become famous for asking the one crucial question that no one else thought to ask and for providing help before we knew we needed it. We can't think of a name for that skill, which means we're probably going to need your help with a new book. (Run while you can!)

Jennifer Pesci-Kelly, Marketing Manager—Bringing concepts to market can be difficult enough, but when dealing with three highly opinionated psychologists in the process, one faces a far bigger challenge. But you have been greater than the task. We have come to depend on your fortitude, optimism, and unconditional support, but even more on your wisdom and insights about how to translate concepts into messages that will resonate and to create a community of accelerated learners who will grow together.

Janet Wiard, Senior Graphics Designer—If a picture paints a thousand words, you have been our Picasso. So many concepts in this book became clearer and more vibrant through the magic of your creativity and design expertise. You wowed us time and again.

Susan Ryan, Creative Director, Marketing—Like most books, this one evolved, and so too did the cover concept as well as many other graphical treatments throughout the book. Thankfully, we had you to translate our fuzzy ideas into brilliant images that tell stories all by themselves. On our cover you captured growth, urgency, speed, and simplicity. You've told our story in a single, beautiful image.

Helen Wylie, Special Assistant to the Chairman—You may occupy the office adjacent to the Chairman (Bill Byham), but more than that, you occupy our hearts. We could never fully thank you for your constant support and eternal grace under pressure. So many edit meetings—prototypically rescheduled, reshuffled, and thrown into chaos by chronic tardiness, version control, and disorganized authors—were always recovered by your steady hand. This book might still be strewn across a conference table if not for you.

Shawn Garry, Editor and Proofreader—After we had combed through the book too many times to count, you gave us not one, but two objective reads from the audience's point of view. Your proofreading was excellent, and your suggestions helped to sharpen the focus of our text. Similarly, your eye for detail tightened consistency in text and formatting.

Also, we'd like to thank:

Matthew Budman, Editorial Support—As we shaped the foundational architecture of *Leaders Ready Now,* you generously shared your time and gave us the gift of sage insight. Your nuggets of tough feedback (which we badly needed) were packaged in your warm and open style, somehow making us forget that we were getting tough feedback and steering us toward a far better book.

Our spouses and families: Ellen, Craig, Carolyn, Rachel, Louis, Lex, Clemens, Felix, Leonie, Josh, Chas, Lance, Robbie, Nick, Erin, Tacy, Spencer, Carter—We lack the words to tell you about the roles you all played in the writing of this book, because, of course, you mean so much more. You didn't just make this book possible, you make us possible. We love you with all our hearts.

About DDI

Who We Are. Development Dimensions International, or DDI, is a leading and innovative global human resources consultancy, specializing in leadership assessment and development. More than 45 years ago, we pioneered the field; today, we remain its chief innovator.

What We Do. We help companies transform the way they hire, promote, and develop their leaders across the entire pipeline. The outcome? Leaders who are ready to inspire, understand, and execute business strategy and address challenges head-on.

How We Do It. If you have ever had a leader you revered or marveled at how quickly a new hire came up to speed, you might very well be experiencing DDI at work. Annually, we develop 250,000 leaders worldwide. Often, we are behind the scenes, creating custom training or assessments that clients can roll out on their own. Other times, we are more visible, helping clients drive big changes in their organizations, such as succession management. Always, we use the latest methods, based on science and the test of time.

Who We Do It With. Our clients are some of the world's most successful companies. They are Fortune 500s and multinationals, doing business across a vast array of industries, from Shanghai to San Francisco and everywhere in between. We serve a diverse roster of clients across 94 countries.

Why We Do It. The principles and skills we teach don't just make people better employees; they are at the heart of what makes for happier, more-fulfilled human beings—better family members, better neighbors, better friends.

Visit **www.ddiworld.com** for more information.

About the Authors

Matthew J. Paese, Ph.D.

 Matthew J. Paese, Ph.D., is Vice President of Succession and C-Suite Services for Development Dimensions International (DDI). He began his career at DDI in 1994, at a time when succession management and accelerated development were much different endeavors than they are today. Most of what is written in this book reflects lessons that Matt and his coauthors have learned since then from courageous, innovative client partners who have pioneered cutting-edge approaches to closing leadership gaps.

Matt's work has centered on the application of succession, assessment, and development approaches as they apply to boards, CEOs, senior management teams, and leaders across the pipeline. He consults, coaches, speaks, and conducts research around all those topics and more. He is coauthor of *Grow Your Own Leaders* along with many other articles and research papers.

Matt lives in St. Louis, MO, with his wife, Ellen, and children Rachel (14) and Louis (11). He currently is attempting to accelerate his growth as a husband, father, fly fisherman, pianist, and barista. He hopes to one day be *ready now* in one or more of those areas.

Audrey B. Smith, Ph.D.

Audrey B. Smith, Ph.D., is Senior Vice President for Global Talent Diagnostics at Development Dimensions International (DDI). Since joining DDI in 1989, Audrey has had a mission to learn what truly sparks leadership growth across ever-changing business realities. She's done so through deep collaboration with boards, executives, and Talent Management professionals around the world.

Audrey's customer-driven innovation and global consulting insights have helped shape DDI's succession, selection, and development offerings, from the C-suite to the front line. She has been a key strategist and solution architect, encompassing technology-enabled virtual assessments and development offerings aligned to contemporary business challenges. She also is a coauthor of *Grow Your Own Leaders* and numerous other publications and research studies.

Audrey's commitment to leadership growth shines brightly through her passion for developing current and future generations of DDI leaders. Speaking of new generations, Audrey and her husband, Craig, are enjoying new life adventures with their wonderful (and growing) family, including Lex, Clemens, Felix, Leonie, Josh, Chas, Lance, Robbie, Nick, and Erin. They reside in Pittsburgh, PA.

William C. Byham, Ph.D.

William C. Byham, Ph.D., is Executive Chairman of Development Dimensions International, Inc. (DDI). He cofounded DDI in 1970 and has worked with hundreds of the world's largest organizations relative to executive assessment, executive development, and succession management. Bill's work on executive succession has been featured in many leading publications.

Bill is author of *Zapp!® The Lightning of Empowerment,* a groundbreaking book on empowerment that has sold more than 3 million copies since its 1988 publication. He has coauthored 23 other books, including seminal books on the assessment center method, which established the effectiveness of assessment centers as a method of executive selection and development-needs diagnosis.

Bill lives in Pittsburgh, PA, with his wife, Carolyn, who has been at his side through each and every moment of his long and fruitful career. His daughter, Tacy (now CEO of DDI), son, Carter, and grandson, Spencer, all make him proud every day.

Other Books from DDI

70: The New 50® Retirement Management®: Retaining the Energy and Expertise of Experienced Employees, by William C. Byham, Ph.D.

Grow Your Own Leaders®: How to Identify, Develop, and Retain Leadership Talent, by William C. Byham, Ph.D., Audrey B. Smith, Ph.D., and Matthew J. Paese, Ph.D.

HeroZ™—Empower Yourself, Your Coworkers, Your Company, by William C. Byham, Ph.D., and Jeff Cox

Inside Teams: How 20 World-Class Organizations Are Winning Through Teamwork, by Richard S. Wellins, Ph.D., William C. Byham, Ph.D., and George R. Dixon

Organizational Change That Works: How to Merge Culture and Business Strategies for Maximum Results, by Robert W. Rogers, John W. Hayden, and B. Jean Ferketish, Ph.D., with Robert Matzen

Realizing the Promise of Performance Management, by Robert W. Rogers

The Selection Solution: Solving the Mystery of Matching People to Jobs, by William C. Byham, Ph.D., with Steven M. Krauzer

The Service Leaders Club, by William C. Byham, Ph.D., with Ray Crew and James H.S. Davis

Shogun Management™: How North Americans Can Thrive in Japanese Companies, by William C. Byham, Ph.D., with George R. Dixon

SPARK! How the Science Behind DDI Transforms Lives In and Out of the Workplace, gathered by Nikki Dy-Liacco, Nancy Fox, and Bob Rogers; edited by Ellen Lief Wellins

Your First Leadership Job: How Catalyst Leaders Bring Out the Best in Others, by Tacy M. Byham, Ph.D., and Richard S. Wellins, Ph.D.

Zapp!® Empowerment in Health Care, by William C. Byham, Ph.D., with Jeff Cox and Greg Nelson

Zapp!® in Education, by William C. Byham, Ph.D., with Jeff Cox and Kathy Harper Shomo

Zapp!® The Lightning of Empowerment, by William C. Byham, Ph.D., with Jeff Cox

Index

Page numbers followed by *f* refer to figures.

role in acceleration, 242*f*
senior-level sponsorship, 250
strategic linkages, 251
three coaching types that catalyze acceleration, 234–238, 235*f*
cognitive ability, 70–71
in acceleration, 70–71
deficiencies in, 70–71
defined as a personal attribute, 66
and emotional intelligence, 71
personal attributes category, 66, 67*f*
in success profiles, 70–71
cognitive tests in readiness assessments, 129–131
Commit (Acceleration Imperative), xvi, 2–46
communication, measurement, and accountability tactics
Acceleration Imperatives key system, 3–7
competencies (success profile), 57–65
in Acceleration Center results (example), 119–123
cascading framework (sample), 62–63
definition with Key Actions (example), 59–60
developing, 56–57, 60–63, 161–180, 185–190, 191–194
and Key Actions, 48, 57–63, 161–180
skill domains, 57–59, 58*f* (sample)
in success profiles, 56–63
and strategies, values, Business Drivers, 24–26, 25*f*, 53*f*

in traditional talent-management, 24
wiring to a Business Driver, 52*f*
competency development, 56–57, 60–63, 161–180, 185–190, 191–194
for high-potential, mid-level leaders, 185–190
for senior executives, 191–194
competency skill domains, 58–59
Business/Management Skills, 58*f*, 59, 63*f*
Interpersonal Effectiveness, 58, 58*f*, 63*f*
Leadership Impact, 58*f*, 59, 63*f*
Personal Effectiveness, 58*f*, 59, 63*f*
and sample competencies, 58*f*
The Conference Board, 172–173
creativity
executive coach characteristic, 257
credibility
executive coach characteristic, 255

D

derailers
in Acceleration Center results (example), 119–123
anticipating and managing, 199–206
common responses to, 202–203
identifying before damage is done, 198
leaders taking pride in, 197–198
as negative attributes, 199
as personal attributes, 66–67, 67*f*